Love Is Never Enough

Love
Is Never
Enough

HOW COUPLES CAN OVERCOME MISUNDERSTANDINGS,
RESOLVE CONFLICTS, AND SOLVE RELATIONSHIP PROBLEMS
THROUGH COGNITIVE THERAPY

Aaron T. Beck, M.D.

HARPER & ROW PUBLISHERS, New York
CAMBRIDGE, PHILADELPHIA, SAN FRANCISCO, LONDON
MEXICO CITY, SÃO PAULO, SINGAPORE, SYDNEY

FIRST EDITION

Copyeditor: Mary Levai
Designer: Barbara DuPree Knowles
Indexer: Auralie Logan

Library of Congress Cataloging-in-Publication Data
Beck, Aaron T.
   Love is never enough.
   Includes index.
   1. Marriage—Psychological aspects.   2. Communication in marriage.
3. Interpersonal conflict.   4. Cognitive therapy.   I. Title.
HQ734.B47 1988   646.7'8   88-45010
ISBN 0-06-015956-1

88 89 90 91 92   DT/RRD   10 9 8 7 6 5 4 3 2 1

To Phyllis

CONTENTS

CONTENTS

ACKNOWLEDGMENTS

I am grateful above all to my wife, Phyllis, whose love and devotion proved that marriage can become more fulfilling and meaningful with each passing day. My friend and colleague Norman Epstein, a pioneer in applying cognitive therapy to the problems of couples, was my major resource when writing this book. His gentle criticisms and numerous suggestions helped to keep the writing on course, and his insights illuminated many obscure problems that couples experience. My former students Susan Joseph, Craig Wiese, Janis Abrahms, Chris Padesky, Ruth Greenberg, David Clark, Kathy Mooney, Frank Dattilio, and Judy Beck provided a great deal of material for the book. Others who read the manuscript and gave me valuable feedback included Connie Sekaros, Vivian Greenberg, Carol Auerbach, and Cal Laden.

I am especially grateful to Carol Stillman, who reviewed the manuscript many times and gave me numerous suggestions for simplifying the complexities of the text.

I was particularly fortunate in having Richard Pine as my literary agent. He was unique in his continuous enthusiasm and confidence in this book. My editor at Harper & Row, Hugh Van Dusen, was responsible for transforming the manuscript into the printed volume.

Barbara Marinelli, Executive Director at the Center for Cognitive Therapy, helped to stage-manage the production of the manuscript, and Tina Inforzato, Gail Furman, and Suzanne DePietro typed it.

To all of the above and to the numerous couples at the Center for Cognitive Therapy and elsewhere, who opened up their minds to cognitive therapy, THANK YOU.

Love Is Never Enough is based on case material, including quotations obtained by me and my colleagues in counseling couples. However, all the names and identifying details have been changed without affecting the integrity of the illustrations. In some instances, I have created composites for the purpose of further disguising the identity of the individuals.

INTRODUCTION

I have devoted much of my professional life to a study of thinking problems in anxiety and depression, and, more recently, in panic disorders. Over several decades I have had the opportunity to treat a large number of people who had distressed marriages and a few who were living together though not married. In many cases, these troubled relationships led to depression and anxiety in one of the mates. In others, the depression and anxiety aggravated difficulties already present in the relationship.

As I turned my attention to the problems of couples, I found that they showed the same kind of thinking aberrations—cognitive distortions—as did my depressed and anxious patients. Although the couples were not so depressed or anxious that they needed therapy specifically for these conditions, they were unhappy, tense, and angry. And as my patients did, they tended to fixate on what was wrong with their marriages and disregard—or blind themselves to— what was good.

The Cognitive Revolution in Psychology

Fortunately, the last two decades have witnessed a rapid accumulation of knowledge about problems of the mind that has direct applications to the difficulties that intimate partners experience. This new understanding of psychological difficulties has also been applied to a wide range of disorders, including depression, anxiety, panic disorders, obsessive-compulsive disorder, and even eating disorders such as anorexia and bulimia. This approach, called cognitive therapy, is

1

embedded within a major new movement in psychology and psychotherapy called "the cognitive revolution."

The word *cognitive*, derived from the Latin word for "thinking," refers to the ways in which people make judgments and decisions, and the ways in which they interpret—or misinterpret—one another's actions. This revolution has provided a new focus on how people use their minds to solve problems—or to create or aggravate them. How we think determines to a large extent whether we will succeed and enjoy life, or even survive. If our thinking is straightforward and clear, we are better equipped to reach these goals. If it is bogged down by distorted symbolic meanings, illogical reasoning, and erroneous interpretations, we become in effect deaf and blind. Stumbling along without a clear sense of where we are going or what we are doing, we are destined to hurt ourselves and others. As we misjudge and miscommunicate, we inflict pain on both ourselves and our mates and, in turn, bear the brunt of painful retaliations.

This kind of twisted thinking can be untangled by applying a higher order of reasoning. We use such high-level thinking much of the time when we catch ourselves in a mistake and correct it. Unfortunately, in close relationships—where clear thinking and corrections of our errors are especially important—we seem to be particularly defective in recognizing and rectifying our misjudgments of our mates. In addition, although partners may believe that they are talking the same language, what they *say* and what their mates *hear* are often quite different. Thus, problems in communication lead to and then aggravate the frustrations and disappointments that many couples experience.

Take the following case: Ken and Marjorie, both busy in their careers (he sold insurance, and she was a secretary in a public relations firm), had decided to spend more time together. One Saturday Marjorie told Ken of her plan to spend the afternoon shopping. Ken, wanting to be close to Marjorie, immediately decided to accompany her. Marjorie, after a particularly frustrating day reviewing the books of a large and complex company, interpreted this as an intrusion (thinking, *"He never lets me do my own thing."*) She nevertheless said nothing to Ken and was quiet during the entire shopping expedition. Ken interpreted her silence to mean that she didn't care for his company, and he became angry at her. Marjorie reacted to his anger by withdrawing even more.

The facts of the situation were that (1) Marjorie *did* want to spend more time with Ken but wanted to shop alone; (2) she failed to communicate this to Ken; (3) she misinterpreted his overture as an encroachment on her freedom; and (4) Ken misinterpreted her withdrawal as a sign that she did not enjoy his company.

Numerous, repeated misunderstandings, such as those between Marjorie and Ken, and the resultant mutual anger will erode the foundation of a relationship. I have observed several times that similar misunderstandings escalate to the point of no return. What is remarkable, however, is that if partners catch the misunderstanding and correct it before it goes too far, they can head off the storm. Cognitive therapy is designed to help couples do just that—to clear their thinking and communication so as to prevent the misunderstandings from arising in the first place.

Dissolution of Marital Ties

Most couples are aware that there is a continuing crisis in marriage; that between 40 and 55 percent of marriages are likely to end in divorce. As they see more and more unhappy marriages and more and more breakups, couples may wonder whether this might happen to them, too.

Newlyweds, riding the tide of love and romance, want nothing more than a successful marriage. They often believe—at least initially —that *their* relationship is "different" and that their deep love and optimism will sustain it. Sooner or later, however, all too many couples find themselves unprepared for the problems and conflicts that gradually accumulate in any marriage. They become aware of a growing unrest, frustration, and hurt—often without knowing exactly where the problem lies.

As the relationship founders in a backwash of disillusionment, poor communication, and misunderstanding, the couple may begin to think that their marriage was a mistake. Nowhere is the "cry for help" a therapist hears more poignant than among those clients who see their once happy marriage begin to dissolve. Even couples married thirty to forty years may feel driven to end a relationship that they now regard as an unending series of mistakes and miseries.

It is surprising in a way that so many marriages do collapse. Consider all the forces that you would expect to keep a couple together. Loving and being loved are certainly among the richest experiences that people have. Add to these the other by-products of the relationship—intimacy, companionship, acceptance, support, to name only a few. You have somebody to console you when you are bereaved, to bolster your spirits when you're discouraged, and to share your excitement when good things happen. And you have the extra bonus of sexual gratification, which nature provides as a special inducement to mate. Nor can you underestimate the satisfaction of having children and building a family together.

The hopes and encouragement of parents and other relatives, as well as the expectations of your community that you will stay together, provide pressures from the outside. With all these binding forces operating to fortify the relationship, what can go wrong? Why isn't love—let alone all the other incentives—strong enough to keep couples together?

Unfortunately, centrifugal forces are at work that can split a relationship—demoralizing disillusionments, labyrinthine misunderstandings, and tortured miscommunications. Love in itself is seldom sturdy enough to resist these divisive forces and their by-products, resentment and rage. Other ingredients of a good relationship are necessary in order for love to solidify rather than start to dissolve.

The media's idealized portrayals of marriage do not prepare couples to cope with disappointments, frustrations, and friction. As the misunderstandings and conflicts combine to ignite anger and resentment, the person who previously had been lover, ally, and companion is now seen as an antagonist.

What Is Needed
To Sustain a Relationship

Although love is a powerful impetus for husbands and wives to help and support each other, to make each other happy, and to create a family, it does not in itself create the substance of the relationship—the personal qualities and skills that are crucial to sustain it and make it grow. Special personal qualities are crucial for a happy relationship: commitment, sensitivity, generosity, consideration, loyalty, responsibility, trustworthiness. Mates need to cooperate, compromise, and follow through with joint decisions. They have to be resilient, accepting, and forgiving. They need to be tolerant of each other's flaws, mistakes, and peculiarities. As these "virtues" are cultivated over a period of time, the marriage develops and matures.

Couples are often adept at dealing with people outside the relationship, but few people enter an intimate relationship with the basic understandings—or the technical skills—that make a relationship blossom. They frequently lack the know-how to make joint decisions, to decipher their partners' communications. When a faucet in the house starts to drip, they have the tools to stop the leak, but when love starts to drain away, they have no idea about how to staunch the flow.

Marriage, or even living together, differs from other relationships in life. When a couple—whether of the same or opposite sex—live

4

together, committed to a lasting relationship, they develop certain expectations of each other. The intensity of the relationship fuels certain long dormant yearnings for unconditional love, loyalty, and support. And the partners either expressly, as in the marriage vows, or indirectly, through their actions, pledge themselves to meet these deeply rooted needs. Whatever the partner does is endowed with meanings derived from these desires and expectations.

Because of the strength of the feelings and expectations, the deep dependency, and the crucial, often arbitrary, symbolic meanings that they attach to each other's actions, partners are prone to misinterpret each other's actions. When conflicts occur, often as a result of miscommunication, partners are likely to blame each other rather than to think of the conflict as a *problem* that can be solved. As difficulties arise and hostilities and misunderstandings proliferate, partners lose sight of the positive things their mate provides and represents— somebody to support them, to enhance their experiences, to share in building a family. Ultimately they may doubt the relationship itself and so foreclose on the opportunity to unravel the knots that twist their understandings.

Untangling the Knots

Working with my students—psychiatrists, psychologists, and social workers—at the Center for Cognitive Therapy at the University of Pennsylvania, I found that we could help these distressed couples by correcting their misinterpretations, untying the knots that twisted their communication, and tuning up their abilities to see and hear their partners' signals accurately. Further, we found that they profited greatly from being educated about the dynamics of marriage—how to understand their partners' sensitivities and needs, how to make joint plans and decisions, how to enjoy each other more.

The same program can enhance marriages that are not in trouble. It has proved effective with couples living together as well as those planning to marry. In fact, some of the most dramatic successes have occurred in partners who were completely committed to each other but wanted to get still more out of their relationship.

As the cognitive approaches have caught on over the past decade, an increasingly large number of professionals throughout the world have begun using them. On the basis of their careful record keeping and research at our center and at centers elsewhere, it is apparent that this approach has helped large numbers of distressed couples.

Among the graduates of our training program, Drs. Norman Epstein, Jim Pretzer, and Barbara Fleming have been the most active in conducting and publishing research on the cognitive aspects of marital difficulties, and in applying their insights to treatment. Drs. Janis Abrahms, David Burns, Frank Dattilio, Stowe Hausner, Susan Joseph, Chris Padesky, and Craig Wiese are other cognitive therapists who have pioneered clinical treatment approaches in marital therapy.

In view of the success of cognitive therapy as used by psychotherapists and marriage counselors, the time is ripe to share our insights with the public. This book should be useful to mates of every kind—housemates, roommates, bedmates—and of the same, as well as the opposite, sex. People who have kinks in their relationships can use the book to understand them better and to work out solutions on their own. Those couples whose problems require the assistance of a professional should find the book helpful as a preparation for such counseling and, it is hoped, as an incentive to get further help. The material in the book has also proven useful to couples already receiving counseling.

The purpose of this book is not to describe a "marriage pathology" but to define the nature of ordinary marital difficulties in a precise way so as to clarify their primary causes. Once the various components of the problems have been exposed, we can begin to talk about how they can be solved. I emphasize the problems early in this book because that is the way difficulties are presented. Later, as you gain insight into the problems, you can start to solve them.

The Plan of the Book

By first pinpointing problems and then solving them, I have arranged the chapters similarly to the way in which I conduct a series of clinical sessions.

The first nine chapters deal with different problem areas. Almost every partner in a troubled marriage will recognize difficulties in these chapters that resemble those in his or her own relationship. Sometimes the problem is obvious: there is more beneath the surface than meets the eye with respect to what people think and feel and how they act toward each other. In my work with patients, however, I sometimes have to peel back several layers to get to the heart of a problem. And, at times, one problem sends out roots to other areas, some hidden from view.

The cognitive approach gets to the roots of marital difficulties by focusing on hidden as well as obvious here-and-now problems rather than by reviving early childhood traumas.

To help readers determine the nature of their marital problems, I have included questionnaires at the ends of or in the text of several chapters. Readers can use these inventories to pinpoint their specific problems with their partner, such as unrealistic expectations, inadequate communication, and biased interpretations. When we move on to the remedies, they can review their answers to these questionnaires to help identify their problems, a necessary step toward solving them.

In my clinical practice, I first try to understand a couple's difficulty by analyzing their descriptions and their responses to these questionnaires. I then can prepare for each couple a "cognitive profile" that highlights their particular trouble area. As does the physician who attempts to diagnose a medical ailment through physical examination, laboratory tests, and X rays, I use all the information at hand to make a "marital diagnosis."

Readers of this book can follow the same sequence, first understanding and identifying the specific nature of their marital problems, and then selecting appropriate strategies for dealing with them.

After getting a clear picture of a troubled couple's specific self-defeating attitudes and distortions in thinking and communication, I explain the nature of their problems to them. I have done the same in this book, devoting the first nine chapters to each of the problems most common in marriage: (1) the power of negative thinking: how negative perceptions can overwhelm positive aspects of a marriage; (2) the swing from idealization to disillusionment: why the image of the partner shifts from all good to all bad; (3) the clash of differing perspectives: how partners can see the same event—and each other—in completely different ways; (4) the imposition of rigid expectations and rules: how setting up fixed standards leads to frustration and anger; (5) the static in communication: how partners fail to hear what is said and often hear things that are not said; (6) the conflicts over making important decisions and the breakdown of the partnership: how personal bias and incompetence disrupt its operations; (7) the role of "automatic thoughts" that precede anger and self-defeating behavior: how negative thinking leads to provocation and rage; (8) thinking disorders and biases that are at the core of the problem: how cognitive distortions operate; and (9) the hostility that drives couples apart.

In Chapters 10 to 18 I present a variety of cognitive therapy approaches that partners can tailor to fit their own specific needs and to achieve the goals of their relationship. The "help" chapters start with the question of how couples can overcome the resistances and discouragement that keep them from improving their relationships. It is crucial that people recognize that they *do* have choices—that they are *not* simply victims of a bad relationship, no matter how hopeless it may seem. They can and should take responsibility for their relationships. These chapters show how.

I then take up the basic values of marriage, such as commitment, loyalty, and trust, and describe methods to neutralize the forces that undermine these foundations. It is essential to rebuild or reinforce those building blocks that make the relationship solid (Chapter 11). I go on to show how you can increase the sweet, loving parts of your relationship and reduce the sour, irritating parts. What are the things you can do to demonstrate to your partner that you care? I include a questionnaire for you to use as a guide in evaluating how well you and your spouse are doing in demonstrating consideration, empathy, and understanding (Chapter 12). In Chapter 13, I present concrete examples of how you can correct your distortions and adjust your thinking to reality. Then I shift the focus to the way in which partners talk to each other and show how talking can be a source of pleasure rather than pain (Chapter 14). Chapter 15 shows how you can clarify your differences in preparation for your joint troubleshooting sessions, which are explained in Chapter 16.

After you have eliminated the bugs in conversation and have tackled the practical problems of living together, you are ready to confront those characteristics and habits of your mate that infuriate you (Chapter 17). Finally, in Chapter 18 you will be able to apply the insights from the previous chapters to solving special problems, such as stress, sexual inhibition, infidelity, and the conflicts that arise when both partners work.

My assumption is that, at least initially, this book is being read by only one member of a couple. Consequently, my focus is on what he or she individually can do to be helped and so, in turn, help the marriage. Often, changes in one partner can produce remarkable changes in the other. As you become more knowledgeable about the sources of and solutions for marital problems, your changes can favorably affect your mate's behavior.

In sum, in this book I discuss how partners can correct their self-defeating patterns of thinking and counterproductive habits, improve communication, and help to clarify and modify their mate's problems. Finally, I discuss how they can work together to eliminate miscommunication, to make their relationship enjoyable and fulfilling.

In evaluating your relationship, you will find it useful to keep in mind your goals in marriage and how you can best achieve them. As a guide, I have listed what I regard as the aims for an ideal marriage.

First, strive for a solid foundation of trust, loyalty, respect, and security. Your spouse is your closest relative and is entitled to depend on you as a committed ally, supporter, and champion.

Second, cultivate the tender, loving part of your relationship: sensitivity, consideration, understanding, and demonstrations of affection and caring. Regard each other as confidante, companion, and friend.

Third, strengthen the partnership. Develop a sense of cooperation, consideration, and compromise. Sharpen your communication skills so that you can more easily make decisions about practical issues, such as division of work, preparing and implementing a family budget, and planning leisure-time activities.

Also essential to the partnership is setting policy regarding the care, education, and socialization of children. Foster a spirit of collaboration. Marriage is at once a business, a child care and educational institution, and a social unit. It is important that the approach to these "institutional" functions of marriage be carried out with reciprocity, fairness, and reasonableness.

As with most books directed toward helping people with their problems, this one has a guiding philosophy:

▷ Couples can overcome their difficulties if they recognize first that much of their disappointment, frustration, and anger stems not from a basic incompatibility but from unfortunate misunderstandings that result from faulty communications and biased interpretations of each other's behavior.

▷ Misunderstanding is often an *active process* that results when one spouse develops a distorted picture of the other. This distortion in turn leads to the spouse's misinterpreting what the other says or does and attributing undesirable motives to him or her. Partners simply are not in the habit of "checking out" their interpretations or focusing on the clarity of their communications.

▷ Each partner should take full responsibility for improving the relationship. You need to realize that you do have choices—you can (and should) choose to use whatever knowledge and insights you can gather to make yourself and your partner happier.

▷ Partners can help themselves, each other, and the relationship if they adopt a "no fault, no blame" attitude. This approach will allow them to focus on the real problems and solve them more readily.

▷ Actions by your partner that you attribute to some malevolent trait, such as selfishness, hatefulness, or the need to control you, are often most accurately explained in terms of benign (although misguided) motives like self-protectiveness or attempts to prevent abandonment.

Although this book is designed to educate and provide guidelines, it cannot have the same impact on a seriously disturbed marriage as would a counselor using the same principles and methods. However, I am convinced that many couples who would not ordinarily need or seek counseling can be helped by this book. After reading it, some couples may be motivated to obtain professional help themselves, or to use it in conjunction with counseling.

Many people who read this book may not view their marriage as troubled, but still suspect that somehow it could be more rewarding. Perhaps a couple want to regain their former pleasure at being tuned in to each other's thoughts, of being able to make suggestions spontaneously, of arriving at decisions without wrangling. This book offers hints to cut through the underbrush that impedes solving your joint problems, to untwist the knots that frustrate mutual understanding. With an increased understanding of what makes you and your partner tick, you will be able to enrich your relationship.

THE
POWER OF
NEGATIVE THINKING

Karen, an interior designer, described how she came home one day flushed with excitement and eager to discuss some good news with her husband, Ted. She had just been awarded a lucrative contract to decorate the offices of a prominent law firm. But when she started to tell Ted about this unexpected success in her career, he seemed distant and uninvolved. She thought, *"He doesn't really care about me. He's only interested in himself."* Her excitement evaporated. Instead of celebrating with him, Karen went into another room and poured herself a glass of champagne. Meanwhile, Ted—who was feeling somewhat dejected that day because of a setback in his career—had the thought, *"She doesn't really care about me. She's only interested in her own career."*

This incident highlights a common pattern we have observed in people with marital problems. When spouses' high expectations are thwarted, they are prone to jump to negative conclusions about the partner's state of mind and the state of the marriage. Relying on what amounts to mind reading, the disillusioned spouse jumps to damning conclusions about the cause of the trouble: *"She's acting this way because she's bitchy"* or *"He's being this way because he's filled with hate."*

As a result of such explanations, the injured spouse may attack or withdraw from the partner. And the partner, who very likely feels unjustly punished, usually retaliates by counterattacking or withdrawing. And so begins a vicious cycle of attack and retaliation that can easily whirl into other areas of the relationship.

Interpreting a partner's motives in this way is fraught with danger, simply because we cannot read other people's minds. For instance, what Karen did not know was that Ted had been feeling depressed over a reversal in his accounting business and was anxious to discuss it with her. Karen had no way of finding this out because she left the room in a fury. She assumed that he was just too preoccupied with himself to notice her.

But her angry withdrawal in itself had many meanings for Ted: *"She's running out on me for no good reason"* and *"Once again this proves she doesn't care about how I feel."* These explanations added to Ted's sense of isolation and hurt. Ted, on the other hand, contributed to the disconnections in the relationship through his preoccupation with his own problems. In the past, when Karen would become excited about an experience or a new idea, he would start to analyze it rather than tune in emotionally to her enthusiasm.

This kind of misunderstanding and mutual mind reading is far more frequent in relationships than most couples realize. Rather than seeing that there is a misunderstanding, conflicting partners misattribute the problem to the mate's "meanness" or "selfishness." Unaware that they are misreading their spouses, partners incorrectly ascribe base motives to them.

Although many popular writings have focused on the expression of anger in intimate relationships, and how to deal with it, there has been scant attention paid to the misconceptions and miscommunications that are so often responsible for the anger and conflict. How one spouse *perceives and interprets* what the other does can be far more important in determining marital satisfaction than those actions themselves.

To avoid such marital misconceptions, it helps to understand how the mind functions—and malfunctions—when we are frustrated or disappointed. Our fallible mental apparatus predisposes us to misinterpret or exaggerate the meaning of other people's behavior, to make negative explanations when we are disappointed, and to project a negative image onto these people. We then act on these misinterpretations—attacking the very negative image that we have projected.

It rarely occurs to us at that moment that our negative judgment could be wrong, and that we are attacking a distorted image. For instance, when frustrated by Ted's moods, Karen projected an image of him as a kind of mechanical man, incapable of expressing feeling to another person. At the same time, Ted saw Karen as one of the Furies, filled with hate and vengeance. Whenever one of them would disappoint the other, these extreme images took over their minds and fueled their anger.

The Cognitive Approach

By using a set of simple principles that are part of cognitive therapy, couples can counteract the tendency to make such unjustified judgments and to project distorted images of each other. These principles can help each mate arrive at more accurate and reasonable conclusions, and thus prevent the cycle of misunderstanding that leads to marital conflicts and hostilities. Cognitive therapy has shown that partners can learn to be more reasonable with each other by adopting a more humble, tentative attitude about the accuracy of their mind reading, and its resulting negative conclusions; by checking out the accuracy of their mind reading; and by considering alternative explanations for what a partner does.

If Karen had been able to resist her inclination to portray Ted as uncaring and cold, and questioned him about what was preoccupying him, she might have been able to cheer him up to the point where they both could have celebrated her success. And if Ted had allowed himself to find out what Karen wanted, he could have avoided painting a negative image of her as cold and unsympathetic. But to do this, both would first need to realize that their conclusions could be incorrect and their anger could be unjustified or, at least, exaggerated.

The cognitive principles that helped Karen and Ted and other couples eventually to reach this point of self-understanding are the following:

▷ We can never really know the state of mind—the attitudes, thoughts, and feelings—of other people.

▷ We depend on signals, which are frequently ambiguous, to inform us about the attitudes and wishes of other people.

▷ We use our own coding system, which may be defective, to decipher these signals.

▷ Depending on our own state of mind at a particular time, we may be biased in our method of interpreting other people's behavior, that is, how we decode.

▷ The degree to which we believe that we are correct in divining another person's motives and attitudes is not related to the actual accuracy of our belief.

Cognitive therapy, which incorporates these principles, focuses on the way mates perceive, misperceive, and fail to perceive each other, and the way they communicate, miscommunicate, and fail to communicate. The cognitive approach is designed to remedy these distortions and deficits in thinking and communication. Its basic strategies and techniques are described in detail in Chapter 13.

The essence of marital cognitive therapy consists of exploring with troubled partners their unrealistic expectations, self-defeating attitudes, unjustified negative explanations, and illogical conclusions. Through a tune-up of their ways of drawing conclusions about each other and talking to each other, partners have been helped by cognitive therapy to relate to each other in a more reasonable, less hostile way.

Mind Reading

Lois, an attractive young woman who managed a stylish retail clothing store, tried to explain to herself why Peter, her fiancé, was silent on the way home from a party. Usually quite talkative, Peter sold ads for a suburban newspaper, which is how the two had met. When he became quiet, Lois thought, *"Peter isn't saying anything . . . he must be angry at me."* In trying to read his mind, Lois attributed Peter's silence to his anger at her. Her explanation for what she *believed* Peter was thinking and feeling—her mind reading—did not end there. Lois then thought, *"I must have done something to offend him."* Having established—in her own mind—that Peter was angry at her because of something she had done, she made the prediction *"Peter will continue to be angry at me and eventually break off our relationship."* She then felt sad in anticipation of being alone for the rest of her life.

But Lois was off-target. She had gotten caught in a web of inferences about invisible causes and unknowable consequences. A different woman in Lois's situation might simply have said to herself, *"Peter will probably get over it in a few minutes."* The bare fact of Peter's silence could fit either assessment.

Mind reading can produce inaccurate predictions resulting either in unnecessary upset or in what could prove to be a false sense of security. And such erroneous conclusions can lead to even greater troubles. If Lois acted on her mind reading, she could sabotage herself by withdrawing or lashing back at Peter—a reaction that might mystify him, alienate him, or provoke him to anger.

In this instance, Lois had misread Peter's behavior. He was simply in a contemplative mood. She began to sulk and would not respond when he finally spoke. When she failed to respond, he became angry and started to criticize her. Lois, in turn, took the criticism as validation of her accurate mind reading, and she felt even worse. She reasoned that what she had feared was finally happening: Peter was fed up with her.

This kind of self-fulfilling prophecy is typical of problematic relationships. By misinterpreting the behavior of their partners, people help to bring about what they most want to avoid.

Because what people say and do can be ambiguous or misleading, it is not always easy to assess just how they feel about us or what their motives might be. Thus, Lois—because of her fears of rejection—was prone to interpret Peter's silence as a sign of his anger with her. Although it is natural to read signs and look for patterns to tell what is going on in another person's mind, we risk forming erroneous explanations and drawing wrong conclusions.

The Invisible Mind

Take this incident from my own life: While I am earnestly trying to explain my pet theory to my wife, she suddenly smiles. I wonder, *"Is she smiling because she likes what I said? Or is she mocking me? Or is she amused because she thinks my theory is naive?"* Even when I have other information available, such as our past history together, I may be at a loss to understand what is behind her smile.

What is crucial to me is not what I can see and hear—her facial expression and tone of voice—but something that will forever be inaccessible to my senses; namely, her state of mind. Other people's attitudes toward us, their feelings about us, and their motives in regard to us are just as real as their words, gestures, and expressions. As I discuss my work with my wife, the essential reality—what I really care about—is not her overt behavior, not what she says, but her *true attitude* regarding my ideas—and me.

When we interact with others, we rarely have the time to mull over all the evidence to deduce their real thoughts and feelings. Since the clues are so often equivocal, we depend on fleeting observations of unclear messages, some of which may be deliberately contrived to deceive us. It is not surprising that we sometimes err.

Consider our dilemma. Our sense of one of the most important aspects of our reality—how people feel about us—must be based largely on facts that are not directly observable. Since such "internal" states are beyond the reach of our senses, we rely on our inferences about what we can observe. Problems arise because we tend to believe, as does Lois, our inferences—our mind reading—as much as we believe something that we directly observe.

Of course, being able to tell the true causes of what others do is crucial if we are to know when to reach out and when to pull back. Since this understanding is so central to our sense of security and to our intimate relationships, we constantly mind read—as did Karen and Ted—and automatically regard these guesses as facts. Despite the ambiguities, we manage to make fairly accurate guesses much of the time. If we have a trusting relationship with the other person— for example, our spouse—we can check out our guesses by asking that person what he or she is really feeling.

In the incident I have just described, the various guesses that went through my mind were all wrong! When I checked them out with my wife, she enlightened me regarding the real reason for her smile: my explanation of my theory had touched on an amusing experience she had recently had, and it was the memory of this experience—not my theory—that had made her smile!

When we are caught up in an emotional state, the vagueness of what we observe can trip us up. When we are upset or excited, our interpretations of other people's thoughts and feelings, the "invisible reality," are likely to be based more on our own internal states, our fears and expectations, than on a reasonable evaluation of the other person. We are unlikely to consider alternative explanations for what we see and hear, and our conclusions are more unyielding.

The pattern of jumping to conclusions is highlighted in clinical problems such as depression and anxiety. In these disorders there is a shift in the way people process information, a shift which leads to a negative bias in making observations. Furthermore, they tend to form these negative conclusions very rapidly, on shreds and fragments of evidence. A depressed wife, for example, may react to her husband's fatigued look with the immediate thought that *"He's sick and tired of me."* An anxious husband reacts to his wife's consistently not appearing at a specified time for an appointment with the thought that *"She might have been killed in an accident."* In neither case do they pause to consider the alternatives—his fatigue, her chronic lateness.

All too often, the way we think in daily life is similar to the thinking found in emotional disorders such as depression and anxiety: we come to a snap judgment based on a slender thread of evidence—or no evidence at all.

The ways in which people think often get muddled as they move from a specific interpretation to generalizations. For example, Lois proceeded from the interpretation that Peter was angry at her to the broader idea that *"Peter is always mad at me."* She then slipped into an even more serious overgeneralization—*"I always offend people"* —and she felt sad. At this point, Lois was so much in the grip of her negative ideas that she could not see there might be another explanation for Peter's silence.

Lois's generalization about herself not only made her feel worse but interfered with her finding out whether Peter was, indeed, angry at her. Another less sensitive, more secure person in her situation might wonder, *"Is Peter actually mad at me right now? If he is mad, what should I do?"* But for Lois, such logical reasoning was derailed by her hasty generalization that Peter was always angry at her and that she always offended people. Once these negative ideas had diverted her attention from her original question— *"Why is he silent?"* —she sabotaged the harmony of their relationship.

Other generalizations can intrude to aggravate the problem. Lois reached a further conclusion: *"The reason I always offend people is because I have no personality."* This sort of explanation can acquire "fact" status in one's thinking, and become the basis for still more unpleasant deductions and predictions. For example, Lois then thought, *"Since I have no personality, nobody will ever like me and I will always be lonely."* At this point, she was at risk not only of alienating her boyfriend but of becoming depressed!

Lois progressed from an objective observation of Peter's silence to a negative view of herself— *"I have no personality"* —and then to a dismal view of her future: *"I will always be alone."* Although such erroneous conclusions are based on fuzzy clues, they come to acquire the full force of truth, particularly when crucial relationship issues such as acceptance and rejection are involved. What begins as an inference becomes a "fact," just as "real" as the original observation.

At this point, it would be helpful to review the flow of Lois's thoughts, in which we can see the gradual snowballing of negative ideas, leading to her feeling alone and abandoned.

Why is he silent?

▽

He must be angry at me.

▽

I must have done something to offend him.

▽

He will continue to be angry at me.

▽

He is always angry at me.

▽

I always offend people.

▽

Nobody will ever like me.

▽

I will always be alone.

17

How We Misinterpret

If we could evaluate all the evidence in a situation before reaching a conclusion, we would then be less likely to make such mistakes. However, we rarely have the time to make carefully weighed, logical deductions. We have to rely on a quick interpretation, "reading the signs," as in the mystery of my wife's smile and the puzzle of Peter's silence.

Signs are actually bits of data—a string of words, a gesture—that we translate into usable information. A foreign language newspaper, for instance, consists of lines of printed symbols. but these symbols are meaningless unless we can read the language. In order to transform what we see into something comprehensible, we have to apply our coding system. If the printing is wrong, or if our coding system contains errors, or if we don't apply it properly because of inexperience or fatigue, then the result is misinformation and, of course, an erroneous conclusion.

We develop our interpersonal coding sysem early in life. It tells us the meanings of such observations as a person's tone of voice, facial expression, or gesture. From the context and other observations, we weave the meanings into a conclusion. Since we feel more secure when we believe we know other people's motives and feelings about us, we feel more confident about the conclusions we draw than the evidence justifies.

The major advantage of this coding system is that it provides immediate explanations. Its disadvantage is that it can easily be wrong: we may incorrectly read rejection when our partner is distracted; we may mistakenly assume anger when our spouse is tense and anxious; most important, we may erroneously attribute malice when our mate simply forgot to keep a promise.

Even well-intentioned, loving partners can get into fights and hurt each other because of such misinterpretations. Sometimes the misunderstanding is simply based on faulty communication, as in the case of Marjorie's not informing Ken that she preferred to shop alone. At other times—and perhaps more seriously—the misunderstanding arises because the words or deeds of one partner unwittingly pose a threat to the other. The cause of the fight, consequently, is not the words or deeds per se, but the *meaning* that the partner attaches to them. The meaning, of course, is not apparent to the offending partner, who often believes that the spouse "should have known better."

Signals constitute the kind of signs used in communication. Emotions and feelings, for example, are never communicated directly, but instead through the media of words, tone of voice, facial expressions, and actions. The context, of course, is crucial in interpreting the signal. A waitress serving coffee and toast is signaling a business transaction; a husband serving his wife coffee and toast in bed is signaling caring and affection.

Such signals form the fabric of close relationships, yet their importance is often overlooked in marriage. They carry far more meaning than would be obvious from a literal reading of the specific behavior. In the theme song from the movie *Casablanca*, the lyrics "A kiss is still a kiss, a sigh is just a sigh . . ." serve to highlight the fact that a kiss is not just a kiss. Signals like these are symbols of love and affection, and when they fade from an intimate relationship—or operate on different wavelengths, as in the case of Karen and Ted—their absence takes on a symbolic meaning, such as rejection or lack of interest.

Symbolic meanings can draw people together or drive them apart. A wife described to me how deeply moved she had been during her courtship whenever her fiancé took her to expensive restaurants and sent flowers. Even though she realized intellectually that this attention did not necessarily mean that he cared for her, the "deeper" meaning was so strong that she was always greatly moved by the gesture.

But after they were married, she started to react to "negative symbols." Whenever he would come home late without having called her, she assumed that he didn't care about her. Even though he would often cite his legitimate lack of access to a telephone, the symbolic meaning of his not calling was so strong that she could not revise it in her mind. Further, his waning attention to wining and dining her and sending her flowers also symbolized to her that he no longer cared.

Since signs and symbols are not the real thing, they have to be translated. Sometimes the coding system is deficient, and a spouse fails to read the signal: a husband may fail to recognize that his wife's withdrawal is a cry for help; a wife may not identify her husband's mock enthusiasm as a cover for profound disappointment.

Some people are more likely than others to attach symbolic meanings to certain specific situations. Men, for example, are more likely to regard conversation simply as a medium for transmitting facts, while women are more likely to engage in it as an end in itself, as a symbol of caring and friendship. Because of these sex differences in the symbolic meaning of communication, misunderstandings can arise between partners.

In close relationships, we are less flexible in using our coding system than in more impersonal situations. In fact, the more intense a relationship, the greater the possibility of misunderstanding. More than any other intimate tie, marriage presents continual opportunities for the misreading of signs.

Misreading the Signals

Marjorie and Ken met while they were both in college. They had the proverbial storybook romance. He was an outstanding athlete and she was the prom queen. After a whirlwind courtship, they were married. He became an insurance salesman and she became a secretary in a large firm.

From the beginning of their marriage, there were problems. Verbal, competent, overqualified for her job as a secretary but lacking the self-confidence to try anything better, Marjorie wanted more support and nurturing than Ken was willing (or able) to give her. Ken, who was not as successful in his career as he had been in college athletics, depended on her earnings to maintain the kind of standard of living enjoyed by his more successful friends from college.

A typical confrontation occurred after five years of marriage. Following a difficult day in the office, Marjorie started to complain about the working conditions to Ken.

MARJORIE: I'm fed up with the job. I really should quit. Harry [the boss] is always giving me a hard time. He's always picking on me.

KEN: [*She's planning to quit the job. If she quits, we won't be able to manage.* Feels anxious. *How can she do this? She doesn't care about me and the children.* Feels outraged.] You always do things impulsively.

MARJORIE: [*He doesn't trust me. He should know I would not quit the job.* Feels hurt.] I'm just trying to tell you . . .

KEN: [*This is awful. I've got to stop her from thinking this way.*] (Loudly) I don't want to hear any more about it!

MARJORIE: [*He doesn't care about me. That's why he won't listen to me and yells at me.* Feels more hurt and angry. Starts to cry and runs to the bedroom.]

KEN: [*She always does this to make me feel guilty.*] Don't you run out on me!

Consider the crucial importance of the meaning the partners attach to each other's words and deeds. Marjorie wants and expects empathy from Ken. She is saying, in effect, *"I'm in pain and I want you to comfort me."* But Ken translates her complaint (signal) into a threat. According to his coding system, when people complain about something, it means they will take some action, usually a rash one. Thus, in his automatic thinking, a complaint about a job means "will quit."

Such hidden fears often trigger hostile reactions. Because he reads Marjorie's mind incorrectly, Ken not only fails to respond to her wish for sympathy, but he also condemns her. Marjorie reacts to his condemnation with a sense of injustice and isolation. Her reaction when she feels hurt and annoyed is to cry and withdraw. Her withdrawal—which comes from a feeling of being abandoned—is then interpreted by Ken in a still more negative way, as a sign of manipulativeness—that she is trying to make him feel guilty. Consequently, the angry exchange (the criticism and withdrawal) takes on a reality of its own.

This vignette illustrates several features of coding systems. The meaning of a communication, while crystal clear to the sender, is often unclear to the receiver. Decoding the message, in essence, requires reading the sender's mind. However, we often have peculiar ways of decoding the message; consequently, we are often wrong. In addition, the signals can be ambiguous, subject to quite different interpretations. Also, we sometimes read hidden meanings where there are none.

Once people attach a meaning to an event, they are likely to accept it as valid without further confirmation of its accuracy. If Ken had checked out his initial mind reading by asking Marjorie a question (for instance, "Are you thinking of quitting?"), he might have corrected his misconception at the outset. If Marjorie had not been carried away by the meaning she attached to his criticism (*"He doesn't trust me"*), she might have made a more robust attempt to correct his misconception. Further, once the attack-and-withdraw sequence occurs, the meaning each partner attaches to the other's hostile actions thwarts a clarification of the initial misunderstanding.

Partners should check their mind reading, either by asking directly or by making further observations of their mate's actions. They will often find that their mind reading is incorrect. By disproving their interpretations based on mind reading, they have an additional payoff, namely, they can correct their coding system for understanding their spouse—reprogram their computer, as it were. This technique helps them to be more accurate in knowing what their partner is actually thinking and feeling so the relationship can be more harmonious.

Cognitive therapy increases people's awareness of how they form such conclusions, and it encourages them to think of alternative explanations. This kind of therapy explores the signs and symbols that people typically misinterpret and helps them to arrive at more accurate conclusions, a great benefit to couples like Lois and Peter. We will see in later chapters the specific principles that were used to help Karen and Ted, as well as Ken and Marjorie.

Symbols and Meaning

In intimate relationships, certain kinds of situations have especially strong meanings. Such meanings are not based on the actual event but are derived from the important assumptions that one mate makes about the other's actions.

When a person's coding system is put into words, it is found to consist of a hodgepodge of beliefs, assumptions, rules, preconceptions, and formulas. As he discovered in therapy, Ken's underlying assumptions were *"If Marjorie complains, she will take some impulsive action"* and *"She likes to manipulate me by crying."* Marjorie's assumptions were *"If Ken is angry, it means he doesn't love me"* and *"If he misunderstands my motives, we can't communicate."*

The actual interpretations of events are shaped by these beliefs. If Marjorie believes that a loud voice means rejection, then she can only experience rejection when Ken raises his voice. If her belief holds that anger and rejection lead to abandonment, then she feels desolate —all alone—when Ken yells at or misunderstands her.

When an event consistently evokes highly personalized meanings, it becomes a symbol. When a person attaches a symbolic meaning (love, rejection, freedom) to an event, his or her reaction may be *excessive*, involve some *distortion* of the situation, and lead to *multiple meanings*. Lois, for example, perceived Peter's silence as a symbol of rejection. Her symbolic interpretation had a ripple effect: she started to blame herself for the supposed rejection and to project a bleak chain of events into the future.

Though myriad symbols apply to married life, there are two major kinds of symbolic events that trigger excessive reactions. The first group of symbolic events revolves around the theme of caring and not caring. At the positive pole are symbols of affection, love, and consideration. At the negative pole are symbols of rejection, thoughtlessness, and lack of understanding. The specific misunderstandings of Karen and Ted, Marjorie and Ken, Lois and Peter, revolved around these negative symbols.

The second group of symbolic events in marriage involves the theme of pride. The positive symbols center on the theme of respect, while the negative symbols involve the theme of disrespect or even contempt. Spouses who feel loved and accepted can still be hypersensitive to any message that suggests that they are being belittled or depreciated. We will see later how equality became a big issue in the relationship between Ken and Marjorie.

In the following dialogue, the symbolic meaning is *"You underestimate me."*

KEN: I've decided that we need to get a new boiler.

MARJORIE: [Puzzled. *Why didn't he consult me first before he decided?*] Why do we need a new boiler?

KEN: [*She doesn't have much respect for my judgment.*] We're getting it because we need it.

MARJORIE: [*He's annoyed at me for asking. He doesn't think that I can have an opinion.* Feels hurt.] I still don't see why we need a new boiler.

KEN: You never can trust my judgment on anything, can you!

Because of the symbolic meanings they read into each other's remarks, Marjorie and Ken felt slighted by each other. If their words had not triggered these symbolic meanings, the initial statements could have been taken at their face value, or any negative interpretations could have been readily corrected. However, since they each read more into the situation than was intended, they both overreacted, and neither sought to verify the interpretations. Each partner was too caught up in hurt and anger.

In order to understand their hypersensitivities and overreactions, couples need to become aware of the symbolic meanings of the specific events that produce the exaggerated negative reactions. Marjorie and Ken could have prevented their overreactions. But they would have had to catch these reactions *as they occurred,* and then corrected their erroneous symbolic interpretations and conclusions (as explained in Chapters 8 and 13). But Ken was too miffed to accept Marjorie's question ("Why do we need a new boiler?") as a reasonable inquiry, and to answer it as such. The chain reaction of mind reading, attaching symbolic meanings, and misunderstandings had begun.

Bias

Some of the misunderstandings that beset a marriage have their roots in the rigid thinking that underlies prejudice of all kinds. The biased expectations, observations, and conclusions that form a prejudice reflect the frame of mind known technically as a "negative cognitive set." When a husband has framed his wife within this set, for example, he will interpret virtually everything she says or does in a negative way.

Prejudice can twist our interpretations not just of others but of ourselves. There is a form of prejudice in people with low self-esteem; in this instance, the target of their prejudice is themselves rather than others. Such people are intensely concerned with the meanings of their interactions with other people, especially with what others think of them. But because their self-esteem is low, they tend to apply their preconceptions and make unjustified negative interpretations of how others regard them.

Lois is typical of such a person. Before she became so upset over her fiancé's silence, she had had many animated discussions with him. But the one time that Peter was quiet wiped out, for her, these clearly positive experiences. Her assumption was that *"When somebody is quiet, it is a sign that he doesn't like me."* Once this assumption was activated, Lois's view of Peter and herself became dominated by it. It never occurred to her that her assumption might not apply to Peter. Interestingly, Lois came from a family in which the "silent treatment" was used frequently to punish an offending member.

The prejudice that people with low self-esteem direct against themselves includes a web of negative attitudes. The thoughts that Lois had about Peter typify her responses to a variety of encounters. Lois's basic assumptions could be articulated as follows: *"If somebody doesn't like me now, he will* never *like me"*; *"If this person doesn't like me, then I am unlikable"*; and *"If I am unlikable, I will always be alone and unhappy."* Her assumptions predisposed her to interpret Peter's silence as she did—as signaling the rejection that would end their relationship.

Although each of Lois's assumptions could be proven groundless, they nevertheless exerted a powerful force on her thinking. Once the episode with Peter had occurred, the assumptions molded Lois's interpretations of their relationship. One of the thrusts of cognitive therapy is to expose such assumptions, to determine whether they have a realistic basis, and to change them accordingly (Chapter 13).

We can see what underlies many of the problems of committed relationships more clearly if we look at the exaggerated versions of these ways of thinking in people who have psychological disorders such as anxiety, depression, and hypochondriasis. Their system of coding particular events is uniformly biased. Depressed people, for instance, are likely to interpret ambiguous events in a way that *reflects badly* on themselves. A housewife, seeing that the children are squabbling, concludes, *"I am a failure as a mother."* An anxious person, on the other hand, sees *danger* in innocuous situations. A nervous husband whose wife is late for an appointment thinks, *"She was mugged."* And the hypochondriac interprets normal bodily sensations as signs of *serious disease:* slight faint feelings signify a brain tumor; heartburn indicates an impending heart attack, and a backache signals kidney disease.

Such people differ from "normal" people in that they ascribe much more importance to their conclusions and hold them far more tenaciously. They are much more likely to spot patterns that fit their own preconceptions, and to ignore information that does not fit these patterns. Paradoxically, they remain mired in their way of thinking even though it brings them great pain. Such "cognitive rigidity" is accentuated in most people when they are under stress.

We can learn a great deal from these psychological disorders because we see the same kind of thinking in distressed relationships when the prejudice is directed toward the partner. Research studies have shown that couples in distressed marriages can be reasonably objective in the motives they attribute to other couples; but, in the same situations, they inaccurately attribute negative motives to their own spouses.

Distressed couples often react to *each other* as though they themselves had a psychological disorder. Their thinking about their spouse shows bias like that seen in people with anxiety and depression. To them, their beliefs are real, their minds are open. Actually, they have closed minds and a closed perspective where their partner is concerned.

Hostile spouses, for example, do not realize that their view of their partner may be distorted by their state of mind and the beliefs that dominate them. When someone tries to correct these distortions—particularly the spouse—that person may well run into a wall of hostility. Angry people do not take kindly to having their views of reality contradicted, and they see the other person not only as wrong but as attempting to manipulate them or even deceive them.

When hostile spouses attempt to divine an invisible state—namely, their partner's emotions, thoughts, and motives—they are as convinced of their conclusions as they would be if they could see right into their spouse's mind. To them, their beliefs are not simply a conclusion but *reality*. To correct these conclusions requires the application of a number of strategies, as explained in Chapter 17.

On the other hand, during the infatuation of courtship and early married life, couples show a positive bias. Almost everything the partner says or does is interpreted in a positive light. He or she can do no wrong. But if the marriage runs into difficulties, the repeated disappointments, arguments, and frustrations lead to a change in mental attitude. Distressed, the partners shift from a positive to a negative bias. Then, much of what either of them does is interpreted in a negative light. He or she can do no right.

The power of negative thinking is demonstrated in our casual observations. How often have we heard a partner complain, "We had a great day together and then one stupid little thing happens and it spoils everything!" The power of the negative is shown in a number of research studies. What most of all distinguishes distressed marriages from satisfactory marriages is not so much the absence of pleasant experiences but the larger number of unpleasant experiences, or ones given that interpretation. The improvements that couples show in counseling are accompanied more by a reduction in unpleasant encounters than by an increase in pleasant events. Happiness seems to come more naturally when the negative experiences and negative interpretations are diminished.

Just as cognitive therapy can help patients with clinical anxiety or depression understand their erroneous thinking, the same principles can counteract the misunderstandings and biases of distressed marriages, such as those described in this chapter. But first it is important to understand the basis for such problems in thinking, and to learn how to identify them. Then, couples can test their interpretations and beliefs about each other, and correct them accordingly—rather than letting negative thinking spoil their happiness.

THE
LIGHT AND
THE DARKNESS

One of the mysteries in our society is how love, which can soar to the heights, can also trail off—leaving behind a cloud of disappointment, frustration, and resentment. One couple, who had anticipated a life of excitement together, drift into indifference and boredom. Another, who had shared all their enjoyments previously, now share only discontent and malaise. Still another, who had agreed previously on almost everything, now agree on nothing.

How does a couple shift from illusion to disillusionment, from enchantment to disenchantment, from supreme satisfaction to dissatisfaction?

Consider Karen and Ted, a couple who consulted me because they "could not get along" together. Karen was the successful interior designer and Ted the accountant mentioned in Chapter 1. They both wanted to understand why they were constantly fighting and to recapture the feelings they had had for each other during courtship and the earlier part of their marriage. They were puzzled by their constant bickering; after all, Karen had a number of good friends and Ted had always gotten along well with other people at school and at work.

Karen and Ted had married when she was twenty-six and he was twenty-eight. Always rather lonely and serious, Ted had been attracted by Karen's lightness and carefree spirit. Her spontaneity amused him and her happy-go-lucky attitude offered an antidote to his seriousness. When Ted was with Karen, her joking, impulsiveness, and gaiety helped to lighten the heavy burden he felt he was carrying; her cheerfulness tempered his melancholy. They laughed together, enjoyed conversing and just being together.

As Ted's affection increased, he sang Karen's praises: "She's wonderful. Everything she says and does is charming. She really makes life meaningful for me." He thought about her constantly when they were apart, and every thought of her aroused in him a sense of longing, coupled with a feeling of euphoria. He wrote her long, passionate letters pledging his total devotion.

Within a few years, however, everything had changed. Ted became hypercritical of Karen. He was continuously annoyed at her: "She's a pain in the neck. She's an airhead. She's irresponsible. She never takes things seriously. She's superficial. She goes around with a vacuous smile. I can't depend on her."

Although Ted's attitude had changed from one of admiration to faultfinding, Karen's personality had not changed in any substantial way. Both Karen and Ted agreed on this point. What had changed was Ted's view of Karen, his "perspective" of her. It was as though he had switched lenses and so saw her differently. He now attached negative labels to the same qualities he had previously described so glowingly. The easygoing manner that he had once attributed to her free spirit, he now ascribed to her "flakiness," and what he saw before as playfulness, he now viewed as childishness.

Ted's responses to Karen illustrate an important principle of relationships. A change in perspective brings a change in feelings. Ted idealized Karen until the inevitable problems of living together arose. He then began to blame these difficulties on the same qualities he had previously admired: her spontaneity ("frivolousness"), lack of seriousness ("superficiality"), and changeability ("irresponsibility"). As his perspective shifted, he began to see Karen's qualities—and Karen herself—in a totally different way. He came to regard her as a drudge rather than a delight.

Ted had grown up in a middle-class family in which great emphasis was placed on correct behavior. Each evening his parents would have intellectual discussions with him that left little room for family fun and games. He matured into a serious, interesting adult. It was not until he met Karen that Ted was able to enjoy the lighter side of life. Initially, Karen's appeal lay in her ability to ease his burdens acquired during a childhood overly constrained by propriety and intellectuality. Later in their marriage, however, he began to judge Karen according to these same values, and he found her wanting.

Karen also underwent a shift in her view of Ted. She had originally seen him as brilliant, witty, stable, reliable, and conscientious. He had an encyclopedic knowledge of public affairs, history, and literature. She had greatly enjoyed listening to his long analyses of the political scene. After she read Robert Pirsig's *Zen and the Art of Motorcycle Maintenance*, she labeled Ted a classicist, directed toward getting things done properly; and herself a romanticist, more concerned with enjoying each moment. She delighted in teasing him about his stuffiness. When she was able to liven up Ted's life and get him to be more easygoing, she felt happy and worthwhile.

But once those qualities of Ted's that Karen found most attractive or challenging threatened to stifle her spontaneity, she started to view them in a completely different way. Instead of being intrigued by his logical, intellectual approach to problems, she now felt oppressed. Karen began to conclude, "I can't be myself when Ted is around. He dissects everything instead of enjoying it," and she became increasingly restless and irritable in his presence.

Karen had been reared in a family in which much dissension occurred between her parents and among her siblings. Her father, who had ongoing financial problems, was strict and remote in his relations with Karen and her two brothers. Although Karen tried to please him by doing well at school and being helpful at home, she received the message that her best was never good enough. Her mother, though nurturing, seemed overwhelmed by the demands of family life. Karen developed a strong need for a mate who, unlike her father, could provide a solid base of security and who would accept her completely —without her having to perform well to win acceptance. She found this solidity and acceptance in Ted. But later, when he started to judge her, she found herself in the same position she had occupied with her father.

Karen and Ted offer a good example of how a couple's thinking shapes their feelings toward each other. When they perceived each other in positive terms, they felt love; when they devalued each other, they felt resentment. This principle was expressed almost two thousand years ago by the stoic philosopher Epictetus in *The Enchiridion*: "Men are disturbed not by things, but by the view they take of them."

The case of Ted and Karen is not unusual. Many couples suffer a similar disillusionment but seem to strike a new balance. Other couples regard their disappointment as unique, without realizing that this experience is common. And just as the same forces that split apart other couples apply equally well to them, so do the principles that can draw couples back together again. Of course, there are couples who do maintain a high level of mutual respect and admiration, and consequently do not have a distressed marriage.

To see what can heal a rift between a couple, we first need to understand more fully how relationships, such as that of Ted and Karen, can dissolve. Paradoxically, the roots of trouble often go back to the very beginning, to the overpowering attraction that brought the partners together in the first place.

The Light: Infatuation

I need you to survive
Without it I'm just half alive. . . .
I'm forgetting all my pride
I couldn't leave you, girl, if I tried.

—Al Hamilton, Herman Weems, William Garrett, "I've Got to Have You"

Love's sweet mysteries have inspired romantic songs and poetry that capture the imperative do-or-die quality, as well as the exquisite rhapsodies, of this mysterious state. Even thoroughly disillusioned couples may still cling to the sentimental romantic notions of love expressed in songs, movies, and novels.

It may seem almost sacrilegious to dissect love, to reduce it to its basic psychological essentials, stripped of its poetry and glamour. Yet, in order to understand why people such as Ted and Karen fall out of love, we need to understand more about how they fall in love in the first place.

The feelings of love are, of course, among the most dramatic and cherished we have. Few people would forgo the intense pleasure, exhilaration, and excitement—despite the dark side of unfulfilled yearning, disappointment, and despair. Love in its most intense form, infatuation (which some regard as a kind of pseudo-love), is more than just intense feelings and yearnings; it also involves an alteration of consciousness. Expressions such as "floating on air," "feeling high," "head in the clouds," bespeak a blurring of focus and a drift from realistic evaluation and response—a euphoric dream.

Sometimes, the enchantment takes on the full force of a psychological disorder. In fact, infatuation has been described as a "kind of insanity." Its derivation from the Latin *fatuus,* "foolish," indicates its kinship with the concept of folly. The infatuated lover's unremitting preoccupation with thoughts and images of the loved person often shows hints of the obsessional neurosis. While she was smitten by Ted, Karen, for example, would repetitively write his name and had an irresistible urge to gaze at his picture.

This compulsion also leads to the irresistible desire to be with the loved one continuously. A student at a southern college, for example, felt driven to leave school in the middle of the term in order to be close to his girlfriend in a northern school. He was happy only when he was able to get close enough simply to watch her, to drink her in with his eyes, as it were, even though she was busy studying and attending classes and tried to ignore him.

Another young man, whose love also was not reciprocated, spent long hours standing outside the house of the object of his affections, hoping to catch an occasional glimpse of her through the window. Further, he ransacked the trash can for any objects associated with her—a piece of paper with her writing, a discarded facial tissue.

Some people find infatuation debilitating. As one young woman described it, "I became totally dependent on him. I had great trouble concentrating on my work. I could not sleep. I lost my appetite. I felt very vulnerable—as though his slightest disapproval would drive me over the brink." Such loss of control indicates the force of the infatuation.

Some aspects of infatuation resemble the thinking and feeling of the manic person. The illusory glow of love, consisting of magnification and idealization of the loved one's positive qualities, and tunnel vision—seeing only positive attributes and screening out negative ones—are found in the thinking typical of mania. The glossy picture of the loved one during infatuation is in stark contrast to the grim negative that emerges with disillusionment. At the peak of her infatuation with Ted, Karen could see in him only what she was looking for—despite her friends' suggestions that some of his qualities were worrisome. After their problems started, she could see only pedantry and restrictions.

Infatuation has been likened to an addiction by social psychologist Stanton Peele. The similarities throw additional light on the nature of love. The "highs"—the exalted, intoxicating, intensely pleasurable feelings—show a striking resemblance in both love and addiction. And the sad, empty feelings when the "intoxicant" (drug or loved one) is withdrawn are similar. Further, the compulsive need to get a "fix," to maintain the "high," is found in both conditions. Early in their relationship, for instance, Ted felt as though he were "taking off" when he was with Karen but would "crash" when they were apart, and he could not bear to wait until they were together again.

Many people in love, as we shall see, are so absorbed in its pleasures that they become oblivious to the possibility that the qualities evoking this high may be illusory. Even if they admit they may be unrealistic about the other person—that, for example, they have glossed over telling differences in personality, intellect, or interests —they seem unable to focus on or give weight to these potentially disruptive factors. When she was infatuated, it never occurred to Karen that Ted's emphasis on intellectual achievement and propriety could someday lead to her feeling judged and controlled. Infatuated lovers are gripped by a fantasy of sailing off with the loved person on a sea of permanent bliss, without being able to see that this could all be a mirage.

Still, infatuation serves a crucial role: it forges a powerful bond that spurs a couple to commit themselves to a relationship. Declarations of undying, eternal love, although often muted after the first few years of marriage, express the expectation of a permanent fusion. The gratification a couple experience by being together, sharing pleasures and problems, offers a strong incentive for forming such a partnership and perpetuating these pleasures.

Moreover, the expectation of regular sexual gratification serves as a major stimulus for the partners to live together and, presumably, to produce offspring. Sexual attraction sometimes is the first binding force in a relationship, and only later progresses into a full-blown infatuation. The staying power of such a sexual attraction frequently diminishes after marriage. Marjorie, for example, was continually turned on by Ken's masculinity—his muscular physique, athletic ability, and aura of authority—during their courtship. She could hardly wait to make love with him. Years later, these same masculine qualities were no longer "turn-ons." In Marjorie's mind they represented Ken's domination and insensitivity, which she found objectionable.

The Infatuation "Program"

What triggers infatuation is highly specific to an individual and depends on his or her particular psychological needs, preferences, and tastes. Thus, one person may respond to conventional criteria of attractiveness and beauty, while another person is drawn only to one type of build or particular coloring.

Although physical attractiveness is an especially powerful excitant, it is by no means the exclusive one. Some people are enchanted by social or personality traits such as grace, conversational skill, and humor. Others are attracted by virtues such as dependability, sincerity, and empathy. Still others are drawn by kindness, strength, or decisiveness.

Despite individual tastes, there is a remarkable universality about the nature of infatuation. The thoughts about and image of the loved person are the directing force. Although the emotions of love are more dramatic, the actual direction of the feelings comes from the view of the loved one.

The perspective of infatuated lovers is an idealization, or positive framing, analogous to the negative framing that occurs when love turns to aversion. The positive frame produces an idealized image of the lover that highlights the desirable features and shades the undesirable ones. At times, the attractive features expand until they fill the frame. In a sense, this perspective becomes "closed," so that not a single unpleasant element can enter the picture.

During courtship, even unpleasant behavior can be turned around and made positive. After a fight with Ken, Marjorie thought, *"His anger at me proves that he loves me."* She found it impossible to fit any negative observations into her image of him. Later, after marriage, when her feelings changed, she found the same angry outbursts to be intolerable.

The inability to modify the idealized perspective, even when the loved one's unpleasant traits become obvious, is a feature of the infatuation "program." Thus, a young man, who had been infatuated with a variety of women over a long period of time, found that during each period of infatuation, it was almost impossible to correct his unrealistic image. Once activated, the positive image controlled his attitude and feelings, even though he recognized intellectually that his partner had many undesirable features and that the relationship could not last.

Indeed, the infatuation program appears designed to prevent or at least downplay negative evaluations. Its thrust is to promote an intimate relationship by fixing all attention on positive images, memories, and expectations of the loved one. The program actively resists a shift in focus to the person's undesirable qualities or to possible deleterious, long-range effects of the relationship. People in the throes of infatuation sometimes realize that they have excessively idealized the object of their affection, that the passionate attachment is inappropriate, and that the long-range consequences could be disastrous. Yet, they find it difficult to attach much significance to this knowledge. Realistic considerations cannot penetrate the capsule of their infatuation.

When married people develop such an intense but inappropriate fixation to somebody other than their mate, they may be driven to jeopardize or even destroy a reasonable marital relationship. In the heat of passion, they seem incapable of attaching any real weight to the potentially disastrous consequences of their infatuation—the possible breakup of their marriage. They cannot "turn off" their infatuation even if they want to! Yet, when enough time has elapsed without their seeing "the other woman (or man)," they generally find that their infatuation dies down.

The "Turn-Ons" (Activators)

To understand further what impels couples to fall out of love, it is useful to examine what brings people together in the first place.

The characteristics that evoke feelings of excitement and the desire for intimacy are subject to the influence of symbols. Symbols convey a meaning that goes beyond the literal or dictionary definition of the object or situation itself. In the sense that we use the term, it refers to a highly personal meaning that produces an *automatic* effect in a person, without reflection or deliberation.

To Karen, Ted's steadiness was a symbol not only of security but of being taken care of by a strong "father figure." Karen's brightness symbolized to Ted the fun and enjoyment that were absent from his childhood.

The symbols that activate the infatuation program are often dictated by cultural fashions. The particular yearnings of a specific age group are also reflected in its corresponding symbols. Thus, we can see why adolescents—a group highly concerned with peer acceptance, but also troubled by doubts of social desirability—place a premium on achieving popularity, whether through personal attractiveness, athletic ability, or charisma. The idea of winning the affections of a socially desirable person is highly stimulating to an adolescent and may persist throughout life.

Other qualities, of course, can acquire the status of a symbol and, given the proper circumstances, evoke infatuation. Some of these qualities are narcissistic in the sense that a person becomes excited at the prospect of being paired with someone who will elevate his or her own status through power, prestige, or wealth. Such an attraction is not necessarily calculated and cold-blooded, as is sometimes assumed. The prospect of expansion of one's own domain, even if vicarious, through such a relationship is in itself exciting and makes the partner appear supremely desirable.

A woman, for instance, described her fiancé as follows: "He has enormous talent. He is going to make his mark on the world. With me to help him, he will be a tremendous success. He is larger than life." Several years later, when her overblown dreams were not realized, she recognized how much she had misled herself, how she had mistaken his ambition for ability, his facile glibness for brilliance. In this case, her own desire to be admired and praised by other people was wrapped up in her inflated evaluation of her fiancé.

The high pitch of excitement and mutual gratification during the early stage of infatuation often serves as a kind of standard by which couples judge the later stages of their marriage. The hurts, quarrels, and petty frustrations stand in stark contrast to the euphoria of the courtship period. Many people are unwilling or unable to relinquish their early image of what marriage should be like—which promotes later disillusionment with both the spouse and the relationship itself. Of course, we know couples who still feel the magic of the relationship for years after their marriage. Their fantasies appear to be realized, but they are in the minority.

The Darkness: Disillusionment

You and me, we wanted it all
We wanted it all
Passion without pain
Sunshine without rainy days
We wanted it always.

You and me, we reached for the sky
The limit was high
Never giving in
Certain we could win that prize
I should have seen it in your eyes.

—Peter Allen, "You and Me"

Disappointment

How do the bright lights of courtship start to dim and go out one by one? What accounts for the refrain *"I am so disappointed in my marriage"*? Ted and Karen are a case in point. To understand their disillusionment, we have to look at the psychological "baggage" that each brought to the marriage.

Once they were married, certain dormant expectations began to rise to the surface. Ted silently expected that Karen would always give him support when he was feeling low; that she would always be punctual; that she would follow his lead in doing things in an orderly, logical way; and above all, that she would always be reachable when he wanted to get in touch with her. He never articulated these expectations to Karen because he regarded them as so normal as not to need spelling out.

Although Karen was frequently punctual, orderly, logical, and available, she was occasionally late, disorganized, and capricious, and unavailable when he tried to call her. Ted felt wounded by each of Karen's failures to meet his expectations, and he saw them as signs of her "flawed character." In searching for explanations, Ted was behaving in a manner characteristic of the wounded partner, who attributes the trouble to some global, negative, and unchangeable trait of the other person.

When Karen did not consistently live up to his expectations, Ted began to believe that his initial attraction to her had been an illusion. Karen's endearing features lost their appeal for him and, in fact, took on a negative tone. Once Ted became disillusioned, he no longer perceived Karen as carefree and entertaining but instead as "flaky."

Ted's reaction reflects a sobering fact. What attracts partners to each other is rarely sufficient in itself to sustain a relationship.

35

Ted's inflexible expectations of Karen illustrate a crucial character-istic of all intimate relationships. When someone fails to live up to our expectations in a non-intimate relationship, we may feel disap-pointed and tend to expect less from the person, or write off the relationship as not worth maintaining. In this kind of relationship, our expectations adjust to fresh experiences—and disappointments lower our expectations.

In a marriage or other committed relationship, however, the re-sponse is frequently different; disappointment does not necessarily lead to a lowering of expectations. In many cases, the husband or wife either cannot or is unwilling to relinquish the original expectations. Ted said, for instance, "I'm *entitled* to have Karen ready when I'm ready. She doesn't have the right to keep me waiting . . . I have every reason to expect that my wife will do what I ask. I always do what *she* wants."

The expectations in marriage are generally less flexible than in an uncommitted relationship. Part of the inflexibility may be explained by the fact that when couples make a lifetime commitment, the stakes are much higher than in a more casual relationship. Marriage implies entrusting your happiness, if not your life, to another person. As a result, the partners build strict rules into the relationship to provide warranties against being abused or betrayed. Further, committed re-lationships are much more likely to revolve around *symbols*—of love or rejection, security or insecurity—which by their very nature are inflexible.

A particularly distinctive aspect of such expectations in marriage is interpreting "lapses" as indicating a *general* failure in the relation-ship. The offended spouse regards these lapses as evidence that the partner is uncaring. Karen, for example, expected that Ted would accept her unconditionally—as he had during the courtship. When he became critical, she believed that he didn't care.

Broken Promises

Sometimes, explicit promises made during the courtship period are not fulfilled after marriage, and they contribute to the "period of dis-illusionment." Such broken promises are cited as examples of a spouse's not caring. One young English physician, knowing that his fiancée was enamored of the theater, took her to the theater district in London. He pointed to a row of theater marquees and said, "See those signs? Someday I will take you to all of these plays." After they were married, however, he never mentioned the theater. To her, his indif-ference represented a betrayal—a symbol that he no longer cared.

Another woman was escorted by her fiancé to a number of travel agencies, where they planned foreign adventures. After marriage, however, he lost interest in travel. His wife believed that he had misled her, and she was bitter about his "dishonesty."

Though some promises are not made explicit, they seem implicit in the courtship, whose nature can be misleading from the start. Each partner is on good behavior and attempts to be agreeable, solicitous, and engaging in order to promote the relationship. They become effective salespeople, trying to say and do things that will enhance their desirability—and so create unrealistic expectations about how they will act after marriage.

Infatuation adds to the deception, albeit unintentionally. It provides the couple with a fusion of interests, even of identity, so that what pleases one automatically pleases the other. There seems to be a vast community of interests, and of sharing—much of which may shrink eventually. One wife commented, "Before we were married, I would be willing to crawl on my hands and knees to Mecca to please him. Now, I don't even feel like walking into the next room for him."

Another source of disappointment in many marriages is the sense of entitlement that partners feel. Ted claimed that he had the *right* to expect certain things from Karen because she was his wife; Karen, he complained, was continually violating the rights due him as her husband. His sense of entitlement left him feeling both frustrated and betrayed.

Because Ted believed that his rights were continually being violated, his image of Karen changed. By seeming to ignore what Ted assumed to be his rights, Karen appeared as insensitive, uncaring, and selfish. Ted was oblivious to the fact that his so-called rights were actually demands and claims on Karen, and that she would experience them as such.

Husbands and wives, or unmarried couples living together, have certain expectations of the return on their investment in the relationship. One mate, for example, may want to feel totally accepted, to be understood, to share pleasant experiences, to receive support when feeling bad, and to obtain help when troubled. In return, he or she is willing to make sacrifices for the partner and to offer similar support. The other partner may expect more practical benefits: somebody to provide enough income for a reasonable standard of living, to share the raising of children, to participate actively in sex, and to arrange for social and recreational activities.

These expectations form an implied contract, "the marital compact"—one that is rarely made explicit. When one partner knowingly or unknowingly violates the compact, however, the partner who holds those expectations will feel let down or betrayed. Keeping the contract is seen as a symbol of caring and trust. But honoring it depends in large measure on whether one mate can sense what the partner expects and has the necessary motivation and skill to meet the expectations. To show consideration and empathy, for example, requires skills such as the ability to listen, ask questions, and provide explanations.

The Grand Reversal

When people are infatuated, they tend to read into the partner all kinds of positive qualities that are not present, or are present in lesser degree than they imagine. The optimistic bride imagines her husband to be considerate and sensitive; her husband expects her to be responsible and reasonable. In successful marriages, partners do develop these qualities increasingly as the marriage matures, and as they mature individually. But in the early years of marriage, many of these patterns are still unformed or in an early stage of development.

The following qualities are viewed as expressions of the deepest hopes and dreams of love and devotion:

Sensitivity

Fairness

Kindness

Consideration

Generosity

Respect

Responsiveness

Reasonableness

Responsibility

If, after repeated disappointments, people recognize that their mates do not hold to the standards embedded in these virtues—if they don't, for instance, offer help, understanding, sympathy, and so on—the image of the mate and the marriage in general starts to change from positive to negative. For instance, because of his "realization" that Karen was inconsiderate, Ted began to think, *"She let me down. I can't count on her for* anything. *I have no confidence in her. She's unreliable."* Karen, likewise, came to see Ted as "a tyrant," and her feelings fluctuated between those of hopelessness and blind rage.

As disillusionment progresses, single episodes of disappointment seem sufficient to justify attaching a negative label to the partner. If a husband does not show sensitivity at a particular time, then he is "insensitive"; if a wife fails to show kindness when her husband expects it, then she is "unkind." A woman who spent a lifetime competently handling her personal affairs and her career felt paralyzed when her new husband would leave every Sunday—the only day he was not working—to play golf. She concluded that he was basically selfish, inconsiderate, and unfair.

Similarly, a man became enraged at his wife when she informed him she would no longer type his business reports. He saw her as unresponsive and unkind. He considered her refusal a kind of abandonment and a betrayal of his trust that she would share with him the responsibilities of generating family income.

In each of these instances, the *symbolic meaning* of the event went far beyond its practical significance, and stirred feelings of desertion and rejection. The absence of a particular pattern of behavior struck at the heart of the yearning for love and devotion. The partner attributed the mate's behavior to some "bad trait." Further, the disappointed partner regarded the trait as permanent.

Thus, the *absence* of a virtue was translated into its polar *opposite*, a vice:

Insensitivity

Unfairness

Unkindness

Inconsiderateness

Selfishness

Rudeness

Nonresponsiveness

Unreasonableness

Irresponsibility

In actuality, people are not split into absolute opposites. If they are not totally responsible, it does not follow that they are irresponsible; they may be carefree, not well organized, absentminded, and so on. People in general are neither all black nor all white, but varying blends of gray.

Such labeling in terms of opposites is similar to the either-or, all-or-nothing thinking that we will be discussing in later chapters. This type of labeling is usually just as unrealistic as the idealizations that go on during the early period of infatuation.

Often a benign explanation, rather than a vice, accounts for a particular frustration. Marjorie, for instance, was often accused by her friends and husband of being irresponsible and selfish because she was frequently late in attending to things she had promised to do. Her problem was that she was *too conscientious*, not that she was irresponsible. She did not like to refuse requests and so committed herself to doing more than she had time for.

Since Marjorie was conscientious about doing the best job she could, she rarely finished in time to meet her next commitment, including those to her husband. Her desire to please Ken and other people blinded her to the impossibility of fulfilling all the promises that she made. For Ken and the others, however, her tardiness obscured her conscientiousness. And since she was not "responsible" in their eyes, she was the opposite—"irresponsible." Marjorie's plight was due in part to the universal tendency of people to fixate on the first explanation occurring to them and not to look for other, more benign reasons.

Making Balanced Judgments

Thinking in opposites, which is common in couples, differs from the kind of thinking we use in most dealings with other people. Our judgments outside our intimate relationships are, for the most part, more moderate and more reasonably balanced. But when we have a large investment in a relationship, we seem to slip into this more primitive, all-or-nothing thinking. Ted illustrates this process. He perceived Karen in extremes, he interpreted her actions by way of his private frame of reference, and he pronounced negative judgments on her.

But the future of troubled relationships is not so grim as this discussion may imply. The so-called vices are not embedded in rock; they are not fixed traits that cannot be modified. With counseling, Ted and Karen and Ken and Marjorie were able to see each other more reasonably, and they learned to meet each other's expectations better.

Important changes *can* occur if couples improve their communication skills, such as listening more attentively, expressing their wishes more effectively, and defining and meeting their problems in a collaborative spirit. Acquiring these basic skills can change marital partners into being more sensitive, considerate, responsible, reasonable, and so on—in short, more "virtuous." Of course, reaching these goals requires considerable application and practice.

But that is only a first step to make a marriage work better and be more enjoyable. Simply learning new ways of communicating may not always be sufficient. Partners have to revise many strongly held, negative beliefs. Remarks like "She's so wrapped up in herself, she never cares about my needs" or "He always does what he wants to do and never what I want to do" often represent, in part, the speaker's own self-centered orientation.

Such egocentric attitudes are discernible in formulas embedded in Ted's notion that *"If Karen is on time, she is responsible. If she is late, she is irresponsible."* Such beliefs become absolute and rigid because they are seen in terms of opposites: virtue and vice, goodness and badness. The logical consequence of Ted's belief was that when Karen was on time, it did not count for much; when she was late, it led to the conclusion that *"She is never on time."* Any lapse on her part was a violation of Ted's rule and led to the absolute generalization "never."

In order to bring about effective change, spouses must be able to state specifically *what types* of actions represent considerateness, kindness, and responsibility to them. Ken needs to make clear to Marjorie that if she calls to say that she will be home from work late, *this* represents consideration to him. Marjorie has to impress on Ken that when he offers to help with cleaning the house, *that* represents a cooperative spirit. Although getting your spouse to act in these ways does not guarantee that he or she has incorporated an attitude of consideration and cooperation, the actions themselves can form the forerunner of such attitudes.

Encouragement and signs of appreciation help. If the husband shows his wife how much he appreciates these actions, she will be more likely to repeat them on her own. Each time the partner behaves in a desired way and is rewarded for it, it increases his or her motivation to repeat that action. This repetition sends down roots to form a new concept in the spouse's mind: *"It is desirable and rewarding to do these things for my partner."* The repeated cycle of constructive action plus *reinforcement* can also neutralize the egocentricity that opposes consideration of the other's needs.

Such self-centered attitudes develop early in life as a way for people to establish independence and achieve goals without taking the needs of others into consideration. In marriage, such unbridled autonomy breeds hurt feelings and resentment. But with clear communication and encouragement, marital partners can help each other learn to shift gears and fuse their own interests with those of their mate. As the new patterns of behavior succeed, they start to replace the egocentric patterns.

The kinds of actions that indicate caring and loving are innumerable. However, they fall into certain broad categories, listed on pages 185–91 in Chapter 12. Some of these are caring, acceptance, understanding, support, and sensitivity. You might want to refer to this list now—to be able to pinpoint those areas in which you or your partner is lacking, and to get a head start on addressing these deficiencies.

THE CLASH OF
PERSPECTIVES

The differences that divide a couple may stem from fundamental differences in the way they view themselves and each other. We have seen such differences in Ted and Karen. Ted, the classicist, values what is orderly and predictable in life, while Karen, the romantic, seeks out novelty and excitement.

Such differences in perspective can make seemingly trivial incidents propel mates toward severing their relationship. A couple planning to get married consulted me after the following episode, only one in a long series of disputes. Let's tune in on their conversation as they replayed it later in my office.

LAURA: Will you stay home tonight? I think I have the flu.

FRED: I'm already committed to visit Joe [a professional colleague].

LAURA: [*If he won't do this small favor for me, how can I count on him when I have a major problem?*] You never want to stay home. I very rarely ask you to do anything.

FRED: [*If she insists on keeping me home for such a small thing, what will happen when something big happens—like when we have children? She is completely unreasonable. If I have to give in to her every wish, I won't be able to breathe.*] I'm sorry, but I really have to go.

LAURA: [*I can't depend on him. I should get out of the relationship while I can and find somebody I can depend on.*] Go ahead if you want to. I'll find somebody else to stay with me.

Very different as people—Laura was an art instructor in a private day school, while Fred worked as a computer programmer—they saw the same situation in totally different ways, and their individual per-

43

spectives were closed to each other's point of view. Each was oblivious to the meaning the other attached to the situation, so they made more negative explanations for each other's actions than they would have if they were more attuned to each other. Since Fred was unaware of Laura's fear of abandonment, he saw her as willful and controlling; Laura, not realizing that Fred felt threatened by this "infringement" on his freedom, regarded him as selfish and insensitive.

Also, they both believed that the reasonableness of their own interpretations would be apparent to anybody, and that the other's attitude was, likewise, *obviously unreasonable*. Laura saw no flaw in her logic that if Fred would not comply with a minor request, then she could not rely on him for help when something serious occurred. Fred believed anyone could see that having to conform to such a trivial request meant being placed in a straitjacket for the rest of the marriage.

Moreover, their minds were closed to any corrective feedback that they could have received by listening to and understanding each other's views. Thus, they were left flailing away in a futile attempt to force each other to accept their own frames of reference. Each partner argued that the other was wrong and, in effect, mean, selfish, and bad —and that the relationship was therefore untenable.

When partners hammer away at each other, they only bolster each other's resistance, strengthening negative beliefs and making them even more extreme. Eventually, the partners' positions become completely polarized, frozen in their own egocentric perspective. Each concludes that the other is "impossible" and "intolerable," and both partners foresee catastrophe if they remain married.

The intensity of Laura's and Fred's reactions can be seen to have deeper roots: their conflict happened to strike at each one's vulnerability. Laura was person-oriented. She received satisfaction and security through social interactions, and so was threatened by Fred's leaving. Fred was more autonomous and so valued freedom, mobility, and self-sufficiency. He was put off by what he saw as Laura's clinging nature. While for Laura, Fred's show of independence symbolized desertion, for Fred, her dependence represented incarceration.

Because of differences in their personality make-up (Laura, sociable and dependent; Fred, autonomous), they could not view the problem in the same way; thus, this kind of clash was inevitable. Moreover, because of their fixed perspectives, each was unable to comprehend the other's interpretation of the situation.

Married people often say, "I just don't understand my husband [or wife]." Generally, each perspective—in the eyes of the husband or the wife—seems correct. Not understanding the differences in perspective, partners tend to ascribe ill will to each other during a conflict. They fail to realize that they are simply perceiving the identical sets of circumstances differently, and that neither is guilty of malice.

Research suggests that the kind of conflict experienced by Laura and Fred is not uncommon. For example, Carol Gilligan, a psychologist at Harvard University, has shown that wives tend to be more involved in personal relationships (sociotropic), whereas husbands are likely to be more independent. Nonetheless, the beliefs associated with these differences may be modified to minimize marital friction. Or, at the very least, partners can take each other's personality into account so as not to be unnecessarily threatening.

The problem of conflicting personalities is illustrated by the clashes between Marjorie and Ken. Marjorie, a college beauty queen, lacked confidence in her ability to do things on her own. But she was struggling to prove that she was a "real person" and could be independent. She tended to see other people as having more confidence, and she felt inferior to them. Ken, a former basketball star, was the reverse—very self-assured and independent. He saw other people, including Marjorie, as weaker and in need of his protection.

The following interchange occurred when Marjorie wanted to hang a picture but had difficulty driving the nail into the wall:

KEN: [*She's having a problem. I'd better help her.*] Let me do it for you.

MARJORIE: [*He has no confidence in my ability.*] That's all right. I can do it myself (angrily).

KEN: What's the matter with you? I was only trying to help.

MARJORIE: That's all you ever do. You don't think I can do anything.

KEN: Well, you can't even drive a nail straight [laughs].

MARJORIE: There you go again—always putting me down.

KEN: I was just trying to help.

The spouses had completely different versions of Ken's intervention. Marjorie's goal in hanging the picture was to assure herself that she could handle manual tasks; in fact, she was looking forward to Ken's praise for her demonstration of competence and independence. His intrusion, though, brought her sense of incompetence to the surface. While each was correct in the belief that Ken lacked confidence in Marjorie's manual ability, Ken perceived himself as kind and considerate, while Marjorie viewed him as intrusive and patronizing. What started as an innocent gesture of helpfulness on his part led to hurt feelings and antagonism.

To add to their upset, each attributed ill will to the other. Marjorie saw Ken as meddling and controlling. Ken saw Marjorie as ungrateful and defiant. (In the past, she had always been dependent on him, and he had enjoyed helping her and demonstrating his superior ability.)

Such negative labeling of the spouse is common in marriage. Research by University of Maryland psychologist Norman Epstein and his colleagues indicates that during misunderstandings, distressed partners are more likely to attribute negative motives to each other than are nondistressed couples.

Open and Closed Perspectives

Our perspective is a composite picture that includes not only the details of a situation but also the *meanings* that we attach to it. In this broader sense, our perspectives are shaped by beliefs and experiences. Thus, Ken's view of Marjorie as needing help stemmed from his belief, based on past experience, that she lacked skill in manual tasks. Her perspective of him, on the other hand, was shaped by her belief that he was heavy-handed, interfering, belittling, and critical. Paradoxically, she had been attracted to him in part because of his superb self-confidence and protectiveness, which made her feel more secure. Yet her sense of incompetence was always near the surface and became a sore spot whenever she tried to assert herself. Though both partners were well intentioned, their conflicting viewpoints caused strife.

In normal interactions, individual perspectives are "open." People form an image of another person and change it as more information is obtained. Their image of their partner is a composite of his or her desirable and undesirable traits. When their partner changes, so does their open perspective. But these changes in perspective are based on a reasonable appreciation of their partner's motives—not on their own preconceptions.

Marjorie's *closed* perspective of Ken was based solely on her growing drive toward independence, and not on his actual motives. Ken's present perspective of Marjorie was based on his previous view of her as a dependent doll, and not on her evolving independence. With an open perspective, Marjorie would have recognized that Ken was simply trying to be helpful, and Ken would have grasped her yearning to be more independent.

Closed or self-centered perspectives are defined by individual frames of reference; people view events only according to how they relate to them. Their images of an event are based solely on its personal meanings and exclude entirely what the event may mean to others. Even when they try to view an event from the other person's perspective, they find themselves stuck in their own frames of reference.

In the picture-hanging incident, for example, Ken believed that he was being considerate and helpful. Actually, however, he was operating out of his own conception—not hers—of what was good for his wife. Similarly, Marjorie interpreted his offer to help solely according to her personal perspective. She saw him as deliberately interfering rather than as being kind. They both had closed perspectives. The next step for both was to assign labels of "badness": Ken was bad for interfering, and Marjorie was bad for being ungrateful.

Clashes are inevitable when both partners operate from a closed, self-centered perspective. Even though Ken had no desire to hurt his wife—and indeed wanted to help her—his egocentric perspective blinded him to Marjorie's real desires. His perspective was centered on his own desire (to help) and not on *her* desire (to be independent). Similarly, Marjorie's perspective was centered on *her* own wishes; consequently, she saw Ken solely as interfering with her wishes and not as merely expressing *his* wish to be helpful.

Marital conflict fosters and exaggerates egocentric perspectives. When mates feel threatened, they are forced into a closed perspective as a kind of defensive reaction. When they view each other through the lens of their egocentric perspectives, they are bound to be out of synchrony. Their interpretations of what happens between them will be susceptible to conflicts of interest, misinterpretation of each other's motives, and hostility. When marital conflict results from closed perspectives, the mates see only negative qualities in each other and jump to conclusions regarding the "disaster" that these negative traits will cause. As we shall see in Chapter 9, the resulting hostility itself becomes a problem that transcends the original clash.

What forces the differences to escalate to serious conflict are the unpleasant explanations for the spouse's actions. These negative explanations often lead to hostility, which in turn generates a new set of even *more* negative meanings, until finally the other person is seen in a completely negative light as a "bitch" or "bully." Since their perspectives are closed, the partners have trouble giving credence to or even recognizing each other's view of the situation. Bear in mind that people do not voluntarily assume a closed perspective. But, once locked into it, it dictates their thoughts and actions.

A person with an open perspective, on the other hand, is able to adopt the frame of reference of the other person, see the world through the other person's eyes, and so relate more flexibly. For example, many parents are open in this way to their child's perceptions, wishes, and feelings. But even "good parents" sometimes shift to closed perspectives and, for instance, see the children in terms of the "burden" they impose on them, or as "rotten kids."

Parents may have less empathy for one another than for their children because they expect each other to be an "adult" (that is, not to have childish responses). Paradoxically, many of a spouse's desires, feelings, and expectations are carried over from childhood and call for the same kind of understanding as they merited in childhood.

Framing

▷ "He likes to see me suffer."

▷ "She is manipulative."

▷ "He is a dictator."

▷ "She is deceitful."

Accusations such as these do not necessarily mean a spouse actually *is* extraordinarily mean, exploitive, domineering, or dishonest, though in some cases of course these accusations may have a core of truth. In my experience with distressed couples, however, such accusations are usually based on global, overgeneralized conclusions that marital partners reach because they have been hurt.

Partners who have been hurt tend to blame and to project negative qualities onto the other person. After repeated occurrences—which are so painful for the partners—the accusations may crystallize into "never" and "always" thoughts. Instead of seeing the unpleasantness as temporary, the partner regards it as permanent—as a personality trait. Such ideas, whether they are openly expressed or kept concealed, evolve into a well-formed perspective on the other person.

If such overgeneralizations are repeated enough, the negative perspective of the "offender" becomes fixed. At this point, spouses who had once waited breathlessly to see each other at the end of the day now face the prospect with fear or loathing. Such a fixed perspective often includes a visual image of the husband, for example, in which meanness and contempt are etched into his facial expression. The same person who once appeared loving and attractive is now perceived as hateful and ugly. The visage that once evoked excitement and pleasure now produces distaste and pain.

This negative, biased, and rigid mental picture then determines what one partner notices—and fails to notice—in the other. In essence, the offending partner becomes "framed" by a biased image that accentuates negative features and ignores the positive ones. Once the partner is framed, almost any action he or she takes will be viewed through that frame. Neutral acts will be seen as negative, and negative acts will appear even more so. Positive acts will be reinterpreted as negative or will be disqualified. If the husband is considerate, for instance, the wife thinks, *"What is he up to now, the hypocrite?"* If his wife treats him kindly, the husband thinks, *"She's acting phony— she doesn't mean it."*

The framed image that people impose on their mate is reinforced continually by newly gathered bits of evidence, while those events that do not fit are soon forgotten. Since the frame admits only information that is consistent with it, it becomes increasingly convincing over the course of time until it is firmly fixed as reality in the spouse's mind. Finally, when offended spouses recite to their friends the accumulated evidence for the framed perspective, the selected data seem so convincing that it persuades even a disinterested third party of the validity of the image.

Laura crystallized her picture of Fred as insensitive when he refused to stay home. She then concluded that he was oblivious to her needs and would someday be insensitive to those of their children; that he was incapable of being a supportive husband and caring father. He was framed in her mind as selfish and irresponsible—not just that one time, but always.

After that, Laura saw Fred in the same negative light, no matter what he did. In fact, when any incident arose that even remotely resembled the original traumatic incident, she would experience a flood of images and flashbacks of it. And each time that she saw the traumatic image in her mind's eye, she would feel more anger toward Fred. The counseling for this couple took the form of "reframing," in which Laura and Fred questioned the basis for their negative perspectives and selected a more benign explanation to account for each other's actions (Chapter 13).

Conflicts of Personalities

Sometimes the friction between a couple in constant conflict cannot be explained only on the basis of differences in perspective or framing. It is necessary in such instances to look for a more permanent quality, namely, the couple's personality traits. Such clashes stem from the differing ways in which their personality make-up dictates how they perceive events. The romantic sees life through rose-colored glasses, the pessimist through dark glasses. The autonomous person may view an offer of help as a put-down or as a lack of confidence, while the dependent one sees it as a sign of caring. The autonomous person equates separation with freedom. For the dependent person, however, separation amounts to abandonment.

Ted and Karen illustrate two bents of personality that are apt to clash. Karen, the autonomous romantic, is self-sufficient and happy to do things alone. Ted, the lonely classicist, is less independent and craves company. Being dependent, Ted wants Karen to be available all the time. At a less conscious level, Ted fears she will abandon him.

What Ted did not realize during their period of conflict was that Karen's personality—in fact, her identity—was centered on her freedom to move from one activity to another, to act on impulse, and to be free of restraints. Ted, who always felt a bit lonely, placed an enormous value on having a partner he could depend on at all times. Karen, on the other hand, did not like to be pinned down. She had her own set of rules based on her desires for freedom, mobility, and independence. She was not concerned about being efficient, punctual, or prepared.

One day when Karen kept him waiting for a half-hour, Ted was plagued by fears that something terrible had happened to her. When she did arrive—and even though she was very pleased to see him— Ted became furious at her for having kept him waiting. His fury was fueled by his hidden fear that she had gotten into an accident. The thought that she might have been killed frightened him and activated his lifelong fear of being alone. Instead of feeling relieved to see her, he was angry at her for having "caused" him to be anxious.

Ted interpreted her breaking his rule of punctuality to mean: *"She doesn't care. She isn't the least concerned with my wishes."* He sulked, hoping that this would drive his message home to Karen. Sulking and withdrawal had little effect on Karen, however, because she was relatively autonomous and could easily handle emotional distance and isolation. Indeed, she simply pulled back from Ted, giving him less support than before, which threatened him even more. Ted became more hostile, seeing her as a "depriver." He couched this in terms of her "being irresponsible" and told himself, *"I can't count on her."*

Ted's strategy to ensure steady satisfaction of his need for dependency was to try to control Karen. Karen desired, on the other hand, to be free of his restraints and control. To guarantee her freedom, she tried to discourage his attempts to control her. As she felt stifled by Ted's demands, she withdrew more to get her distance, leaving Ted feeling abandoned. Ted, increasingly desperate, tried scolding and then verbal attacks—at each step driving Karen further away.

Karen and Ted illustrate how two personalities may seem initially to complement one other but actually clash because of differing sets of rules and attitudes. For example, one of Karen's formulas was *"If Ted really cared for me, he would encourage me to be independent."* Ted's corresponding formula was *"If Karen really cared, she would want to be closer."* Even this dissimilarity need not necessarily preclude a balanced relationship. We all know people with different personalities who get along well with each other. But when the partners cling tenaciously to their own perspectives and are oblivious of or refuse to accept their spouse's perspective, real conflict occurs.

What went wrong between Ted and Karen? As pointed out in Chapter 2, Ted was attracted by Karen's carefree attitude and her joie de vivre, a welcome departure from the controlled and overintellectualized atmosphere of his childhood home. Karen, in turn, was intrigued by Ted's wit, his storytelling abilities, his methodical approach to problem solving, and his breadth of knowledge of politics and history. Above all, she was reassured by his reliability and sense of responsibility—all of which marked him in stark contrast to her own father.

The attractive features of once harmonious partners are real and important enough to be capable of drawing them together again— even for a couple at odds like Ted and Karen—if they can overcome their misunderstandings. But these attractive features are not strong enough in themselves to hold a marriage together when a couple's personalities do not easily blend. Herein lies the answer to the puzzle of why partners who seem so attracted to each other and who appear to "have everything going for them" may fail to maintain a stable relationship. Their individual personalities largely shape their expectations, their view of life, and the way they react to each other. As the initial gratification from the "attractive" features starts to wane, the personality differences achieve more prominence. Their perspectives begin to clash. Finally, their perspectives of each other become warped by the negative explanation they provide for their partner's actions.

As Ted and Karen felt thwarted, they each came up with explanations for the conflicts that assigned the fault to the other. Their mutual views darkened so that they could not appreciate their positive attributes. Ted remained a splendid raconteur, but Karen could no longer enjoy his stories. Karen remained vivacious and cheerful, but Ted was no longer entertained. They could only see each other through the bias of negative frames: Karen appeared rejecting and frivolous; Ted seemed forbidding and ponderous.

Once they were fitted into these frames, considerable work was required to get them out. Some of their conflicting traits and attitudes toward one another had to be modified. How we were able to bring about these changes will be discussed in later chapters. At this point, we can list several steps a couple must take if theirs is a troubled relationship like Ted and Karen's.

1/The partners need, first of all, to realize that much of the friction between them is due to misunderstandings stemming from differences in their perspectives—and is not the result of meanness or selfishness.

2/They have to recognize that certain traits of the other mate are not "bad" but are grating only because of a mismatch with their own traits.

3/It is essential for them to recognize that when their perspectives differ, neither is necessarily right or wrong.

4/They need to reframe their perspective of each other, expunging the negative features they have artificially introduced, and to see each other more benignly—and realistically.

In the course of time, the two personalities can gradually change. As one partner becomes more tolerant of the other's traits, both often find, surprisingly, that their differences begin to blur. In fact, their personalities become shaped to accommodate one another, thus reducing the friction and misunderstandings.

BREAKING
THE RULES

Sybil and Max were happily married for several years, during which time Sybil worked and Max went to medical school. After their children were born, Sybil gave up her position as a teacher and dedicated herself to the children and her husband. Max, a promising medical researcher, was away from home a good deal, although he considered himself a devoted husband and parent. A critical event in their marriage occurred when Max called Sybil from a distant city where he was attending a medical convention:

MAX: [*Sybil will be glad I'm getting on so well, meeting a lot of people, learning a lot.*] I'm having a great time. How are you?

SYBIL: [*He's having a great time while I have two sick kids on my hands.*] Joan and Freddie are sick.

MAX: [*Oh no, she's going to lay something on me.*] What's the matter with them?

SYBIL: [*Will he respond? Show a sense of responsibility?*] They have chicken pox. They're running a fever.

MAX: [*Chicken pox is usually not serious. She's exaggerating the problem.*] You don't have to worry. They'll be all right.

SYBIL: [*Why doesn't he offer to come home?*] All right.

MAX: [*I hope she's reassured.*] I'll call tomorrow.

SYBIL: [*He's never around when I need him.*] You do that! [sarcastically]

Max and Sybil see the same situation in completely different ways, and so evaluate each other's actions—and each other—totally differently. This difference in perspective is typical of distressed marriages and often leads to more serious problems.

Max does not view the children's illness as serious enough to warrant his immediate attention. He knows that if Sybil really *needed* him, he would "come running," but in his own mind he glosses over the fact that Sybil seems deeply concerned. He believes that Sybil is overreacting and tries to reassure her that everything will be all right. In any event, he doesn't want to be controlled by her "worrisomeness."

Sybil, on the other hand, views Max as derelict in his duties. He "gets a free ride" while she is left with all the family responsibilities. The following list summarizes the differences in their attitudes:

Sybil's Attitude	*Max's Attitude*
1 / Max should offer to come home.	1 / Since Sybil doesn't really need me, there's no reason to make the offer.
2 / I should not have to ask him.	2 / I'm not a mind reader. If she needs me at home, she should say so.
3 / He should know I need him. He can make this sacrifice for me.	3 / She's overreacting. She can handle the situation without my having to make a sacrifice.
4 / He's selfish and irresponsible. He places his advancement before everything else.	4 / She's demanding and controlling. She's jealous of my career. She can't stand to have me enjoy myself.

In their dealings with others, both Sybil and Max are considered very nice. Socially they appear to be a happy couple, yet they have reached a serious impasse in their marriage, as their conversation reveals. Much of their exchange—the most important part—is unspoken: Sybil wants Max to *offer* to come home, and Max avoids making such an offer. Because of these unspoken thoughts, they both start to attribute negative qualities to each other. Max becomes selfish and irresponsible in Sybil's eyes; Sybil becomes demanding and jealous to Max.

On further analysis, there are deeper currents in the interaction. Although Sybil is, indeed, worried about the children, she does not feel completely helpless. What she really wants is a sign from Max that he really cares about what she is going through and that he is responsible enough to be willing to pitch in. She recognizes that it would be a sacrifice for Max to come home, and she wouldn't even consider the possibility if it weren't important to her. But she wants —and expects—him to make such an offer. His willingness to make the sacrifice would show that he cared, was responsible, and made the family his top priority. If he should make such an offer, then she might let him off the hook and tell him to stay. In this context, his not offering to come home is a *negative symbol* that he doesn't care and is irresponsible.

Max, on the other hand, sees the family problem in purely practical terms. He is oblivious to the symbolic meaning of his not offering to come home. His only thought is that an immediate return is unnecessary because Sybil is capable of managing without him. Since he thinks only of the practical considerations and not of the symbolic meanings to Sybil—her worries about the children and her wish for him to be present—he alienates her.

Setting Expectations

This conflict between Max and Sybil had much earlier roots. At the time of their courtship, Max was attending medical school and Sybil was working as a teacher. The courtship was a wild romance enlivened by their dreams of a glorious, untroubled life together.

Sybil identified herself with Max and his career, and was euphoric when his peers referred to him as "the young genius." Max was pleased that Sybil idealized him and anticipated a happy future, with him the successful researcher and Sybil providing the backing and support he needed.

Sybil had a number of expectations, which became apparent only later. For instance, she anticipated that she would give up her career so that they could raise a family together. When she was pregnant with their first child, she looked forward to the realization of her fantasy of a "happy family," in which Max would participate fully.

When she found, over the course of time, that Max was not fitting into the role that she had imagined, she was hurt and disappointed. At this point, she became aware for the first time of what her other, silent expectations had been:

▷ Max will always place me and the children first.
▷ I will not have to ask him directly for help.
▷ My needs will be apparent to him.
▷ He will be willing to make sacrifices.

Max, in turn, had his own expectations:

▷ Sybil will respect my career, identify with it, and share it with me.
▷ She will do her job taking care of the children and running the household.

In other words, Max expected they would both be partners and both be providers. She would be the "inside" partner and he would be the "outside" partner. They would each support the other, but their roles would be distinct: she would take care of the home, and he would provide the family income. Sybil, on the other hand, expected that since she had given up her career, Max would be her full partner at home—and not an occasional husband and parent.

As happened with the other couples in conflict, the counseling for Sybil and Max focused on their differing expectations and perspectives. Each partner had to honor the legitimate concerns of the other, but both had to work on an acceptable formula for carrying out these joint responsibilities—specifically, the care of the children. Sybil had to be more "up front" about her expectations of Max, while he needed to be more sensitive to her fears and desires.

Making the Rules

A wife who wants to spend the time talking to her husband may become reconciled to his watching TV football games most of the weekend, or to his having a few drinks with his buddies after work, or to his spending evenings poring over printouts from the office. A husband may accommodate himself to his wife's being less interested in sex than he, or to her not sharing his job, sports, or political interests. Such disappointments generally cause spouses to lower their expectations of each other. As they adapt their dreams and fantasies to the realities of marriage, they usually learn to live with the situation, though they may feel sad at times.

Sometimes, however, the expectations—the hopes and dreams—are not scaled down but escalated. The wish that a spouse would place the family first is replaced by a *demand*. The word *would* is replaced by *should*: "He [or she] *should* place the family first." What was a wish becomes an absolute rule. While people feel sad when their wishes are unfulfilled, they are more likely to feel angry when their rules are broken.

If we tried to judge the conflict between Max and Sybil impartially, it might be difficult to render an absolute decision. Should Max come home, or at least offer to? Is Sybil right in expecting such an action? A simple verdict would be that neither is totally right or totally wrong. But such a verdict would miss the real conflict, which is broader and more complex than simply whether Max returns home. The real issues in their minds are: *"Will Sybil support me at work?"* and *"Will Max support me at home?"*

When we overlook the more abstract issues in marital conflict, we may be misled into thinking of overly simple solutions to the problems. The concrete question of Max's coming home is of significance largely because it represents a broader principle: what Max does or does not do when Sybil wants his support has *symbolic meaning*.

The broader principles that marital partners subscribe to, but are often not aware of, have been described in Chapter 2 as "virtues." These virtues have to do with fairness, caring, consideration, responsibility, respect, and the like. Thus, a single, concrete action stands for a broad, abstract principle. In Sybil's mind, if Max offers to come home, then it means that he *cares*, is considerate, responsible, and fair; if he does not make the offer, it means that he doesn't care, is inconsiderate, irresponsible, and unfair. For Sybil the choice is cut-and-dried.

In general, the need for a rule does not become obvious until some important principle is violated. Laws concerned with hiring practices or voting rights, for example, were passed only *after* the principle of nondiscrimination had been violated. Similarly, it is only after the occurrence of a number of incidents—in which mates clash on important principles—that they are likely to formulate rules in their minds. When Ted was disappointed several times by Karen's tardiness, he arrived at a rule regarding her lateness. Whenever she was late, he applied his rule and could feel justified in being angry and wanting to punish her for her "misdemeanor."

The problem with such rules is that they do not take into account the other person's needs and wishes. Indeed, if they were expressed openly (which they rarely are), the rules would seem arbitrary or even irrational to the other mate. Much of the anger in distressed marriages springs from such broken rules rather than from objectively bad actions on the part of one of the mates.

The rules derive from certain "formulas" that operate as coding systems to define the personal meaning of a particular behavior, and to determine whether it is "lawful" or "unlawful." Some of these formulas are:

▷ If my spouse cared, he or she would offer to help when I am upset.

▷ If my spouse respected me, he or she would not have me do all the dirty work.

▷ If my spouse was considerate, he or she would do what I wanted without being asked.

When a mate does something—or fails to do something—that fits into a formula, then the partner feels hurt. For example, both Laura and Sybil were disappointed that their partners did not respond to their pleas. They then unconsciously applied the third formula: "If my spouse really cared, he [or she] would do what I want." Since the partner did not respond to the wish, it meant he or she did not care. This meaning was devastating to both wives. In the future, they vowed to set up the rule "My mate *must* respond to my need. If not, I will leave him."

Typical rules emanating from these formulas are:

▷ My spouse should help when I get upset.

▷ My spouse should share in the household chores.

▷ My spouse should do what I want without being asked.

These rules protect partners from being hurt or disappointed. Subsequently, when Max broke Sybil's rules and did not meet her need, she became angry instead of feeling great pangs of disappointment, and she wanted to punish Max or leave him.

Applying the Rules

In a way, the rules are just as binding on the partner as a tax levy. When such an obligation is not fulfilled, the partner is seen as an offender, and so a penalty seems warranted, usually in the form of a scolding. Problems arise because this line of thinking is rarely made explicit. Such marital rules are unrepealable, non-negotiable obligations that are often imposed without the spouse's knowledge of their existence—and certainly without his or her ever having agreed to them.

These rules become seen as rights, and then easily evolve into demands. A partner may demand—often tacitly—that the spouse be helpful, concerned, and considerate without ever realizing that the *definition* of what actions constitute helpfulness, concern, and consideration varies enormously from person to person. The rule-making partner assumes that his or her own formula for helpfulness is universal.

Sybil claimed, "Everybody knows that a husband should be available when his wife wants to discuss a problem with him." In Sybil's home, her mother always called her father at work when she wanted to discuss a household problem, so Sybil assumed that this was a totally reasonable expectation in marriage. Max, however, came from a family in which problems of any kind were rarely discussed. Thus, Sybil considered Max uncaring when he failed to discuss her problems with her during the day. Also, since her father had been very indulgent of all her mother's wishes, Sybil came to expect the same from Max. The mismatch that results when one partner's expectations of a spouse's role do not fit those of the other partner occurs frequently in marriage.

The assumption that one's expectations are universal leads to another problem. One partner will believe that the other should know what he or she wants *without being asked.* This expectation that the mate should be psychic is found frequently in distressed marriages. Karen, for example, was hurt when Ted did not assist her with the housework. He would stand by while she set the table, washed the dishes, put away the laundry—without offering to help. Though she would think, *"He should know that this is a burden to me,"* Karen would never ask Ted for help. She assumed that since her "need" was obvious and universal, he was deliberately resisting the normal tendency to be helpful.

Rules that seem perfectly reasonable and obvious to the rule maker often seem unreasonable to the other person. For example, when Karen told Ted that he should have "known" to assist her with the household chores, he complained, "You always expect me to read your mind. If you want something, why don't you just come out and ask for it?" Karen replied, "It was so obvious. Why do I always have to ask for everything? Can't you ever do anything just because it's the right thing to do?"

A crucial feature of the "marital code of rights and wrongs" is that a mate should *never*—willingly or unwillingly—violate a rule. A young man, for instance, was enraged by his fiancée's accidentally blowing smoke in his face. He thought, *"She knows that I can't stand smoke and she should be more careful. She's thoughtless and doesn't care about my feelings."* He was not as offended by the smoke itself as he was by the fact that his fiancée had violated his rule. If somebody else had accidentally blown smoke in his face, he might have been slightly annoyed but not enraged, because no rule would have been broken.

The actual loss or hurt experienced by a spouse when a rule is violated is often trivial, particularly when compared to the intensity of his or her angry reaction. One reason the reaction is so pronounced is that the rule is sacred to the one who holds it. If it is broken, the spouse assumes that he or she will become more vulnerable, as though a small breach now will lead to major breaches later on. The man who disliked smoke, for instance, said of his fiancée, "If she can't follow a simple rule, like not smoking in my face, she can disregard everything that bothers me and ignore everything that matters to me."

Rules That Sabotage

Typically each partner in a distressed marriage believes that he or she has made the most adjustments; or both partners believe that they have given more to satisfy the mate's needs than they have received. Their sense of betrayal is accentuated when the mate becomes critical or abusive. For instance, a wife complained, "My husband never mentions all the good things I do for him. The only thing he notices is if I make a mistake."

Often the notions of being loved and being happy are fused in people's thinking, so that they believe a lessening of love means they will become unhappy. Many people operate, for example, according to the following formula: *"If I am loved totally and unconditionally, then I can be happy. If I am not loved totally, then I must be unhappy."* In equating love and happiness, such people are led to dwell on the painful feelings that result when their mate seems less loving or caring. They anticipate that a transient coolness in their partner means prolonged unhappiness is on the way. Some people, in fact, may slide into a depression when they believe that a love relationship is slipping. They conclude that they face a lifetime of unhappiness because they now have no chance of ever being loved again.

To guard against such suffering, partners in a marriage tend to build up a system of controls to ward off the specter of the relationship's demise. These protective devices assume the form of imperatives levied on the mates—the *shoulds* and *should nots*—which are reassuring to the spouse who makes them. These rigid rules, formulated as a kind of wall to prevent the ultimate suffering of a breakup, often serve to fence in the other partner and restrict his or her spontaneity. Paradoxically, these rules may bring about precisely what is being guarded against: a dissolution of the relationship.

When one of these laws is violated by a spouse, the other spouse—the lawmaker—feels threatened, becomes angry, and wants to punish the offender. It is not just the rule but its author that has been violated. In close relationships, anger obstructs constructive problem solving. In the heat of anger, problems seem beyond negotiation.

The rules, which may seem arbitrary, unreasonable, or trivial to the spouse upon whom they are imposed, typically deal with reassuring symbolic rituals like punctuality, politeness, and present-giving. They also often involve more subtle processes like anticipating a mate's desires and tuning in to his or her feelings: *"He should know that I will need his help"* or *"She should know that I am feeling down."*

People are inclined to punish their partner for any breach of rules, even when such an infraction in itself brings no real loss or pain. The "offender" becomes angry because the infraction seems trivial and the spouse's reaction is so far out of proportion to any real hurt. Besides, the "offender" feels constrained by the implicit rule. The "offender" thus becomes the offended and may counterattack, so that the spouse actually *does* experience the pain that the rule was supposed to prevent. Thus, we see one of the paradoxes of disturbed relationships: the rules that are carefully constructed to prevent unhappiness actually lead to unhappiness.

Many couples believe that problems should not occur in marriage in the first place. People often complain, if only to themselves, *"If she [or he] truly loved me, we would not quarrel."* When problems do occur, they seem to violate the implicit rule that couples should not argue; mates therefore become angry over the very existence of conflict. They have devised a formula that reads: disagreement = lack of acceptance, respect, and love. Since the combination of anger and recrimination distracts the couple from solving their problem, the result can be an escalating cycle of hostility.

Enforcing the Rules

Knowing what to expect from a spouse provides a sense of stability in planning, handling crises, and making decisions. These shared expectations, moreover, serve the vital function of providing the marriage partners with guides as to what each is expected to contribute to the relationship.

Hidden expectations, however, disrupt a relationship rather than stabilize it. These unspoken rules often revolve around a symbolic act, such as a husband's offering to take care of the children while the wife takes a break, or a wife's preparing precisely the right kind of meal. Some symbolic rules apply to other members of the family: "If you care for me, you will be considerate to my parents and siblings" is an example.

Even these symbolic rules need not necessarily cause serious problems. But when they are wrapped in the trappings of *absolute* imperatives—injunctions and prohibitions, *shoulds* and *should nots*—they are particularly troublesome.

There are several kinds of *shoulds* and *should nots*, many of them useful. The most obvious *shoulds* have to do with carrying out a particular job properly, for example, fixing the washing machine. Another kind of imperative protects against danger. For instance, "safety first" rules are especially important in families; members should lock doors, turn off the stove, drive carefully, and so on.

Other rules apply to social situations. It is a given that one spouse is expected to do nothing to diminish the other's social image. Thus, in public, the spouse should be concerned, helpful, respectful, and should avoid being callous, uncooperative, and disparaging. Finally, rules regarding the financial security of the family, such as not overspending, are vital to its existence.

These rules are quite reasonable, but they can cause trouble if improperly applied. If people treat them as absolute and inviolable, and if infractions are regarded as warranting punishment, a conflict is inevitable.

Ted, for example, believed that Karen *should know* her tardiness bothered him, that she should therefore always be on time. Rather than discussing his sensitivity with her, he simply criticized her for being late, as though tardiness were a mortal sin in itself. Karen, on the other hand, saw nothing wrong in being a little late. She believed that Ted knew his nagging upset her and that he should appreciate all the things she did that he wanted her to do—he should not pick on her for the few things that she overlooked.

The *shoulds* may go beyond simply coercing another person to comply with our wishes. Dominating and controlling another person through *shoulds* may be a source of satisfaction in itself. What people forget is that agreeing to their partner's wishes is also a source of satisfaction.

Tyranny of the *Shoulds*

When we strip away the veneer of ingratiation in our dealings with others, we can expose hidden threats. We may use honey to get our way but hold in reserve the iron fist. If we encounter resistance, we can insist that others comply . . ."or else." The obligations we impose carry with them a strong hint of punishment in the form of criticism, threats, anger, or sulking.

The absolute nature of the *shoulds* poses problems in marriage because, in actuality, to comply totally with another person's imperatives means to submerge one's own personality, goals, and needs. An exaggerated or rigid set of *shoulds* can tyrannize others, as well as ourselves.

Psychoanalyst Karen Horney, in a series of books on the "neurotic personality," introduced the concept of the "tyranny of the *shoulds*." She saw the neurotic person as making unreasonable claims and demands based on an assumed right. These claims took the form of an insistence that others follow one's dictates, regardless of their wellbeing or needs. When these demands were thwarted, the person would become enraged. Other claims were leveled against the world, fate, or God: "I deserve to be happy," "It's unfair that life is so difficult," "People should treat me better." These people were so caught up in outrage over their own apparently disproportionate share of difficulties that they could not enjoy—indeed might ruin—the pleasures available to them in life.

Such demands and claims cause trouble in marriage. As the psychologist Albert Ellis noted, people not only want their mates to treat them with kindness all the time, but *demand* that they do so. When the mate does not live up to their expectations, they then become enraged. They think, *"He has no right to treat me this way," "I deserve better than this," "She let me down."*

Such people become very upset when they are thwarted or disappointed, a reaction expressed in thoughts or statements like "I can't stand to be treated this way." Related to this mechanism is what Ellis calls "awfulizing": "It's awful to be married to a person who is unfeeling." A short step away is "devilizing": "He's a terrible person— a bum" or "She's hateful—a real bitch." In "devilizing," diabolical characteristics are attributed to the spouse, who may be seen as malicious, manipulative, or deceitful. An inevitable outcome of these steps is "catastrophizing": "I can never breathe as long as I am stuck in this marriage" or "I will always be unhappy." Further examples and definitions of these mental mechanisms are found in Chapter 8.

Consider how absolute these statements are. The spouse is a "terrible person," without any redeeming qualities; his or her behavior is inexcusable, unforgivable, and incorrigible. The pain of frustration and disappointment is total and intolerable; the future of the relationship is bleak, without a ray of hope.

The demands and claims described by Horney and Ellis are transformed into self-defeating mental (cognitive) distortions. People's demands that their mate *always* treat them with kindness, for example, inevitably lead to a letdown. Even the most loving spouse is incapable of constant kindness. Hence, a single lapse could be distorted into the conviction *"She always ignores my wishes."*

Breaking the Rules

Shoulds and *should nots* form a wall that protects the partner from feeling vulnerable. If the wall is penetrated at any point—i.e., if a rule is broken—then the partner reacts as though he or she has been attacked: "An attack on the rule is an attack on me."

Sometimes a violated *should* represents real damage to the partner.

Most often, though, a partner perceives an offense when the damage is only potential or hypothetical. Consider the following instances:

▷ A child did not show good table manners at home when there were guests. His mother became so angry she "felt like shaking him."

▷ A husband did not mail a letter when he said he would. It made the later pickup anyway, but his wife became angry. She thought, *"What if it was important to get the letter out?"*

▷ A wife went through a traffic signal just as it was turning red. Her husband became furious. He thought, *"Suppose a car had been speeding the other way. We could have been killed!"*

These kinds of reactions fall into the realm of *what-if* rules. People who are particularly vigilant, keyed to the possibility of attack or offense, are especially dominated by such rules. Their mode of operation is directed by a variety of *shoulds* and *should nots* designed to minimize danger. When one of these injunctions is violated, they react as though they are endangered. Their sense of vulnerability, heightened by a rule's infraction, leads them to lash out at the offender. And then, having done what they believe is necessary to prevent a recurrence of the violation, they become content that their vulnerability has been protected.

Punishment

Another kind of imperative is what might be called the "double *shoulds.*" Most people are not usually aware of the *shoulds* at all, just as they are not aware of other automatic thoughts. But they can catch the *shoulds* and the double *shoulds* in action if they focus on their thoughts as they begin to feel angry. The double *shoulds* consist of an initial thought, a negative evaluation like *"My spouse should not have refused to listen to me"* or *"She should not have gotten angry at me."* This gives rise to a second *should,* an instruction to retaliate: *"If I don't do something, she'll get away with this. I should yell at her."*

Max demonstrated the double *shoulds* clearly. Whenever Sybil made a mistake, he would think, *"She should be more careful."* (First *should.*) His next thought was an instruction to himself to criticize her: *"I should tell her that she's careless and negligent."* (Second *should.*) When Sybil made a wrong turn or ran over a rut while driving the car, for example, Max would think, *"It's awful that she messed* up." He had the insistent thought, *"I must tell her she's not driving properly."*

What is curious about these reprimands is that they persist despite repeated evidence of their uselessness—and even destructiveness. They have the force of the thoughts of obsessive-compulsives, who go through such rituals as washing their hands continually to prevent an imaginary infection.

If people can check their internal commands to punish, they can break the habit of reproaching and criticizing to control their partner's actions. But a much better point at which to stop this chain reaction would be the moment when people first feel offended (*"She shouldn't have done that"*). If they decide that their anger is justified, then the chain reaction proceeds; however, if they determine that becoming angry is not warranted, they can stop the chain reaction at that point. It takes a very rapid reappraisal of a situation, however, to see that a reprisal is uncalled for. Once the hostility begins to form, it is difficult to stop an emerging criticism (Chapter 17).

Emergence of Rules

Where do the rules in a marriage come from? Why do they seem to acquire full force only after a total commitment? There are several kinds of expectations that operate at different stages of a marriage. The early, romantic expectations concern loving and being loved—continuously. One of life's cruel deceptions is the myth that the intense idealization and infatuation that draw a couple together will guarantee a loving relationship over the years. Sometimes this romantic notion is fortified by the belief *"If I am a good spouse, I will surely be loved and be happy."*

Although the notion that couples have to work at their relationship has become commonplace, it is surprising how few people actually follow this precept—or know what to do. In the early phase of marriage, the idealization and passionate attachment tend to smooth over differences. As time goes on, many partners may avoid facing their emerging differences out of a futile hope that things will work themselves out. Moreover, one of the mates may be oblivious to the fact that there are real difficulties or may believe that the partner is only manufacturing problems or is a chronic complainer. When the partners finally do attempt to solve their problems, they may have accumulated so many memories of slights and injustices that they can no longer approach their difficulties in a dispassionate way.

Expectations in the early years of marriage are shaped in part by a person's conception of the roles of wife and husband. Spouses bring to marriage their own special notions that are often derived from their own familial experiences.

People do not necessarily copy their parents in deciding how a husband and wife should behave. A husband, for instance, may regard his father as an appropriate example of "husbandhood," or he may react against what he sees as his father's "weakness" or "tyranny" by assuming opposite characteristics. These assumptions are rarely expressed openly, discussed, or agreed on by the partners. Further, the silent assumptions of each mate about the roles of husband and wife rarely match.

The basic contract of a marriage is *"I will take care of my husband [or wife] and, in return, he [or she] will provide for my basic needs."* But the partners may have very different definitions for these two components of the contract. Further, mates may lack the one ingredient that could make their partnership effective—flexibility.

A major epoch in the emergence of rules begins after a child is born into the family. Some studies have shown that at this time, husbands as well as wives are prone to experience symptoms of depression and increased irritability. The spouses' differing childhood experiences shape different strategies for child rearing, with different expectations regarding the role each parent should play. These differences may lead to conflict.

The first child usually has a strong impact on the young mother, who generally assumes a heavy set of obligations for parenting. But in addition to the responsibility she accepts for herself, she also increases her expectations of her husband, with respect to care both for their child and for herself. If her husband does not respond to her unspoken *shoulds*, she is likely to become resentful or even depressed.

The husband, on the other hand, may blithely assume that he will continue to receive the same attention and support from his wife that he received before the child was born. If his wife is less "giving" than previously, he may see her as *deliberately* withholding the affection or attention to which he is "entitled."

Each spouse seems to operate according to a similar set of entitlements: *"I'm putting more into the family. I'm entitled to as much affection, attention, and support as I got before."* But given the physical and psychological demands of pregnancy and the postnatal period, the new parents generally have fewer resources to draw on and offer as support, and so each is likely to feel deprived. A relationship that had been relatively tranquil can easily become unsettled after the birth of a child.

Dealing with
Rules and Attitudes

This section contains a questionnaire listing various formulas that shape partners' reactions to specific situations. Also included in the questionnaire are some attitudes that may affect relationships adversely. When people have such attitudes or believe very strongly in these formulas, they may lose the flexibility essential for a harmonious relationship. Rigid adherence to these attitudes leads to clashes, making compromises and ordinary give-and-take behavior more difficult. Psychologists Norman Epstein, James Pretzer, and Barbara Fleming have found that individuals in distressed marriages tend to get high scores on questionnaires like this one.

Complete the questionnaire. If you have particular problems in your marriage, look at the items in which you have a high score. These may give you some clues as to the pressure points in your marriage. It is particularly helpful when both spouses participate, because they can then educate one another, as well as themselves, regarding their specific sensitive points. Note that this questionnaire is not designed to give you an absolute score by which you can determine whether your relationship is in trouble. The scores for each item should be used simply to help you identify potential problems. To repeat: a high score suggests a possible counterproductive belief or attitude.

Beliefs about Your Relationship

INSTRUCTIONS: For each of the following fifteen statements, select the number (1 to 7) of the category that best fits how much you agree or disagree. Enter that number on the line next to each statement.

AGREE: *completely* (7) *a good deal* (6) *somewhat* (5)

NEITHER AGREE NOR DISAGREE (4)

DISAGREE: *somewhat* (3) *a good deal* (2) *completely* (1)

_____ 1 / If a person has any questions about the relationship, then it means there is something wrong with it.

_____ 2 / If my partner truly loved me, we would not have any quarrels.

_____ 3 / If my partner really cared, he or she would always feel affection for me.

_____ 4 / If my partner gets angry at me or is critical in public, this indicates he or she doesn't really love me.

_____ 5 / My partner should know what is important to me without my having to tell him or her.

_____ 6 / If I have to ask for something that I really want, it spoils it.

_____ 7 / If my partner really cared, he or she would do what I ask.

_____ 8 / A good relationship should not have any problems.

_____ 9 / If people really love each other, they should not have to work on their relationship.

_____ 10 / If my partner does something that upsets me, I think it is because he or she deliberately wants to hurt me.

_____ 11 / When my partner disagrees with me in public, I think it is a sign that he or she doesn't care for me very much.

_____ 12 / If my partner contradicts me, I think that he or she doesn't have much respect for me.

_____ 13 / If my partner hurts my feelings, I think that it is because he or she is mean.

_____ 14 / My partner always tries to get his or her own way.

_____ 15 / My partner doesn't listen to what I have to say.

NOTE: This questionnaire has been adapted in part from the Relationship Belief Inventory of Epstein, Pretzer, and Fleming.

STATIC
IN COMMUNICATION

▷ "My husband is deaf. He never hears what I say."

▷ "She talks every subject to death."

▷ "He always gets defensive when I ask him something."

▷ "She makes everything into an argument."

▷ "He is stubborn . . . he won't even consider what I have to say."

▷ "He never says what he means."

▷ "That's not what I meant."

Such statements are typical of troubled relationships. While they may simply reflect inadequate communication, they may also point to profound problems. Even couples with only mild difficulties in communicating can have important misunderstandings. These often lead to frustration and hostility—and consequently to a further impairment of communication. In the worst cases, even simple conversations become the forum for competitiveness, power struggles, and mutual depreciation. Far from promoting clarification and understanding, words become weapons; discussions become battles.

Indirectness
and Ambiguity

Any couple is faced with making dozens of decisions large and small: division of domestic duties, budgetary matters, social and recreational activities, where to live, whether to have children, how to raise children, and on and on. Clear, precise communication helps facilitate such decision making, while ambiguity confounds it.

It is distressing to observe how poorly some otherwise articulate people fare when it comes to communicating their thoughts, desires, and feelings with their own partners. Some state their wishes in a way that defies understanding. They express their opinions vaguely, talk around the point, get lost in trivial details—all under the bland assumption that their partner grasps what they are trying to say. One partner may swamp the discussion with excessive verbiage while the other impoverishes it with a paucity of words—both erroneously believing that they are contributing to mutual understanding.

Sometimes, they seem to be speaking different languages; they use the same words, but the message sent is totally different from the message received.

It is not surprising, given such faulty communication styles, that both partners feel frustrated. Since each is oblivious to his or her own contribution to the murky exchange, blame is laid at the other mate for being obtuse or bullheaded.

Marjorie, for example, wanted Ken to invite her to a favorite cocktail lounge overlooking a bay to celebrate their anniversary. She archly asked him, "Ken, do you feel like going out for a drink tonight?" Ken, who was feeling tired, missed the hidden message contained in her question. He responded, "No, I'm too tired." Marjorie was extremely disappointed. Only after feeling hurt and sorry for herself did she realize that she had not communicated to Ken her real desire—to celebrate their anniversary. When she later made clear her true wish, he readily agreed to celebrate.

Consider the following exchange between Tom, an architect, and Sally, a pediatrician, an unmarried couple who were busy restoring their first home, a handsome Victorian townhouse in the heart of the city. Note how personal fears and doubts can lead one partner or the other to skew a message, thus making it vague and misleading. Inevitably, misunderstandings arise. In this case the ambiguous first statement triggered a row over a simple social decision:

SALLY: The Scotts said something about dropping over to their house on Thursday.

TOM: [hurt] They invited *you?* [meaning: *Only you and not me?*]

SALLY: [testily] I just told you. [*He's challenging my veracity.*]

TOM: [hurt] How come they invited *you?* [meaning: *You and not me also.*]

SALLY: [hurt] Obviously they like me. [*He doesn't think I'm likable enough to be invited on my own.*]

TOM: Well, go, I'm sure you'll have a wonderful time. [*I hope you have a terrible time.*]

SALLY: [bitter] I'm sure I will. [*He doesn't want to go because they issued the invitation to me.*]

Something is obviously askew in Sally and Tom's communications. Their problem, however, lies behind the words, not in what is said. Tom and Sally are out of step with each other because, in an attempt to protect themselves, each is holding back significant information, leading each to misinterpret the other's statements.

To start with, Sally is pleased that the Scotts invited her because she believes that she has been in Tom's shadow; she fears people find Tom more desirable, and that she just tags along. She knows that when the Scotts issued the invitation to her, they meant a plural *you* —including Tom. But in telling Tom, she is purposely ambiguous because she is afraid that he might refuse.

The Scotts are basically Tom's friends, but Sally wants to be liked by them. She is concerned that he might resent their having issued the invitation to her and not to him. To protect herself against being rebuffed by Tom, Sally relays the information in such a vague way that he misinterprets her statement. He thinks she is bragging that only *she* was invited, and he feels hurt. Consequently, Tom emphasizes "invited *you?*"—instead of asking whether the invitation was issued "to us." His emphasis on *you* leads Sally to believe that he is skeptical that the Scotts regard her as desirable enough to invite on her own. Missing Tom's point, Sally responds to the presumed challenge with a flip statement—"I just told you."

Tom, still operating on the premise that he was specifically excluded, interprets her response as a gibe and retaliates by sarcastically wishing her "a wonderful time." Sally counterattacks with a further jab, without even clarifying whether Tom will accept the invitation.

The obvious drawback of indirectness is that it leads to misunderstandings. For example, Sally is generally very concerned about crossing Tom. Therefore, when she sends out her "feelers," she says things in a way that she hopes will elicit a positive signal from Tom; then, based on this, she will either pursue the idea or drop it.

On a separate occasion, for example, she wanted to invite another couple over to their house. She started off tentatively, testing the waters, as it were: "I wonder what the Richards are doing these days?" Tom, missing the hint, responded, "I have no idea," and changed the subject. Sally interpreted his answer as a signal from him that he didn't want to see the Richards. (It later came out that he actually would have been pleased to entertain them.)

After being thwarted a number of times when she made suggestions in an indirect way, Sally began to think, *"He's antisocial"* and *"He never wants to do what I want to do—he's just interested in himself."*

Later, when her anger built to a high pitch, Sally accused Tom of being antisocial and never caring about what she wanted. Tom was mystified. When she claimed that she had been telling him this all along, he angrily disagreed. He then accused her, "You never know what you want and you never say what you want." Sally considered his accusations unfair because, in her mind, she had been forthright in her suggestions. To Tom, on the other hand, she seemed incapable of making up her mind and was unfair in blaming him for her own inadequacies.

When relationships are working well, partners are often able to communicate with hints and allusions such as Sally was using. Their own private language and special idioms can carry the message. But when the relationship is strained, the private language is no longer adequate and can promote misunderstanding.

Defensiveness

People like Sally and Tom often are imprecise to protect themselves from being put down or rebuffed. The likelihood of misunderstanding further increases when they allow their personal agenda—such as the wish to prove something about themselves or the desire to thwart rejection or ridicule—to muddy what they are trying to convey. Such defensiveness obscures their messages so that they are bound to be misinterpreted.

The fear of being rejected for voicing a certain opinion or making a request increases defensiveness. Such defensiveness not only led to the confusion between Tom and Sally but also made it harder for each to decipher the hidden meanings in the other's statements.

In the following exchange, their positions are reversed, with Tom in the vulnerable position.

TOM: Are we going to visit my mother this weekend?

SALLY: I don't think so—I've got a lot of things to do.

TOM: [angry] You never want to visit my mother.

In this interchange, Sally chose to take Tom's question at its face value, as simply asking for information rather than making a request. She disregarded Tom's true meaning: *"I'd like to visit my mother this weekend."* Tom, wary of stating his wish outright, became annoyed and reproachful when Sally refused.

Of course, beneath the surface, there are more complex problems in Tom and Sally's relationship than their ambiguous and defensive ways of communicating. Sally's conversation about the Scotts' invitation contains her hidden problem: her sense of being socially inferior to Tom and her consequent drive to prove that she, too, can be liked by Tom's friends. At the same time, she is defensive because of her fear that Tom will denigrate her attempts to build up her own image. Tom, in return, interprets Sally's talk as a sign that she is competing with him (by showing that she is more desired than he), and he feels impelled to "put her in her place." In the interchange regarding Tom's mother, Sally asserts her power in the relationship by ignoring Tom's implied request and, in effect, invites him to retaliate.

Although such patterns may tax a relationship, there is often enough strength in the bond to absorb the strain. Tom and Sally did indeed enjoy each other's company a great deal; one of the strong points in the early years of their relationship was the pleasure they took in talking with each other. However, as awkward communications led to mounting misunderstandings, their exchanges became bogged down by covert accusations and recriminations. Even the shared pleasures of conversation became tainted and lost their binding power. Even minor issues that could be relatively easily settled became a source of conflict because of the indirectness and defensiveness of one partner in "sending a message," and the "deaf spot" of the other in receiving it.

The problems posed by Sally and Tom were not very difficult to solve: they needed to practice having clear, straightforward discussions. Although they initially conducted these discussions in the presence of a counselor, they could have begun this program on their own. Guidelines that couples can use to improve their ways of communicating are described in Chapters 14, 15, and 16.

Missing the Message

Good communication involves more than getting your own ideas across; it also means understanding what is being said by the other person. People who are consistently vague or indirect in their speech lead their partners either to jump to incorrect conclusions or to ignore what they say. Others have difficulty in understanding their spouse's messages and thus misinterpret what they hear.

A study by psychologist Patricia Noller showed major differences in the understanding of communications between couples who have a good marital adjustment and couples with a poor one. The couples with unhappy marriages were less accurate in decoding what their spouses meant than were the happily married spouses. It is especially revealing that the unhappy couples performed as well as the happy spouses in decoding messages from *strangers*.

This finding suggests that the whole process of communication, which can work well outside the marriage, is somewhat derailed in distressed couples. Their misunderstandings are generally not rooted in some chronic communication deficiency with everyone; they are specific to the disturbance in the marital relationship.

Monologues, Interruptions, and Silent Listening

Some problems in communication arise because of differences in partners' speaking styles, such as timing, pausing, pacing, and so on. In a typical case described by Deborah Tannen, a professor of linguistics, a woman was annoyed at a male colleague because he answered all the audience's questions at a workshop they were conducting. She blamed him for dominating her, hogging center stage, and having no respect for her views.

Actually, the "domination" resulted from differences in the *timing* of their answers. By habit, she took much longer to respond to questions than he did. Consequently, while she was getting around to answering a question, he would become restless and concerned. To avoid what he feared would be an uncomfortable silence and the impression that neither of them could respond to the question, he would take the initiative and answer himself. His colleague interpreted this behavior as a form of sexist domination.

Such differences in timing and pausing can cause difficulties in a marriage. A husband, for example, who pauses for a long time between sentences may be interrupted by his wife, who pauses only briefly. He then becomes angry because he hasn't finished his train of thought and, in fact, may lose track of it thanks to his wife's interruption. He may make the accusation "You always interrupt me . . . you never want to hear my opinion" without realizing there is a more benign explanation for her actions.

A similar problem can arise when the briefly pausing spouse is talking. She may be expressing a point of view interspersed with what seem to her to be reasonable pauses for her husband's responses. Her husband, however, being a long pauser, may not recognize these

breakpoints and conclude instead that their discussion
by his wife.

Some people are temperamentally "long talkers" an
to keep talking far beyond the point of diminishing retu
around a subject, or they flood the listener with a pleth
essary detail. It often seems almost impossible for them
point or to complete a topic. When I have noted this co
style to these people, they have generally responded with astonish-
ment—because they have believed they were indeed communicating
effectively.

The kinds of complaints leveled against "overtalkers" are issued,
too, against "inanimate listeners." It is not uncommon for a wife to
tell me, "My husband never pays attention to what I am saying." The
husband, though, is able to repeat back verbatim what she has just
said. Actually, her observation stems from the fact that her husband is
listening too quietly—he is not responsive in his listening. He pays
attention impassively without giving her any feedback, such as nod-
ding, gesturing, changing his facial expression, or uttering important
listening sounds like "mm-hmm," "uh-uh," or "yeah."

A number of studies suggest men and women tend to listen in
different ways. Men generally utter listening sounds comparatively
infrequently and, when they do, they are generally meant to indicate
"I agree with you." But as anthropologists Daniel Maltz and Ruth
Borker point out, women take these feedback utterances to mean *"I
am listening."* Thus, women are more liberal than men in sending
these nonverbal signals, and they also expect to receive them: a wife
may believe that her husband is not paying attention at all, even
though he may be carefully, if impassively, listening.

Many people attach a symbolic meaning to these signals, which
indicate not only *"I'm listening"* but also *"I enjoy what you're saying"* or *"I care about what you are saying."* Ultimately, the symbolic
meaning may be *"I care for you."* In contrast, the absence of such
signals may have a negative symbolic meaning: *"I don't respect you"*
or *"I don't care for you."*

Partners are generally unaware of the power of this subtle aspect
of marital conversation. But this ingredient laces their exchanges,
even seemingly innocuous ones, with implicit meanings of acceptance, respect, and affection—or rejection, disrespect, and hostility.

If mates could become sensitive to these hidden meanings, much
of their frustration would be reduced. The mismatch of conversational
styles, for instance, could be alleviated by their agreeing on a set of
"rules of conversational etiquette." Once the problem is identified,
long pausers can learn not to take offense at being interrupted and

train themselves to pick up the threads of their story after an interruption. Interrupters, likewise, can learn to judge whether a pressing observation or remark justifies an interjection or is simply a sign of their impatience. Overtalkers can train themselves to be more concise and undertalkers, more expansive. And unresponsive spouses can give more signals of paying attention, while their mates should recognize that silence is not necessarily a sign of indifference.

Deaf Spots
and Blind Spots

Deaf spots and blind spots become apparent when one partner does not mentally register what the spouse is really communicating in words, gestures, and the like. This lapse leads to complaints such as "You don't know what I want or what I'm asking" and "You don't know me at all." Couples with deaf spots often have difficulty with even simple decisions. Although both partners may want to cooperate, their lack of a meaningful exchange of information handicaps their agreeing on important issues, such as the division of duties and the rearing of children.

Although a partner's deaf spots or blind spots may be caused by insensitivity, they can frequently be traced to hypersensitivity and defensiveness. People may tune out what they don't want to hear, because the message may be directed toward a vulnerable area. Apparently benign discussions can present a threat to the self-esteem of the partners. In order to protect themselves against damage to their pride, or against rejection, they set up defenses that block their view of the practical problem. Sally's long-standing sense of inferiority and Tom's sensitive pride, for example, set up a barrier to communication and understanding.

Sometimes one mate may be totally blind to the impact of his personality on his spouse. Consider the following couple, for example. Harvey, a sharp, aggressive attorney who didn't know how to confine his adversarial tactics to the courtroom, delighted in "putting down" Stacey, his wife, a homemaker with an empty nest who had gone back to school to finish her B.A. In social situations he would ridicule what she said; in private, he was likely to dismiss her complaints. Stacey was unable to tell Harvey how distressed she was about this. On the few occasions when she was able to express herself, Harvey would dismiss her complaints by labeling her "hypersensitive." At other times he called her "neurotic" and advised her to get professional help. Harvey was oblivious to the pain he was causing his wife.

After twenty-five years of marriage, Stacey announced to Harvey that she could no longer live with him and was leaving. He was completely floored by her action. He had been unaware of how miserable she had felt all those years from his put-downs. Stacey explained that she had stayed with him only long enough for their children to reach an age at which they could more easily sustain the breakup of the marriage. Since the children were now grown, she would no longer live with him.

It is a pity that they did not seek counseling early in their relationship, or have access to a useful guidebook on marital misunderstandings and miscommunications. They both remarried. In their second marriages—which were successful—Harvey was very circumspect with his wife, and Stacey was far more assertive in informing her husband about what she did not like. They both had learned their lessons well.

Differences in Pacing

Deborah Tannen describes the following case: Sandy complains that Matt really doesn't listen to her. He asks her a question, but before she can answer, he asks another question—or starts to answer it himself. When they are together with Matt's friends, the other people talk so fast that Sandy can't get a word in edgewise. Afterward, Matt complains that Sandy was too quiet, but she knows that she isn't quiet with her own friends. Matt decides that Sandy's quietness means she doesn't like his friends. But the reason that Sandy is uncomfortable with them is that she believes they ignore her—and she can't find a way to participate in their conversations. This is a prime example of how a difference in conversational style leads to misunderstanding, anger, and criticism.

How does this misunderstanding arise? Matt's friends follow a different code of etiquette than do Sandy and her friends. Matt's friends talk a good deal—sometimes in parallel conversations, sometimes in a monologue—and they frequently interrupt each other. Sandy and her friends, however, consider it rude to talk in this way. Their code of politeness calls for discrete interchanges, without one person's talking over another. The result of this difference in conversational style is that Matt erroneously sees Sandy's quietness as meaning she dislikes his friends. For Sandy, their "shutting me out of their conversation" means to her that they don't think she has anything useful to contribute.

Use of Questioning

Asking questions would seem a very normal way to carry on a conversation. We ask questions not only to get information but to get support, to find out what the other person wants, to negotiate, and to make decisions. Nonetheless, questioning can lead to misunderstanding and distress. Questions are obviously worthwhile, but the person who is asked may regard the questioning as a challenge to his or her competence, knowledge, or honesty. Since we expect conversation to proceed under its own steam, asking too many questions, or the wrong sort, may in itself send a message of no confidence, or at least indicate a lack of rapport.

When Sally questions Tom, for instance, he starts to bristle, thinking that she is challenging his veracity, questioning his ability, or doubting his intentions. Some people may regard questions as a threat. They perceive the questioning as a kind of probing, a working through their defenses to discover soft spots (in somewhat the same way as a dentist probes for tooth decay). Indeed, some spouses *do* probe more deeply than they need to because it satisfies their own emotional needs.

One woman, for instance, told me, "I like to get inside people's minds and see how they are ticking. I want to understand everything about them." But when she used this approach with her husband, he was irritated at what he perceived as a relentless interrogation.

A person may resort to questioning when the conversational partner is being indirect. For example, when Ted, the intellectualizer, is not clear about what Karen is saying, he often tries to pin her down. Karen responds by saying, "Why are you always cross-examining me? You always put me on the defensive." Ted, of course, is hurt by her complaint, because he is simply trying to ferret out what Karen means or desires. Karen, however, feels hemmed in by his line of questioning. Ted has a special problem in wanting to be absolutely sure of his facts. Karen's problem is related to her concern about being pressured and controlled.

A particular type of problem may be created when *why* questions are employed: this kind of question can make the other person defensive. Although the questioner may be quite innocent in asking the questions and is sincerely seeking information, the use of *why* at the beginning of a question may remind the partner of reproachful questioning by a parent: "Why did you come home so late?" or "Why are you still watching television?" Further, *why* questions sometimes imply a distrust or even suspicion. For example, when Marjorie asked

Ken why he was replacing the boiler, he took this as a vote of no confidence in his ability to make decisions—even though she simply wanted to find out the reason for his decision.

There are ways to ask questions that circumvent the use of the word *why:* Here are two examples:

▷ "Could you explain to me your decision about the purchase of a new boiler?"

▷ "Is there some problem about your getting home on time?"

The differences between husband and wife in their use of questioning may hark back to their upbringing. In some families, parents are continuously asking for explanations, and it seems second nature both to ask for explanations and to give them. In other families, explanations are rarely asked for or given. A spouse from the first type of family may ask questions quite often, whereas somebody raised in a more taciturn family is not accustomed to being asked questions—or answering them. Such a person may therefore consider his spouse's question as a challenge or invasion of privacy.

There are also dangers in asking too few questions. Spouses who never ask questions are likely to proceed according to their own hunches, which may be wrong a good part of the time. Moreover, one spouse may interpret such reticence in his or her mate as a lack of interest.

The important point about conversational styles is that they are *learned*—and if they interfere with effective communication, they can be *unlearned.* Many people believe that their own style is the natural one but find that they can "unlearn" it and assume a more adaptive style.

Differences
between the Sexes

Daniel Maltz and Ruth Borker summarize a number of findings that shed light on why marital partners have problems communicating. One reason is that men and women tend to have different conversational styles. Although a given person may have essentially the same style as the spouse, in most instances where there is a difference in style, the wife adopts a culturally defined, "feminine" conversational style; the husband, a "masculine" style.

Characteristically, women show a greater tendency to ask questions. In observations of female-male conversations, a question-answer pattern was found, with the females asking most of the questions. Some researchers believe that women's propensity for question asking indicates their investment in maintaining routine interactions between people. Their questioning is a sign they take responsibility for facilitating and sustaining the flow of conversation. This conversational device may also represent their greater involvement in personal relations.

Men are less likely than women to ask personal questions. Men are prone to think, *"If she wants to tell me something, she'll tell me without my asking."* A woman might reflect, *"If I don't ask, he'll think that I don't care."* For men, questions may represent intrusive meddling and an invasion of privacy; for women, however, they are a sign of intimacy and an expression of caring.

Women use more utterances to encourage responses from the other person. As was mentioned previously, they are more likely than men to use listening signals like "mm-hmm" to indicate that they are paying attention. A man, typically, will use this response only when he is agreeing with what his wife is saying, whereas his wife will use it simply to indicate she is listening. Thus, a husband may interpret his wife's listening signals as signs that his wife agrees with him. Later, he may feel betrayed when he discovers that she was not agreeing with him at all. He does not realize that she was simply indicating her interest in what he was saying and "keeping the conversational ball in the air." The wife, on the other hand, may feel ignored and let down because her husband is not making any of these listening sounds, which she then interprets as his lack of interest.

Men are more likely than women to make comments throughout the stream of conversation rather than wait until the other person finishes speaking. Women appear to be more troubled—and apt to make a "silent protest"—after they have been interrupted or have failed to evoke a listening response. This difference lies behind the complaint of many wives that "My husband always interrupts me" or "He never listens." Women also show a greater use of the pronouns *you* and *we,* which acknowledge the other speaker. This conversational style promotes a sense of unity.

Drawing on these research findings, a couple might keep in mind the following observation about the husband's conversational habits. First, as indicated earlier, men are more likely to interrupt their conversational partners—male or female. Second, they are less likely to respond to the comments of the other speaker; frequently they make no response or acknowledgment at all, give a delayed response at the end of their partner's statement, or show a minimum degree of enthusiasm. Third, they are more likely to challenge or dispute statements made by their partners, which explains why a husband may seem to be eternally argumentative. Finally, men make more declarations of fact or opinion than do women. Some wives resent the "voice of authority"—not realizing that their husband's assertions may represent a masculine style rather than a sense of superiority.

Given the contrast between conversational styles among men and women, the conditions are ripe for conflicts to arise. A wife, for example, could easily perceive her husband as uninterested, controlling, or unresponsive when his way of speaking simply reflects the style that he has learned to use with everyone, not just her. Judgments such as "My husband never listens" or "My husband disagrees with everything I say" most often reflect the husband's habits of speech rather than any insensitivity or ill will toward his wife. Knowing that such differences between the sexes exist and that they are not caused by bad faith, lack of respect, or lack of interest can help couples to note their partner's style without taking offense, and to provide a safeguard against misinterpretation.

Despite these differences in communication styles, there is no question that husbands and wives can improve their relationships by learning to synchronize their styles. In view of the important symbolic meaning of his speaking style, a husband could facilitate communication if he, for instance, became more active in listening and interrupted or disputed his wife less. It would also help for him to pay more attention to the spirit of the conversation and recognize that signals of his attention (such as active listening signals or gestures) are often just as powerful as the words themselves—if not more so. Finally, he has to recognize that his dogmatic statements are "conversation stoppers."

Explanation for
Differences in Style

Although it is tempting to attribute the differences in conversational styles to asymmetrical power relationships between men and women, or to the existence of personality differences between them, there are also other explanations. A great deal of evidence supports the notion that, with respect to conversational style, men and women behave as though they belong to two different subcultures. Maltz and Borker point out that there are highly specific differences between men and women in their concept of friendly conversations, their rules for engaging in conversation, and their rules for interpreting what the partner is saying. This sociological approach sees conversational problems as arising either from differences in the way people talk and listen, or from how they hear what the partner says.

Origin of the Sex
Differences

THE WORLD OF GIRLS

Maltz and Borker point out that to a large extent friendships among girls, in contrast to boys, are based on their talking together. Systematic observations indicate that girls learn to give support, to let others speak, and to acknowledge what other girls say as a way of maintaining relationships of equality and closeness. Thus, talking represents a bridge, a binding force, among girls.

Girls both form and end friendships through talk. Best girlfriends share secrets that bind them together. And girls are much freer than boys in discussing their feelings—love, hate, anxiety, sadness.

Girls also learn to criticize and argue with other girls without being perceived as "bossy" or "mean." They are less inclined than boys to order others around because this behavior runs contrary to their concept of equality. Shifting alliances within girls' small peer groups lead them to pay much more attention to reading the intent of other girls. Thus, girls become increasingly sophisticated in divining one another's motives, detecting nuances, and interpreting what people mean.

THE WORLD OF BOYS

Boys tend to play in larger, more organized groups, and these groups place a higher premium on status and dominance. Boys who are less dominant have a relatively low status within their group and are made to feel the inferiority of their status position. In contrast to that of girls, the social world of boys consists of posturing, asserting dominance, and trying to command the attention of an audience. Their conversation is filled with orders like "Get up," "Give it to me," and with ridicule: "You're a dope." They also are inclined to threats or boasts, such as "If you don't shut up, I'm going to bust you in the mouth." Further, they tend to be much more argumentative than girls.

While girls use words as a bridge, boys more often than girls use them as weapons or instruments of dominance. The most powerful boy in a group is not necessarily the most physically aggressive but rather the boy who is most effective and skillful in his speech. Boys who tell tales are frequently faced with mockery, challenges, and sarcastic side comments. And boys are given to put-downs and verbal tricks to "catch" another boy.

Given these large differences in conversational style between boys and girls, it is not surprising that friction arises when a boy is paired with a girl rather than another boy or group of boys. A boy's conversation revolves around dominance and competitiveness, whereas a girl looks for intimacy and equality.

A poll by *Family Circle* magazine had illuminating results: the respondents indicated that women are much more willing to talk about the intimate details of their lives with other women than they are with men. In fact, 69 percent said that if unhappy, they would rather reveal this feeling to their best women friends than they would to their spouses or boyfriends.

SUMMARY OF DIFFERENCES

Key conversational differences between men and women, which seem to be derived from the different subcultures of boys and girls, can be summarized as follows:

▷ Women seem to regard questions as a way to maintain a conversation, while men view them as requests for information.

▷ Women tend to connect "bridges" between what their conversational partner has just said and what it is that they have to say.

▷ Men do not generally follow this rule and often appear to ignore the preceding comment by their partner.

▷ Women seem to interpret aggressiveness by their partner as an attack that disrupts the relationship. Men seem to view aggressiveness simply as a form of conversation.

▷ Women are more likely to share feelings and secrets. Men like to discuss less intimate topics, such as sports and politics.

▷ Women tend to discuss problems with one another, share their experiences, and offer reassurances. Men, on the other hand, tend to hear women (as well as other men) who discuss problems with them as making explicit requests for solutions, rather than as simply looking for a sympathetic ear.

DIFFERENT MEANINGS OF TALK

These variations in the meaning of talk lead husbands and wives to have very different expectations. Women frequently want their partners to be a new, improved version of their best friend. They warm up when their husband tells them secrets, they enjoy being his confidante, and they are disturbed when their husband holds in his feelings.

Even though many husbands do not meet their wives' standards of intimacy, the fact remains that they are more likely to confide in their wives than in other people. When I have asked couples, "Whom do you most frequently confide in?" the husband generally responds, "My wife" and the wife says, "My best friend."

When it comes to talking out conflicts, again there is a sex difference. Many women, for example, take the attitude "The marriage is working as long as we can talk about it." Many husbands, on the other hand, have the view "The relationship is not working as long we keep talking about it."

Talking about problems makes some people (especially husbands) more and more upset; they would prefer to arrive at a quick, practical solution. But many people (especially wives) want to talk the problem out, because that is the way they get a sense of empathy, intimacy, and understanding.

Men and women tend to differ, too, in the way they respond to each other's problems. A wife, for example, may share a problem with her husband, hoping he will give her understanding and sympathy. Not infrequently, however, the husband fails to offer consolation. Instead, he is all business, trying to give his wife a practical solution; indicating areas in which she may be distorting or misinterpreting the situation; suggesting that she might be overreacting; and advising her how to avoid these problems in the future.

In these circumstances the wife may feel hurt or slighted. She is put out that her husband does not realize she knows perfectly well what to do about the situation, but merely wants his understanding—perhaps to tell her about similar experiences that he had. If the husband questions her interpretation of the problematic situation, she may read this reaction as criticism, indicating that there is something wrong with her. Instead, she wants him to convey to her in some way that she is not peculiar or wrong for reacting the way she does.

Husbands and wives frequently differ over what they consider important in what their mates tell them. For instance, a lawyer friend of mine, whose wife works in an art gallery, complains that she always wants to tell him "the trivial details about who said what to whom," while he would like to hear more about the kinds of paintings she is dealing with, her evaluation of them, and specific business details, such as purchasing strategies. He wants the facts and does not see the importance of his wife's conversations with her colleagues. To his wife, however, what happens between her and her associates at the gallery constitutes the fabric of her working life. Only a small proportion of her on-the-job attention is focused on details of the paintings themselves. Because she focuses on her interpersonal experiences—which strike him as trivial—the husband tends to cut her off. She is then hurt, because he seems to be telling her not only that what she says is unimportant and that her job is unimportant, but that *she* is unimportant.

The husband's chief satisfactions, on the other hand, come from talking about his law practice, politics, and sports. When he starts to discuss any of these areas, his wife thinks that he is lecturing her and is being condescending. Indeed, when I listen to his tone of voice, it is clear to me that there *is* a note of condescension, of which he is unaware. (Such sexist attitudes may be prominent among husbands and may become accentuated when their wives embark on their own careers.) In such a situation, the husband requires some consciousness raising in order to appreciate the importance his wife places on narrating her interpersonal work experiences. At the same time, he needs to modify his condescending way of instructing her, and to correct his estimation of her as intellectually inferior to him.

Partners will find it helpful to review the following checklists as a first step in determining whether impediments to their marital conversations exist. Ideally, each partner should complete the checklists and then compare their ratings. The first checklist concerns the styles of talking and listening that can hinder the exchange of ideas and information. The second checklist deals with the psychological difficulties that impede the flow of conversation. If after completing these checklists you would like concrete guidelines for improving communication, you might skip ahead to Chapters 14, 15, and 16, which contain a number of problem-solving approaches.

Problems in the Style
of Communication

Below is a list of behaviors that may cause problems. In the left-hand column, rate the behaviors your partner uses with you. Use the following numbers to indicate frequency:

(0) *does not apply*   (1) *rarely*   (2) *sometimes*   (3) *frequently*   (4) *all the time*

In the middle column, indicate how much the problem bothers you:

(0) *not at all*   (1) *slightly*   (2) *moderately*   (3) *a great deal*

In the right-hand column, rate the behaviors you use with your partner. Your partner should also complete this questionnaire.

	Communication Style		
	YOUR PARTNER WITH YOU	THIS BOTHERS ME	YOU WITH YOUR PARTNER
1 / Doesn't listen	_____	_____	_____
2 / Talks too much	_____	_____	_____
3 / Doesn't talk enough	_____	_____	_____
4 / Interrupts	_____	_____	_____
5 / Too vague	_____	_____	_____
6 / Never gets to the point	_____	_____	_____
7 / Doesn't nod or indicate agreement	_____	_____	_____
8 / Doesn't utter listening signals (for example, "mm-hmm")	_____	_____	_____
9 / Doesn't give mate a chance to talk	_____	_____	_____
10 / Won't discuss touchy subjects	_____	_____	_____
11 / Talks too much about touchy subjects	_____	_____	_____
12 / Asks too many questions	_____	_____	_____
13 / Doesn't ask enough questions	_____	_____	_____
14 / Shuts mate up	_____	_____	_____
15 / Withdraws when upset	_____	_____	_____

NOTE: There is no absolute score that indicates when you need to be concerned about communication. However, if you are aware of difficulties in this area, this checklist will enable you and your partner to pinpoint them and start to improve them. Keep in mind that your perception of your partner's behavior may be incorrect or exaggerated.

Psychological Problems
in Communication

Read the following statements. Next to each, enter the number (o to 4) that best indicates the frequency of your feelings. Your partner should also complete this questionnaire.

_____ 1 / I feel inhibited in discussing my problems with my partner.

_____ 2 / It's hard for me to express my feelings to my partner.

_____ 3 / I'm afraid to ask for what I want.

_____ 4 / I don't believe what my partner says.

_____ 5 / I'm afraid that what I have to say will make my partner angry.

_____ 6 / My partner won't take my concerns seriously.

_____ 7 / My partner talks down to me.

_____ 8 / My partner doesn't want to hear about my needs and feelings.

_____ 9 / I'm afraid that if I begin to express my feelings to my partner, I'll lose control of my emotions.

_____ 10 / I am concerned that if I open up with my partner, he or she will use this information against me in the future.

_____ 11 / If I expressed my true feelings, I'd regret what I said later.

NOTE: This checklist will help you to focus on the specific psychological or interpersonal problems that block effective communication. In later chapters, as we describe the negative influences of automatic thoughts and suggest specific training techniques in communication, you will have some clues to help you overcome these barriers.

6

BREAKDOWN
OF THE PARTNERSHIP

Threats to the
Marital Compact

Why do bitter arguments break out between people who presumably love and care about each other? During courtship, a natural self-centeredness of the partners dissolves in the fusion of their concerns and even identities. The penetrating rays of love that melt differences in temperament, interests, and goals help to generate altruism and empathy.

The partners *want* to please each other. They are gratified when they can make each other happy, and sad when their partner is sad. In seeking to please, they try to look at everything from their partner's point of view.

For many people, no doubt, part of the pay-off for this self-sacrifice and subordination of self-interest is relief from loneliness. For others, the sheer pleasures of intimate sharing are paramount. It is as if no price can be too great to pay for the sense of belonging and intimacy.

Because the partners' self-interests are closely linked during courtship, they experience little sense of sacrifice of self-interest. And the rewards for fulfilling one's partner's wishes are plentiful. Not only is there direct reinforcement from the satisfaction of pleasing the partner, but indirect as well, through imagining the partner's pleasure. With this continual reinforcement, the motivation to suspend one's egocentricity is strong. A woman in love is altruistic because she wants to be—not because she "should" be. An infatuated man makes sacrifices for his lover because it pleases him to do so.

FROM FUSION TO FISSION

What, then, happens to loving altruism? A variety of forces can cause its erosion after marriage. Fortified by the security of marriage, those who felt lonely while single no longer experience the relationship as an antidote to loneliness. Partners may discover that their needs are not well met; they may decide that they are better served by satisfying their own desires, even when these are in opposition to those of their mate. As the gratification from altruism wanes, partners come to be driven more by *shoulds* than by genuine desires to please one another. And once the partners feel obliged to give priority to one another's wishes, the compromises or concessions necessary in any close relationship may appear burdensome to them.

Inevitably, as partners begin to assert their own desires and conflicting interests, disagreements arise. Each mate may regard the other's desires as signs of a resurgent self-centeredness. The mates may then come to regard each other (but not themselves) as selfish, pigheaded, or stingy.

Of course, this sequence does not occur in all marriages. In fact, many couples find that over the course of time their self-centeredness is reduced and evolves into reciprocity, sharing, and caring. But distressed couples I have treated showed, consistently, the progression from altruism to egocentricity.

A crucial aspect of egocentricity in marriage is a genuine difference in the way partners perceive the same circumstances. Whatever the topic, their perspective is filtered through their own special lens, frequently leading to dramatically opposing views. Since people tend to regard their own opinions as reality, a different interpretation can seem unrealistic to them. A wife with a diverging perspective may appear to her husband as "contrary" or "arbitrary." When a husband's views differ, his wife may perceive him as "dumb" or "childish."

When one spouse presses a "wrong" opinion about an important issue, such as child rearing or finances, this action constitutes a challenge that can stir conflicts over who is right and who is wrong, whose view of reality will prevail, who has the dominant voice in the relationship. Some mates respond to such a challenge with an automatic put-down: "You don't know what you're talking about" or "You're full of it." Others may simply dig in their heels and refuse to listen. As will be shown in Chapters 14 and 15, you can apply special techniques for resolving these differences in perception, thereby restoring a working partnership.

THE SELF-SERVING BIAS

A more insidious problem is the "self-serving bias." Without realizing it, people have a tendency to interpret events in a way that puts them in the most favorable light, or serves their own self-interest. This self-serving bias exerts a strong influence on their perceptions, making them believe they look better in the eyes of others, as well as themselves. Thus, when mates argue over who is the better spouse or parent, who has contributed more to the marriage, or who has made more sacrifices, they will portray their own roles in such a way as to enhance their self-esteem and prove their moral superiority.

The self-serving bias widens the gap in understanding between spouses. Obviously, there can be substantial self-deception in such a process, and it requires an extraordinary amount of effort for us to see ourselves—stripped of pretense—as others see us. As much effort is also required to recognize how, without our realization, we select and assemble the "facts" in a given situation to serve our own interests.

As differences in viewpoint become pronounced, a spouse's image starts to change; he or she may assume the specter of a foe, representing a serious threat. Then, even a small disagreement can easily escalate into a fight. The partners may disparage each other with thoughts or statements such as "You're contradicting me just to put me down," "What do you know about it?" or "You're just plain dumb." They fail to realize that their own point of view may be just as biased as that of their partner, and that they appear to be equally thickheaded or self-serving. This combination of egocentricity and intolerance easily leads to arguments that wound and seem incapable of resolution.

Because the marriage bond is such an emotional one, it is much harder for partners to implement the goals of their compact than for them to forge the bonds in other working relationships, such as a business partnership or close friendship. At first, marital partners are usually attracted to one another by qualities like appearance, personality, charm, humor, and empathy—not by their potential to function well as a team. While these personal qualities may cement a solid emotional bond, they have little to do with how well a couple makes decisions and takes care of the essential details of married life. Even the most attractive spouse may prove deficient in the skills necessary for meeting the obligations of marriage. Those skills that turn out to be crucial in maintaining an effective partnership—defining problems, negotiating, assigning responsibilities—often have little relevance to the couple's initial attraction.

A lack of the necessary skills and appropriate attitudes weakens the working relationship, which must be strong if the partners are to carry out the practical goals of marriage (fulfilling the day-to-day requirements of living, maintaining a household, managing finances, raising children) as well as the emotional goals (enjoying leisure time, sex, sharing experiences). All of these goals require a spirit of cooperation, joint planning and decision making, a rational division of labor, and efficient follow-through.

When couples are unskilled and have little background in partnership techniques, disagreements about policies and their execution are likely. When these disagreements occur in a setting of egocentricity, self-serving bias, and competition, they lead to clashes and hostility.

SETTING STANDARDS AND JUDGING YOUR SPOUSE

Even when mates want to work together, they are apt to judge each other more harshly than anyone else in other working relationships in their lives. The tendency to impose more stringent standards on the mate seems ironic when we consider that marriage grants people the freedom to let down their hair and expose their vulnerable points. These strict expectations are typically concealed in phrases like "You should know" or "It should be obvious." In addition, these hidden standards are particularly high, as shown in the following exchange between Robert, who had just painted some chairs, and Shelly, his wife, who had asked him to complete the chore. He left the brushes soaking in turpentine instead of cleaning them all at once. This bothered Shelly. She had put in a long day looking after toddlers in a day care center, and she tended to be very sensitive to any sign that Robert, who made much more money than she did as a loan officer in a bank, did not really respect what she did or felt too superior to help around the house.

SHELLY: You didn't finish the job.

ROBERT: I did just as good a job for you as I would for anybody else.

SHELLY: [angrily] But I'm not just "anybody else."

While Shelly might not have felt angry at a painter who left brushes soaking, she interpreted Robert's failure to clean up completely as evidence that he was not pulling his own weight. It was not the specific act but its *symbolic meaning* that bothered Shelly. Because of the symbolic meanings attached to ordinary failings such as being late, one spouse may attach a great deal of significance to the other's tardiness: *"Something may have happened to her"* or *"If he really cared about my feelings, he would be on time."* Fears or self-doubts like these generally lurk behind exaggerated reactions to minor events.

The impact of symbolic meanings may be understood if we examine the unspoken provisions of the unwritten marital compact. In it, as in many other implied compacts at work or in organizations, there is a tacit agreement about the nature of the goals and the procedures for reaching them (for example, setting policy or assignment of tasks). In addition to having vaguely defined rules and provisions for carrying out practical mandates, the marital compact also contains a set of promises and expectations regarding the nature of the relationship (love, caring, devotion, loyalty, and so forth). What complicates the practical component of the compact is that day-to-day performance may be judged for its ability to meet the values and expectations of the emotional provisions of the compact ("Your interests will always come first") rather than for its ability to achieve practical results. Thus, what might be labeled as an "oversight" on the part of a less than meticulous painter becomes an accusation of "unfairness" or possibly "gross negligence" on the part of a spouse.

To repeat, many partners judge one another's actions according to personal, symbolic meaning rather than practical importance. Thus, we hear: "Everybody has a job to do—if my husband doesn't do his job properly, it's because he's trying to get away with something" or "If my wife doesn't do her job, it shows she doesn't care for me."

It is because of the *personal meanings* they attach to each other's actions that spouses are so often less tolerant of each other's lapses than they are of other people's failings. While they accept lapses by service personnel or co-workers, they view what their spouse does as a reflection of the marital relationship.

These lapses in marital standards trigger a sequence of evaluations: Is he acting responsibly? Is she really devoted? Is he entitled to behave that way? If he slips up on his job, he is bad. If she doesn't pull her own weight, she is wrong. If a husband, for example, catches his wife skipping important details, he experiences moral indignation. If a wife suspects her husband of shirking his duties, she experiences righteous rage.

Most spouses are unaware they are rating each other according to moral standards. Interestingly, judgments like those their parents made seep into their own reactions; they see an erring spouse as "bad," just as they were labeled by their parents, and they respond the same way as their parents did—with punishment.

THE INTRUSION OF SYMBOLIC MEANINGS

Symbolic meanings, perfectionism, and moralistic evaluations greatly compound the difficulties created by poor communication and hidden expectations. The net result is that difficulties the couple could easily resolve in other relationships are so emotionally encumbered in marriage that the practical problem doesn't get worked out. This breeding ground for conflict leads to anger and mutual recriminations: "She won't listen to my side—she just insists I do it her way. If I don't, she goes nag, nag, nag."

The everyday mechanics of living together take on meanings that go far beneath surface realities. How well a husband does his chores at home, for example, is evaluated by his wife not just in terms of quality, but also in terms of what she presumes it reveals about his attitudes and feelings toward her. For example, at a counseling session, Shelly said she was furious at Robert.

SHELLY: [sarcastically] Robert never attends to things properly. Some men were working on the roof. I asked him to come home to inspect it before they left. He wouldn't do it. He's always so trusting of people.

ATB: What thoughts did you have about his not coming home when you asked him to?

SHELLY: He doesn't really care. If he cared for me, he would attend to these things because I ask.

ROBERT: She's always bugging me to do things. I have to do them my own way. If she had confidence in me, she wouldn't bug me all the time.

SHELLY: If you really cared for me, you'd do it because I asked.

Actually, Robert had confidence in the roofers but, based on past experience, Shelly had reason to believe they might do a careless job unless their work was inspected.

A "clash of the symbols" is likely when the same event has different—and highly personal—meanings for each partner. Robert's acceding to Shelly's wishes symbolizes to her that he really cares. But being nagged about the roofer symbolizes to Robert that Shelly lacks confidence in him and must interfere in his business. If Robert had agreed to check the roof, as she requested, Shelly would regard such compliance as a positive symbol. But his negative response made her feel helpless and abandoned, and his further accusation "nag, nag, nag" only exacerbated those feelings. For Robert, doing things his own way—without interference—was a positive symbol, whereas being coerced against his better judgment was a negative one. When

Shelly "interfered," he sensed not only her no-confidence vote but also her desire to control him.

People like Shelly and Robert enter into marriage with fixed beliefs about the meaning of certain actions, or non-actions, by their spouses. These beliefs lead them to attach exaggerated significance to those actions. When one spouse's actions take on an importance that leads the other to overreact, that act is symbolic of some deeply held values of the reacting mate. When, as in the case of Robert and Shelly, an action has opposite symbolic meanings for each partner, then a clash is likely. When such clashes occur frequently, the working partnership, as well as the general relationship, is weakened.

In this type of conflict, some resolution is possible if the partners can objectively explain, at a time when neither is angry, how they each felt and how they interpreted the other's actions. As they see each other's perspective—sometimes with considerable surprise— the symbolic insult and rejection are defused, leaving them better prepared to agree on guidelines for handling further disagreements.

After they were able to peceive their controversy through each other's eyes, Shelly and Robert were able to arrive at a set of operating principles: Robert agreed to explain, before starting a project, what was involved and to answer any questions Shelly might have along the way; Shelly agreed to ask questions and inform Robert how the project was proceeding, but not to tell him what to do. (See Chapters 15 and 16 for more information about how couples can work together to resolve conflicts.)

DIFFERING EXPECTATIONS
ABOUT ROLES IN THE FAMILY

The eye of the storm in many marital disputes centers on the expectations that partners have of their respective family roles: what it means to be a wife or mother, husband or father. Spouses often differ in their beliefs about earning and spending the family income, parenting, social and leisure activities, and the division of labor in the household.

Partners enter marriage with many preconceptions about both practical and emotional matters. These expectations are usually formed early in life, based on childhood experiences. A husband, for example, may model himself after his own father, and expect his wife to assume the role his mother did. Or, if he disliked his parents' behavior, he might try to act differently from his father or expect his wife to be different from his mother.

Often, such expectations about practical arrangements are camouflaged early in the relationship by the aura of love, dreams of permanent happiness, excitement, and romance. As a result, the couple never sit down to deal with practical matters until they have become frustrating problems. Frequently, at this point, the true differences in their expectations surface.

Areas of Conflict

There are many areas in which a couple—no matter how devoted and loving—can have disagreements that threaten their partnership. In the following pages, I have selected a few of the more common areas that require collaboration in planning, setting policy, and making and implementing decisions. It will be clear how poor communication, rigid expectations, and the intrusion of symbolic meanings all conspire to disrupt the marital alliance.

In order to pinpoint the specific problems you may be experiencing in your relationship, you will find it helpful to review the checklist "Problems in the Partnership," on pages 105–107. It contains various items that will enable you to focus on concrete difficulties that can be remedied, rather than to get bogged down by vague generalities like "We just can't get along," "We never make decisions together," or "We have irreconcilable differences."

QUALITY OF TIME TOGETHER

Although couples often complain that they don't spend enough time together, I have often found that the problems lies more in *how* they spend their time. Though heated disagreements may be harmful to a partnership, what may be even more destructive is the lack of attention mates pay to pleasing each other at meals, at parties, or in bed.

Harriet and Len are a couple who never had an open discussion about what each wanted out of the marriage; thus, they could not agree over important issues like time spent together, sex, or social events. When a conflict occurred, they both responded by throwing their energies into their careers—Len was an orthopedic surgeon and Harriet was a graphic designer who also taught a high school class in art. In the early years of their marriage, when they were raising their daughter, they seemed to have more in common, but after she left for college, the relationship began to drift. Their initial consultation with me focused on this problem:

LEN: Harriet never takes my feelings into account. She teaches her art class in the afternoon and never has dinner ready on time. When she makes social plans, she never invites my friends. She just invites her own friends—who, by the way, are very boring. Also, she never wants to have sex.

Len had a certain mold that he tried to fit Harriet into. Specifically, he had predetermined that she should:

▷ provide his dinner on time.

▷ provide an entertaining social life for him.

▷ be available for sex whenever he wanted it.

Now, let's hear the other side:

HARRIET: Len always has to have things his own way. He knows that the class is very important to me, so he could wait until I get home or invite me out to dinner the days that I teach the class. . . . He is very mechanical about sex. He thinks he can just snap his fingers and I should roll over. At dinner he announces, "We'll have sex tonight" and then goes back to his newspaper. I'd like to have a little romance, candles, music—that sort of thing. . . . I *have* asked people over but he's very critical of them. He's annoyed because they're my friends. But *he* doesn't have any friends. So I stopped having people over.

Harriet believed a husband should:

▷ communicate with her and not bury his head in the *Wall Street Journal* all the time.

▷ encourage her and take an interest in her class.

▷ think about her social needs—for example, take her out to dinner the night of her class.

Although Harriet and Len were considering a separation, they had not considered precisely what their dissatisfactions were; their expectations were never clearly expressed. Their presumed marital incompatibility was actually a combination of poorly expressed wishes and a lack of follow-through on those desires that were expressed in the form of complaints.

Their difficulties might have been alleviated, for instance, if Harriet could have confronted Len over his habit of reading the paper at breakfast instead of talking to her. Further, if she let him know that she would prefer a more romantic approach to making love, he might have complied. And Len could have helped by being more explicit about his wishes regarding their social life—instead of just being critical.

Their problems were so long-standing that they required professional assistance in sorting them out. With some help from me, it was still possible for them to see the problems from each other's perspectives. Len agreed to read his newspapers at work instead of at meals and to be more romantic. They also arranged to have dinner together at home or at a restaurant. And they cooperated in preparing a list of people whom they both wanted to entertain. Although these changes did not make the relationship perfect, they did make it more satisfying.

DIVISION OF LABOR

Many marriages become mired in conflict over which partner is supposed to attend to what duties in the family. As traditional roles have blurred, there is less precedent to draw on in determining the specific areas of responsibility for each partner. Traditionally, the husband's defined role was providing the family income while the wife attended to domestic duties and child care. When both husband and wife worked, the wife would usually have double duty—her job plus the household chores. The present trend toward sharing both domestic work and providing income has done much to forge closer bonds, but it has also opened new possibilities for conflict in areas in which roles are blurred.

At its best, division of labor is a smooth operation coordinated with an eye on getting the job done. But couples who lose sight of the goals can get lost in evaluating each other's contributions. Getting the job done becomes subordinated to abstract doctrines—fairness, equality, reciprocity. Even when the goal is reached, the partners may become mired in mutual recrimination over their relative contributions, each believing the other has violated the marital compact.

One of the chief sources of such friction is the doctrine of fairness. Partners in a conflicted marriage may, for instance, declare that they are doing more than their share: they fight over who should do the marketing or wash the dishes or put the children to bed. Underneath this kind of squabbling lies a medley of attitudes, concerns, and fears that feed into the conflict.

Marion, for example, had suffered silently for many years under what she perceived as David's domination. In their early years, she had taken complete responsibility for raising the children and keeping house, while he had advanced in his law practice to the level of senior partner in the firm. Marion was more intimidated than proud of her husband's success. She felt ineffectual and thought that was how David saw her, too—partly, perhaps, because that was how her mother had felt in her marriage. She believed that, in his self-assumed role as "Lord of the Manor," he was entitled to push her around and she had no choice but to submit to his wishes, lest she incur his wrath. This meant always having what he wanted to eat ready for him at dinnertime, keeping the children quiet when he came home, and planning social events with people whom he liked. In the background was a deep fear: if she should displease David, he would leave her and she would have the burden of supporting herself and the children. Although this fear was farfetched, she never thought to question it.

By the time their youngest child entered school, Marion realized a long-standing ambition—to return to college to get a degree and then a paid job. By the time she began to earn a salary, she started to view her relationship with David in a different light. She decided that she would no longer allow him to tyrannize her. He would have to agree to change his role in the family and do his share of the household duties.

As it turned out, David accepted the new role with little friction. Marion, however, did not trust his apparent compliance and was continuously on the lookout for signs of shirking or cheating. Her previous sensitivity to being dominated by him now was replaced by a sensitivity to being "used"—a fear that in some way he once again would take unfair advantage of her.

Her hypervigilance toward his "cheating" led to a blowup. On the day after they had given a large party, Marion asked David to put away the lawn furniture and clean the living room and dining room while she was out. David agreed. When Marion returned, she became furious when she discovered that David had recruited two of the children to help with the work. The agreement, as she had interpreted it, was that *he* would do the work and not farm it out. Then she discovered that while they had superficially cleaned these rooms and straightened out the furniture, they had not vacuumed the floor or dusted the furniture. Marion became angry; to her, this "negligence" symbolized David's trying to "get away with something." They then got into a heated argument over whether his definition of cleaning the house allowed for the recruitment of the children, and whether it included vacuuming the floor and dusting the furniture.

Although phrases like *clean up* are often poorly defined, the real problem in this case was Marion's long-standing resentment of the unfairness during her early married years and her resolution "never to be taken advantage of" again. The intrusion of these past hurts and present sensitivities—and not the task of assigning duties—undermined the working partnership. She perceived it not as a joint endeavor but as a struggle to keep David from being manipulative and from shirking his responsibilities.

In cases like this, a number of practical solutions could be applied to handle the problem of distributing duties. Counseling enabled Marion to loosen her single-minded insistence on fairness and equality, and to adopt a more flexible attitude toward the partnership—to switch from thinking in terms of "me" to thinking in terms of "us." Marion had to rethink her perspective of David—to see him as he was *now*, not as he had been during the early years. At the same time, David had to demonstrate his good-faith effort in carrying out his duties and in avoiding the easy way out.

CHILD REARING

Many of the attitudes that guide people in child rearing were formed long ago by the way they themselves were treated as children. Some people follow their parents' example while others repudiate their parents' practices. Either way, they are positively or negatively influenced by their own upbringing.

Although they worked together very well in running the neighborhood pharmacy Frank had inherited from his parents, Mary and Frank experienced considerable conflict over the discipline of their teenage son, Stan. Mary saw Stan as lazy, self-indulgent, and irresponsible. She believed that his friends were a bad influence on him and disapproved of their manner of dress and lackadaisical attitude toward school. She believed Stan should work harder in school since he had such "great potential." Stan was unresponsive to his mother's cajoling and demands that he work harder and find other friends. They had frequent fights.

Frank perceived Stan differently. He admired Stan's casual, easygoing manner, his carefree attitude, and his friendliness. Frank regarded Stan's friends as fun-loving and had the attitude "Since you're only young once, you might as well enjoy it." In contrast to Mary, who pressed for more discipline, Frank advocated a hands-off policy. His major concern was that Stan was shy in social situations and was inhibited in the presence of adults, especially teachers.

Not only did Stan's parents disagree in their attitudes toward disciplining him, but they also perceived what he did differently. Such divergent views of children's behavior often create conflict themselves. Mary blamed Frank for ignoring their son's difficulties and accused him of being an unconcerned parent. Frank thought that

Mary overlooked Stan's many fine qualities and was much too authoritarian. The parents had reached an impasse and, as a result, their perceptions of each other became increasingly negative. Mary saw Frank as negligent and irresponsible; Frank saw Mary as a "dragon lady."

To understand the stalemate between Mary and Frank, we have to explore further their concerns. For Mary, the crux of the problem was a *hidden fear*—namely, that her son would get into serious trouble. Although not fully cognizant of the fear, she was driven to treat him in such a way as to prevent the danger she dreaded. When Stan did not respond to this treatment, his mother began to see him even more negatively—as not only weak and indulgent but also stubborn and rebellious. As a result of being thwarted, Mary grew angry and became even more strict with Stan. Her efforts to enforce cooperation had backfired—leading to Stan's further defiance.

The best-intentioned parents can sabotage their own efforts by trying too hard to correct certain problems in their children. We can see the chain with Mary and Stan: from hidden fear to excessive discipline to frustration to anger. But how can we account for the fear in the first place?

To understand Mary's reactions, we need to probe into her own past history. Mary's parents were easygoing and let her shirk her studies. She did not do well enough in high school to go on to college. Mary often thought that if her parents had applied more pressure on her, she would have done better in school. More significant, however, was the fact that her younger brother had had a series of difficulties with the law during adolescence, first by getting traffic tickets and then by being arrested for possession of a large quantity of marijuana. She blamed her parents for her brother's troubles and attributed them to his lax upbringing. Although Mary's brother eventually straightened out, this family secret came to mind whenever she visited him. At these times, she feared that Stan would fall into the same pattern, and she resolved anew to crack down on him.

Frank came from a different family background. His parents were strict disciplinarians, and he believed that their stern training had fostered his inhibitions and anxiety in the presence of authority. Frank resolved early in life that if he had a son, he would treat him differently; he would want him to be free and uninhibited, and decided that this could best be accomplished by "giving him as much space as possible." Frank's main concern was that Mary's heavy-handedness would force their son into the same mold that had formed him.

We can see a progression in both parents from fear (stemming from childhood experiences) to measures to reduce the fear and, finally, to anger at being thwarted. The parental views of Stan were warped by private fears: Mary's, that he was weak and rebellious; Frank's, that he was weak and inhibited. Their child-rearing theories—authoritarian vs. laissez-faire—arose from these fears. Their conflicting views of their son made each angry and led them to see each other negatively, which further intensified their conflict over Stan.

Another common factor in parental distress is hidden doubt. A mother, for example, doubts that she is a good parent. Her self-doubt leads to the belief she is a failure as a parent. In such a case, when her child misbehaves, the mother overreacts with excessive anger.

Hidden between the child's misbehavior and the mother's over-reaction is another "event," namely the automatic thought *"His misbehavior is my fault. I have failed him."* Such self-doubts drive her to *prove* to herself that she is a good parent. She imposes rules on the child to promote her "good" image of herself and to ward off the "bad" image.

When her child does not live up to the rules, she is again threatened by her self-doubts and retaliates against the son as a way of forcing him to be good. If, at this point, her husband chides her for being too harsh, the fear of being a bad parent again surfaces—which she may attempt to dispel by attacking her husband.

Since mutual antagonism frequently arises from fears of spoiling or neglecting the child, of doing irreparable harm, or from doubts about one's competence as a parent, it is valuable for distressed parents to look behind their anger for the presence of such fears or doubts. Simply exposing the fears may loosen their grip; in addition, discussing them with one's spouse can help evaluate whether there is some basis for them. If there is, then the spouse's help can lead to some constructive, united action.

SEXUAL RELATIONSHIP

Although sexual union is sometimes touted as the acme of a marital partnership, it often dissolves in a flood of tears, or ruptures in a flash of anger. Nowhere in an intimate relationship are symbolic meanings more active—contributing to anxiety, disappointment, and anger. A wife, for instance, may feel disappointed that she doesn't satisfy her husband. She may worry over not wanting to have relations frequently enough to please him and may have the belief (sometimes reinforced by her husband) that she is sexually inadequate. A husband, similarly, may be concerned that his sexual performance is below par and that his wife downgrades his manliness. Such concern over performance can lead to sexual dysfunction.

Problems typically center on the frequency, timing, and quality of sex. Each of these carries—and is in turn affected by—symbolic meanings. Husbands and wives often differ on how frequently and when to have sexual relations. The frequency and timing can have strong symbolic meaning. "Having sex when I want it" may represent being loved to the husband while, to the wife, "giving sex when he wants it" may represent being dominated or used by him. Insisting on sex more frequently than the other spouse desires may suggest the same demanding expectations and sense of entitlement that we have previously discussed regarding day-to-day interactions. One mate (Len, for example) may believe he is entitled to have sex on demand, whereas his spouse (Harriet) may expect preliminary expressions of warmth and tenderness.

Pride is often involved in sex. A wife's concept of her femininity and a husband's view of his masculinity are often wrapped up in how responsive the mate is. One wife regularly felt crushed whenever her husband rejected her overtures. She had always prided herself on being sexually attractive to men, and her husband's apparent indifference was taken as an insult. A husband was incensed at his wife's lack of enthusiasm for sex and her unresponsiveness during love making. To him, this behavior suggested that he "wasn't a man."

The surplus meanings cut both ways. The sense of intimacy, total acceptance, and reciprocal pleasure can serve to turn on a couple; the diminution of the sense of love, intimacy, and acceptance can weaken the passion. If sexual desire—and, consequently, performance—wanes, the symbolic message may be decoded as a loss of intimacy and affection. That sets up a vicious cycle: a loss of feelings of mutuality leads to decreased sexual attraction and satisfaction, which further undermines the mutuality.

Chapter 18 takes up the problem of what to do about sexual disagreements. For now, however, mates can begin to think about the exaggerated labels that they apply—such as "oversexed," "frigid," "inconsiderate," "not caring"—when the frequency, timing, or quality of their sex is disappointing. When things calm down, they can evaluate the validity of those labels, as well as of thoughts like "She uses sex as a weapon" or "That's all he's interested in."

BUDGETARY PROBLEMS

The family budget is an area in which, because of their common interest in financial stability, one would hope for a couple's cooperation. One might imagine that budgeting would help unite a couple through the necessity of working together, pooling their resources for the basics of living, and enjoying the fruits of their labors. But here, too, what could bond a couple in a joint venture often serves to separate them.

When we look at the ways in which couples spend their money, all too often we see at work the sense of entitlement, the preoccupation with fairness, control and competition, and the other kinds of symbolic meanings that subvert joint activities. How many couples have spent tedious hours working out a detailed budget only to discover that one of the partners has gone off on a spending spree! Understandably, the other spouse responds with consternation and indignation. This common divisive event occurs when one partner, generally the chief income producer, tries to control the other through allowance rationing; the other spouse rebels against the control by overspending.

Another kind of problem arises when neither spouse has a business head. Managing the family finances is like running a small business, and partners need to work together to make projections of their expendable income. They need to catalogue expenses for necessities of living and to agree on what extras they can allow for bonuses—entertainment, recreation, vacation—as well as for savings.

Unfortunately, the extra spending often gets worked into a tit-for-tat game that undermines the budget. Harriet signs up for an expensive series of art lessons, so Len retaliates by ordering a case of ten-year-old Scotch.

Partners need to recognize how they use budgets and spending to restrict each other, to defy and punish each other. Working out the meanings behind these fiscal power struggles—crime and punishment—involves applying a number of techniques, which can be found in later chapters.

PROBLEMS WITH IN-LAWS

The total emotional investment of one partner in his or her family of origin can strain the marital relationship, with the other spouse resenting the attention paid to the partner's parents or siblings. This problem was exacerbated for one couple who consulted me because the husband's family lived only a few miles away, while the wife's parents spent most of the year in their Florida condo. Helene described it as follows:

He seemed to think that the sun rose and set on his relatives. He insisted on going over to his parents' house every Sunday. He never asked me whether I wanted to go. He just *assumed* that I would go. When we got there, he completely ignored me, as though I was a piece of furniture. If I said something, he would glare at me as though I was way out. If I said I didn't want to go, he would become furious.

In listening to the stories told by Helene and her husband, Herbert, I wondered whether they were talking about the same circumstances. Herbert gave a distinctly different account of their controversy:

Helene never wanted to visit my parents. She resented my mother and I always had to push her to visit them. When she went there, she would make biting remarks. So I learned to ignore them. I always placed Helene first. I just wanted to see my parents once in a while.

Each spouse suffered from tunnel vision. Neither viewed the situation from the perspective of the other. In terms of decision making, Herbert erred in making a unilateral decision to see his parents. But Helene was wrong in assuming that his insistence on seeing them meant she was less important to him than they were. When Herbert realized that the basis for Helene's recalcitrance was not "bitchiness," he was pleased.

Of course, relatives themselves can and do cause problems for their married children. They can fall prey to the same sense of injustice, overgeneralization, and symbolic thinking as do their married children. For example, Cal's elderly mother liked to visit him and Gail periodically, but she would usually arrive when both were at work. It was of great symbolic importance to Cal's mother that one of them be home to unlock the door and get her settled. From a practical standpoint, though, it would have been easy for her to let herself into the house. But because of the symbolic meanings, she interpreted having to do that as a sign "nobody cares"—a complaint that made Cal and Gail feel a combination of guilt and anger.

Thus, we see the hidden power of symbols: when someone jumps to a highly personalized, overgeneralized conclusion, it is a sign that a deeply valued symbolic expectation has been violated.

The problem with Cal's mother, of course, produced a clash between Cal and Gail: who should go home to let Cal's mother in? Cal insisted it should be Gail, because her schedule was more flexible than his. Gail asserted that it should be Cal, because it was his mother.

From their personal frames of reference, both were right; however, as partners, it would not be constructive for them to take positions based solely on their own views. To function as a team, both partners have to incorporate the viewpoint of the other into their own perspective. Then, the final decision can be made from a joint perspective, in which they weigh the merits of a particular course of action as it affects the *team* rather than the individual. As a real estate agent, Gail could easily find time to run home for a few minutes, while Cal's job as chemist in a large medical lab left him very little free time. Since it was easier for Gail to leave work, a solution in this instance would be for her to go home. At times it might be appropriate for Cal to be inconvenienced.

The resulting sacrifice and inconvenience are far preferable to the upset and the damage to the relationship when partners let problems such as these become a source of friction.

The following checklist details some of the areas in which coordination between partners is important. If you have problems in any of these areas, the list will help you to be more specific in determining friction points and weaknesses. In this way, *you will be able to translate general complaints into specific, solvable problems.* You can also use the checklist as a scorecard to document improvements in your relationship.

Problems in the Partnership

In the left-hand column, rate the following items according to frequency of occurrence:
(0) *does not apply*   (1) *rarely*   (2) *sometimes*   (3) *frequently*   (4) *all the time*
In the right-hand column, check whether you consider the item a problem.

Making Decisions

When we have to discuss a problem or make a decision:

		This is a problem
_____	1 / We disagree.	_____
_____	2 / My partner gets angry.	_____
_____	3 / I get angry.	_____
_____	4 / I give in.	_____
_____	5 / My partner gives in.	_____
_____	6 / We don't compromise.	_____
_____	7 / I make the decisions.	_____
_____	8 / My partner makes the decisions.	_____
_____	9 / We avoid making decisions.	_____
_____	10 / My feelings get hurt.	_____
_____	11 / My partner's feelings get hurt.	_____
_____	12 / We argue about trivial issues.	_____

Finances

This is a problem

_____ 1 / My partner overspends. _____

_____ 2 / My partner won't spend. _____

_____ 3 / My partner begrudges my spending. _____

_____ 4 / We have no plan regarding monthly spending. _____

_____ 5 / We have no agreement about savings. _____

_____ 6 / We have no understanding of where the money goes. _____

_____ 7 / My partner conceals debts or where the money goes. _____

_____ 8 / We have no agreement on setting priorities. _____

_____ 9 / We have no responsibility for spending. _____

Sex Relations

This is a problem

_____ 1 / My partner is more interested in sex than I am. _____

_____ 2 / My partner is less interested in sex than I am. _____

_____ 3 / I find it hard to talk to my partner about sex. _____

_____ 4 / Our sexual relationship is not fulfilling. _____

_____ 5 / I am reluctant to behave affectionately because my partner becomes too amorous. _____

_____ 6 / We differ in the kind of sex we each prefer. _____

_____ 7 / My partner uses sex to control or punish me. _____

_____ 8 / My partner is much too interested in sex. _____

_____ 9 / My partner is not sensitive to my sexual wishes. _____

_____ 10 / We don't agree on birth control. _____

Recreation and Leisure Activities

This is a problem

_____ 1 / We don't spend as much leisure time together as we'd like. _____

_____ 2 / My partner spends too much time on his/her own leisure-time activity. _____

_____ 3 / My partner has no time or energy for leisure activities. _____

_____ 4 / My partner cannot enjoy recreation with me. _____

_____ 5 / I feel compelled to do things I'd rather not. _____

_____ 6 / We don't enjoy the same activities. _____

—— 7 / My partner doesn't have enough hobbies or   ————
recreational interests.

—— 8 / There is no balance between our recreational   ————
time spent together or separately.

—— 9 / My partner has no balance between work and   ————
recreation.

——10 / We have different ideas as to what constitutes   ————
a good time.

7

SILENT THOUGHTS:
THE EYE OF THE STORM

▷ A wife became angry at her husband when he came home early from work. When he greeted her enthusiastically, she glared at him.

▷ A husband became annoyed at his wife when she told him she had returned his overdue books to the library.

▷ A wife became furious at her husband when he bragged in front of friends about how good a cook she was.

In each instance, a spouse's positive gesture triggered anger. Why? The angry people were surprised at their own reactions. Their mates were befuddled—they had expected appreciation, not an attack. Since the angry spouses were receiving cognitive therapy, they knew how to go about deciphering the symbolic meanings of the events. By a careful review, each was able to recall certain thoughts triggered by the other's well-intentioned act. These thoughts were so fleeting that, without practice, the angered spouses would not have been able to catch them.

▷ The wife whose husband came home early thought, *"Why did he have to come home so soon? Is he trying to check up on me?"*

▷ The husband whose wife returned the library books had thought, *"She's trying to show me up. She wants to prove that she attends to things better than I do."*

▷ The wife whose husband praised her culinary skills had thought, *"Why does he have to brag about my cooking? Our friends must think he's fishing for compliments for me."*

Such puzzling reactions become clearer as we begin to monitor these fleeting thoughts. Once we can tune in to our automatic thoughts

—our internal monologue—we can understand better *how we react* and *why we overreact.*

At first glance, it seems that *what other people do* leads directly to our reactions of anger, anxiety, sadness, and the like. We say (or at least think) things like "You make me angry" or "You're getting on my nerves." But these statements are not strictly accurate. They are true only in that we would not experience the specific emotion (anger, anxiety, sadness) if the other person had not acted that way. But the person's actions simply represent facts that we interpret. *Our emotional response follows from our interpretation, rather than from the act per se.*

If we did not first interpret what happens, our reactions would be chaotic. Depending on the circumstances, for instance, a raised fist might be a threat, a call for solidarity, or a gesture of success. The way we decode this act gives it the appropriate—or inappropriate—meaning. However, because of flaws resulting from bias, inadequate attention, fatigue, and the like, we too easily misinterpret other people's motives and so respond inappropriately or even destructively. Such misinterpretations are particularly common in close relationships.

But we can catch our misinterpretations as they occur by focusing on our automatic thoughts. Once we are primed to identify these thoughts, we can examine them and correct them if they are unrealistic.

Because automatic labeling occurs so rapidly, a wife, for example, may be aware only of feeling offended by her husband and, perhaps, of some fleeting, irksome image of him. Her subsequent criticism may not reflect the actual "offense" so much as her reaction to it—her wish to attack, more than her reason for attacking. To uncover the true meaning of the "offense," she would need to pinpoint her automatic interpretation.

To understand why you are angry, it is usually enough just to catch the automatic thought, which frequently tells it all—revealing what significance the event really has for you. For instance, the common denominator in the automatic thoughts listed on page 108 is the partners' sense of being wronged in some way:

▷ The housewife felt pressured by her husband's apparent checking up.

▷ In the library book incident, the husband felt wronged by being "shown up" by his wife.

▷ The angry wife thought her husband's bragging had implied a devaluation of all her other capabilities except cooking skills.

In the course of therapy, we occasionally find that the more obvious automatic thought does not tell the whole story: there is still another hidden meaning that prompts the more obvious indignant thought, and this subtle meaning usually involves a threat that stirs up a painful feeling—like anxiety or hurt. These hidden meanings are what I previously described as hidden fears.

The concealed thought and its associated feeling, the hurt or anxiety, are rapidly overtaken by more obvious, hostile thoughts that mask the original hurt. In the preceding examples, the indignant thought of one spouse—*"Is he trying to check up on me?"*—displaced an earlier, anxiety-inducing thought—*"He will be critical of me because the house is a mess."* I have labeled this silent thought a "threat thought," and one exists hidden behind each fleeting, anger-producing indignant thought. Unless people train themselves, they are likely to miss this thought, which provides the real key to their anger.

▷ The first wife's threat thought was *"He will see that I haven't done the housework yet today, and he'll criticize me."*

▷ The husband's threat thought was *"She doesn't trust me, so she took the books back herself."*

▷ The second wife initially had the threat thought *"They will get the idea that he thinks I'm not good for anything else besides cooking."*

The relationship between the situation and the secondary (angry) and primary (fearful) thoughts is summarized below.

Situation Leading to Anger	Secondary Obvious (Angry) Automatic Thought	Primary Subtle (Fearful) Automatic Thought
Husband comes home early.	Is he checking up on me?	He will be critical because the house is a mess.
Wife returns library books.	She's trying to show me up.	She doesn't trust me.
Husband brags about wife's cooking.	He's fishing for a compliment.	They'll think that's all I'm good for.

The common denominator in these situations is the following: the spouses believed their public image would be threatened by the exposure of some weakness, real or imagined; these presumed threats pained the spouses, and thus led to their thoughts of being wronged and a desire to punish the mates.

You can usually determine an automatic thought with the technique of "filling in the blank": note your anger and then reflect backward on what went through your mind during the interval between the triggering event and the anger itself—as in an instant replay during a ball game on TV.

Automatic thoughts may take the form of words, of images, or both. While waiting for Karen, Ted had the automatic thought *"Something could have happened to her"* and had a mental picture of her being killed in an automobile accident. Karen, knowing that she was late, imagined Ted with a flushed face and bulging eyes—yelling at her.

Automatic thoughts are similar to what Freud called "preconscious" thinking. Albert Ellis refers to them as "self-statements." Automatic thoughts are brief bursts at the fringe of consciousness. Although their rapidity helps galvanize us into action, their brevity makes it difficult to identify them. Once our anger flares and we start to attack, we no longer recall the fleeting automatic thought that provoked us. We focus our attention, instead, on attacking.

The content of the automatic thought is usually condensed, so that an idea such as *"He's trying hard to show me up in front of all these people"* may be compressed into a kind of shorthand: *"Trying . . . show me up . . . people."* However, when people capture their automatic thoughts, they can reconstruct the entire sentence. Series of automatic thoughts form an internal monologue.

Martin, a big, burly man with a self-confident air (he was a football star in college), was exquisitely sensitive to any apparent slight by his wife or co-workers and had difficulty understanding and controlling his sudden bursts of anger. On one occasion he had a seemingly immediate flash of anger and was later able, in several instances, to catch the automatic thought that linked the event to the anger: he had learned to fill in the blank. In each instance, Martin was offended but did not know the reason until he replayed the action and captured the automatic thought.

In one instance, he became furious when his wife, Melanie, did not respond to his conciliatory overtures following an argument over how much support to provide for their two children in college. His automatic (primary) thought was *"She's giving me the cold treatment."* That thought produced a transient hurt followed by his explanation of her motive: *"She's trying to punish me"* (secondary thought). By attributing a hostile motive to her, he triggered his own outrage.

On another occasion, Melanie went out without leaving a note. Martin felt hurt and then angry, and he wanted to reproach her. His painful automatic thought had been *"She doesn't care about me,"* which was immediately replaced by *"She's inconsiderate,"* which led to the anger.

On still another occasion, Melanie cut Martin off while he was talking to a group of friends, and he felt a surge of anger. His primary, painful automatic thought was *"She doesn't think I have anything to contribute."* His secondary, angry automatic thought was *"She always tries to shut me up. She has a need to put me down."*

In each case, a sequence of thoughts intervened between his wife's actions and his emotional flare-up. But once Martin had identified his primary and secondary automatic thoughts, he actually understood the source of his anger. This is especially important in marital misunderstandings, because an automatic thought may be corrected if it is inappropriate or erroneous. And once it is corrected, the anger it prompts usually fades.

Of course, because these thoughts occur so rapidly, you may not be able to catch them unless you are prepared. And once you are able to identify automatic thoughts, they may seem very plausible at first. It is only after you start to look at the evidence that you can tell whether they are exaggerated, biased, and wrong—or reasonable and realistic. Most often, people initially assume that their fleeting thoughts are valid and so are not inclined to question them. But later, after their anger wanes and they have a little perspective, they can recognize, on reflection, that their automatic thoughts were misleading.

Fortunately, Martin decided to check his automatic thoughts with Melanie. What he learned was sobering.

▷ He discovered that the reason she had not responded to his conciliatory remarks ("the cold treatment") was that she was too choked up to speak without crying.

▷ He discovered that her second "offense"—neglecting to leave a note— was unavoidable: she was late for an appointment and had to leave the house in a hurry.

▷ He discovered that Melanie had interrupted him in order to change the subject, not to cut him off: unknowingly, he was treading on a sensitive area that was upsetting one of their friends at the gathering.

Each time, aided by this additional information, Martin was able to see that his anger was not justified but based on misinterpretation. He would not have realized this, however, unless he had first recognized his automatic thoughts. Even if Martin had understood that his anger was inappropriate to the situation, he would simply have apologized without knowing its *real* cause—his own fleeting feelings and thoughts. Unless he could pinpoint his automatic thoughts, he would still be susceptible to feelings of inappropriate anger when similar situations arose in the future.

In almost any interaction between spouses, each will formulate automatic thoughts that influence what they say and how they say it. Even though not openly expressed, automatic thoughts affect tone of voice, facial expression, and gestures. Consider the following dialogue and accompanying internal monologue:

	Automatic Thought	Says	Nonverbal
MARTIN:	She's too easy on the kids. They're getting on my nerves.	Dear, don't you think the kids could quiet down?	Sharp tone of voice
MELANIE:	There he goes again, complaining all the time [feels enraged].	The kids are having a good time. Anyhow, they'll be going up to bed soon.	Taut facial muscles
MARTIN:	She opposes me on everything. I'd better take over [feels enraged].	Should I put them to bed now?	Loud voice, clenched fists
MELANIE:	He is getting out of control. He could hurt the kids. I'd better give in [feels defeated].	No, I'll put them to bed right away.	Limp all over

In this case, both parents carried on a civil conversation, but their thoughts indicated the real friction. Melanie correctly read the signals that Martin was furious, and she decided to appease him in the end. The nonverbal signals—posture, facial expressions, tone of voice— reflected their automatic thoughts more accurately than did their words. Automatic thoughts reflect the "latent content" of a message —what is hidden—in contrast to the "manifest content"—the actual words. Although Melanie, for example, was diplomatic in her choice of words, her automatic thoughts centered on criticism of Martin, then fear, and finally submission. These thoughts were reflected in her feelings and muscular tone (from taut to limp).

Secret Doubts

On another occasion, Martin was offended when Melanie changed the subject while they were talking. But he caught himself in the middle of a series of automatic thoughts, such as *"She always does this to me. I can't let her get away with this. She has no right to treat me like this."*

His anger was way out of proportion to Melanie's actual "offense." In playing back his stream of thoughts, Martin was able to recognize the automatic (primary) ones that *preceded* his critical thoughts: *"She isn't interested in what I have to say. She considers me boring."* Martin was also able to pinpoint the emotion he experienced immediately after this thought: *sadness,* not anger. His critical (secondary) thoughts followed and blotted out his sadness; he went on to blame Melanie for her—in his mind—"offense."

Martin doubted his ability to express himself well; Melanie's apparent indifference or impatience with what he had to say triggered this doubt. However, his train of thought quickly retreated from the painful implications of being boring and socially undesirable, and shifted over to focusing on his wife's "wrongdoing."

Most overreactions could be alleviated if spouses would transfer their attention from a preoccupation with the partner's "injustice" or "impropriety" and zero in on the preceding, hidden hurt. They might recognize when their anger is fueled less by their partner's misdeeds than by their own sensitivities. They might then become less reactive and respond constructively to their spouses—instead of blaming them.

Another common scenario that illustrates how pain leads to anger starts with a spouse's doubts about his adequacy, as illustrated by Mike and Sue, a well-meaning young couple whose differences in background—the men in Mike's working-class Irish family were all policemen and firemen with high school educations, while Sue's people were Waspish college graduates—contributed to their frequent clashes.

Mike is having an argument with Sue, who is truly bossing him around and "intimidating" him. His initial thoughts center on his sense of inferiority and vulnerability. As he shifts the blame to Sue, his sadness is replaced by anger.

Automatic Thought	Feeling
1 / Why am I such an inhibited jerk? She always gets the upper hand. She out-talks me and threatens me with leaving if I open my mouth.	Sad
2 / She's a bitch.	Angry

Sometimes the hidden feeling is *guilt,* often instigated by self-criticism. Note Mike's thoughts after Sue has accused him of being too strict with their children:

Automatic Thought	Feeling
1 / Maybe she's right. I may be too hard on them.	Guilty
2 / Why does she always try to make me feel bad? She enjoys picking on me.	Sad
3 / She's undermining my relationship with my kids.	Angry

Another frequent, hidden thought that triggers anger is expressed overtly as an *accusation* against the partner: *"You are irresponsible. You don't care about me."* Although these thoughts are aimed at the spouse, they are preceded by earlier ones that are often directed against oneself. These are typically "self-critical" thoughts or "alarmist" thoughts.

For example, Cindy went to a social gathering with her lover, Jeff. During the party she became increasingly angry at him, although she was not sure why. She then became openly critical of him. The following sequence illustrates how Cindy's initial self-criticism (*"What is wrong with me?"*) produces pain, which she then deflects by blaming Jeff and feeling angry.

Automatic Thought	Feeling
1 / Nobody is paying attention to me. What is wrong with me? Why can't I be as popular as Jeff? He is having a good time with everyone.	Hurt
2 / Nobody is interested in me.	More hurt
3 / He should be paying attention to me.	Angry
4 / He never pays attention to me.	More angry

The initial automatic thoughts were barely noticed by Cindy. She felt hurt for a moment or two, and then angry for a long time. Her anger and hostile thoughts toward Jeff were so pronounced that she lost sight of her initial "wound." A later argument with Jeff did nothing to ease her anger or end her accusations directed at him because it did not touch on the *source* of her primary, hidden pain: *"Nobody is interested in me."*

With practice, you will find it becomes easier to fill in the blanks and identify these hidden thoughts. If you are vigilant, you should also be able to pinpoint the hurtful thoughts that precede the critical ones. Techniques for uncovering automatic thoughts are discussed more fully in Chapter 13. In addition, I will show how you can correct these thoughts and, thereby, reduce—or eliminate—the hurt and angry feelings.

Origin of Doubts
about Self and Spouse

Some of the doubts that people experience are derived from rules (*shoulds* and *should nots*) they heard their parents state and from memories of how their own parents behaved toward each other. They take these memories as models and expect themselves and their own spouse to follow them.

If the partner falls short of the parental models, then they feel let down, sad, and angry. If they themselves fail to live up to the parental standards, they may be filled with self-doubt and guilt. This was the case with a couple who had married very young and had trouble breaking away from the models presented by their own parents. For instance, Wendy absorbed her mother's rule *"The role of a wife is to take care of her husband."* This traditional mold shaped her reactions to her husband, Hal. When she failed to live up to the rule, Wendy felt inadequate and became very critical of herself.

But Hal's parents had different attitudes. His father had emphasized perfectionism so much that Hal had developed the belief *"I can never do anything right."* And Hal's mother had a demeaning attitude toward men that only strengthened his insecurity: *"Men can't do anything—they're weak and helpless."* For Hal, these rules generated serious self-doubts when things went wrong.

In one fateful encounter, Wendy noticed that Hal looked worn and tired after a day at the office.

WENDY: [*I am a failure if I don't take care of him.*] You are working too hard, dear.

HAL: [*I am inadequate. I haven't been paying her enough attention. That's why she's complaining.*] You don't appreciate me. I can't do anything right. I've never done anything right. You're never satisfied [looks and sounds depressed].

WENDY: [*Maybe I've done something wrong. Probably I shouldn't have said anything to him. I should reassure him.*] Look at all the good things you've done. You've provided for us. You always do things around the house. You're successful. You've been a good husband.

HAL: [*She's being sarcastic.*] Why don't you get off my back!

WENDY: [*He's mad at me. There's no reason for him to act this way. Maybe he's crazy.* Withdraws and starts to cry.]

HAL: [Feels guilty. *I've failed.*] Damn it, there you go again!

WENDY: [Feels guilty. *I was very wrong. I'm not supposed to upset him, and I was trying not to. I guess I'm a failure.*]

Wendy, believing she had "broken" her mother's rule about not upsetting her husband, was filled with remorse and fear. Hal, meanwhile, had gotten caught in internalizing his father's perfectionistic standards and pronounced himself a failure because his wife was upset.

The Secret *Shoulds*

People rarely give voice to their *shoulds,* which most often occur as automatic thoughts. What they voice instead is the *outcome* of the *shoulds:* complaints, scolding, and blaming. Consider the operation of these mental mechanisms in an encounter that took place between Mark and Sarah.

When Mark returned from work, he was greeted with several complaints from Sarah about her difficult work day. Mark, though, had been feeling good because he had picked up a new advertiser for the radio station where he worked, and he was looking forward to telling Sarah about his good day. His silent expectation was *"Sarah will be happy when I share the news."* Sarah, however, was preoccupied with her own problems because her boss had blamed her for a mistake *he* had made in handling a customer.

	Thinks	*Says*
SARAH:	[I *should not* have all these difficulties at work. Mark *should* listen and sympathize.]	I had a terrible time at work.
MARK:	[I *should not* have to carry Sarah's burdens. She has no right to lay them on me. I'm entitled to have a wife who is cheerful when I come home. She always has to spoil my day.]	Can't we talk about something else?
SARAH:	[I *should* be able to talk to my husband when I'm down. He *should* be supportive.]	You never want to hear about my problems. You only like to tell me your problems.
MARK:	[I *should not* have to put up with her criticisms.]	All you ever do is bitch and moan. If you can't handle the job, why don't you quit?
SARAH:	[He has no right to be angry at me and criticize me.]	You always put me down when I have a problem. You're so self-centered you can't stand to listen to anybody else.

MARK: [She has no right to attack me. If you're going to be bitchy,
I can't stand it.] I'm getting out of here [leaves
the house].

The *shoulds*, rights, and entitlements in the left column were not
stated aloud. But as automatic thoughts, they were *mental signals to
attack*. The attack began with the flash of a negative image of the
partner, which then prompted Sarah and Mark to say what each perceived as the cause of the problem, namely, the other's actions. The
offended partners are angry at the mental image of the other, but they
attack the real person.

Sarah's attack is her way of punishing Mark for his supposed misdemeanor—not supporting her by listening to her—but it is her own
negative image of Mark that she actually attacks. It is the "real" Mark,
however, who simply wants to change the subject—who feels the
pain. Mark does not really know why Sarah is attacking him, nor does
Sarah know what truly is bothering Mark; but, by counterattacking,
Mark lends credibility to Sarah's picture of him as unsympathetic and
self-centered.

Both Sarah and Mark believed strongly that their implied requests
(Mark: *"Listen to my good news"*; Sarah: *"Listen to my bad news"*)
were obvious and reasonable. Thus, they believed that their partner's
obliviousness to their requests—indeed the hostility evoked by the
interchange—was unreasonable. What they did not realize is that
their implied requests were actually invisible claims that they insisted be honored—but which neither stated openly. As soon as their
claims were "unjustifiably" thwarted, each conjured up a negative
mental image of the other, selecting negative evidence that seemed
to justify the image. The various distorting processes at work here—
such as overgeneralization, negative attribution, and "catastrophizing"—will be described in the next chapter.

Even when partners mean to be kind to each other, such silent
thoughts can undermine their intentions, producing angry misunderstandings. Many fights between spouses start because tacit expectations are thwarted. Since the mates do not realize the actual source of
the problem, they attribute their discomfort to some negative qualities in their partner rather than to a *mismatch in their expectations*.
Because of their disappointment, they have negative thoughts about
the other (*"She's going to lay a trip on me"*; *"He should be supportive"*) that spur them to scold the mate. The attack brings a counterattack, thus confirming the negative image each has of the other.

If Mark and Sarah had only stepped back to recognize that they
were "out of synch," they could have avoided yet another destructive

confrontation and offered the kind of support they had given in the past. By "rolling with" their disappointment, they could, for example, have taken turns telling their good and bad news. Mark could have listened to Sarah instead of trying to change the subject. Sarah could have restrained her wish to scold him, and Mark could have checked his wish to counterattack. A constructive intervention *at any one of these points* could have halted the chain reaction. Instead, they allowed themselves to be goaded by their *shoulds,* and their sense of violated rights.

Among their friends, Mark and Sarah were considered kind and sympathetic. When these friends wanted to share their successes or problems, Mark and Sarah showed a high degree of tolerance, flexibility, and patience. But these qualities had atrophied in their interactions with each other. The couple's belief in their divine right to be heard when they wanted to—regardless of the other's concerns at the moment—made them rigid, intolerant, and impatient when they were frustrated.

TRICKS
OF THE MIND

FRANCES: I can't stand my husband. I just have to get divorced. . . . I have to do everything he wants. Right now, his brother and wife are visiting. I have to wait on them hand and foot.

FRIEND: You can say one two-letter word—NO!

FRANCES: I can't do that . . . he'd make my life miserable.

FRIEND: I thought you said you were going to divorce him anyhow, so what do you have to lose? You say you either have to give in completely or you are going to leave him. Isn't there anything in between?

FRANCES: No.

Frances's responses illustrate the kind of polarized, all-or-nothing thinking that I have seen in many troubled marriages. The mates, a salesman and a schoolteacher who first began to experience trouble in their marriage after his employer transferred him twice in six years, view their situation in only one of two ways: it is either all good or all bad—there is nothing in between. They have the same response to any problems that arise between them: either the problem can be solved easily or it can't be solved at all. Frances, for example, was unable to consider a reasonable solution, even when one was suggested by her friend.

This thinking in extremes leaves couples with an exaggerated, unpleasant view of each other and their marriage. Since they cannot define their problems accurately, their difficulties can take on momentous proportions. And because they do little to solve these seemingly formidable problems, their sense of helplessness—and rage—builds, further thwarting their efforts to tackle the problems.

At first glance it may seem that Frances is deliberately exaggerating her predicament—that perhaps she gets some perverse pleasure in boxing herself in. This is not so. The thinking traps that couples fall into reflect involuntary distortions in the ways in which they process information, not in their conscious or unconscious intentions.

Thinking problems have nothing to do with intelligence. Couples who show high levels of intelligence in dealing with people outside their family, or in solving demanding problems at work, can revert in their married life to the most primitive, erroneous thinking under the pressure of demands, threats, or frustrations. Of course, twisted thinking in itself sets people up for further frustrations.

When people experience extreme feelings, such as rage, fright, or despair, in their intimate relationships, they are very likely thinking in extremes. To be sure, sometimes the situation is extreme in reality, in which case the emotional reaction may well be appropriate. But for the most part, these intense reactions are based on distortions of normal thinking processes: all-or-nothing thinking, mind reading, overgeneralization.

How Symbolic Meanings
Twist Our Thinking

Since many of our thinking problems occur in situations that have specific symbolic meanings, it will help to review the kinds of situations that lend themselves to symbolic interpretations—and misinterpretations. Some people make typical errors in their thinking when they perceive threats to *vital aspects of their lives:* to their security, safety, and close relationships. They may, for example, exaggerate the consequences of a family member's minor illness—he or she may get sicker and die, they tell themselves. Others may magnify the consequences of bills not being paid on time—they fear bankruptcy. Still others become alarmed when their spouses are angry at them—they envision an end to the relationship.

Because of the huge symbolic importance people attach to these types of situations, they see themselves in a do-or-die position. This perception facilitates the kind of absolute thinking that Frances demonstrated.

Recall Ted's insistence that Karen always be prompt. For Ted, punctuality was akin to godliness. When Karen kept him waiting, even if only for a few minutes, he would become very upset. He had a deep, hidden fear of being abandoned. Karen's lateness aggravated the fear that something might have happened to her—*and he would be left all alone.* Another symbolic meaning for Ted was that Karen didn't care enough about his feelings to arrive promptly. He thus would be angry at her when she did appear—for having caused him unnecessary worry.

Karen could not fathom Ted's insistence on punctuality. To her, it meant that he was restricting her freedom of action; in short, Ted's demands had a symbolic meaning for her. Even when she decided to accommodate him, Karen harbored resentment. She was unable to strip Ted's insistence on punctuality of its meaning: a wife being unfairly controlled by her husband. Thus, what might seem to be a minor event for most couples acquired—because of symbolic meanings—highly magnified, distorted, and troublesome proportions for Ted and Karen.

Often, it is easier for a spouse to recognize the telltale signs of a symbolic reaction in the partner: the hair-trigger, exaggerated response to a specific situation and the tenacity with which the mate clings to his or her interpretations, contrary to all logic. Once mates know this, they can take their partner's sensitivities into account. For example, knowing Ted's concerns, Karen could try harder to be on time without having to feel that she was sacrificing any of her autonomy.

With some effort, it is possible for people to realize when they are reacting to a symbol invested with inflated meaning; in this way, they can take measures to lessen the extremity of the reaction. But it takes considerable time, and persistence, to alter psychological habits—to strip symbolic situations of their power to trigger the same extreme reactions.

Ted, for instance, had to recognize the inappropriateness of his fear that some disaster was imminent whenever Karen was late. But by applying reason and logic to his fear, he managed to assuage it and to see that Karen's tardiness was an expression of her personality—not a sign of indifference. Karen, for her part, was able to understand that making an effort to be punctual did not signify a curtailing of her freedom or her domination by Ted. As Ted and Karen were able to grasp the symbolic meanings, their thinking became more reasonable and they experienced fewer overreactions. They did not reach this objective totally on their own: it took several counseling sessions to get them on the right track.

The Spreading Factor

As distress mounts in a marriage, the twists and turns in a couple's thinking begin to spread. Where previously a husband may have become angry over his wife's interruptions or reproaches, he now reacts with irritation or even fury to almost anything she does. He shows the same negative, black-and-white thinking in response to the way she greets him, the type of meal she prepares, and their social engagements. Family issues like domestic chores, finances, sex, and leisure time become sources of conflict. While problems in these areas may once have been solved through discussion, they now become magnified, prompting either hot debates with no resolution, or mutual withdrawal, or both.

As the negativity becomes more pervasive, the spouses' perspectives of one another begin to change. Whereas Karen originally saw Ted as kind and sympathetic, she later viewed him as mean and inconsiderate; Ted, who previously regarded Karen as lively, affectionate, and understanding, began to see her as detached and unresponsive.

Once couples get caught up in symbolic meanings, still other problems may arise. Partners may begin to make generalizations, or overgeneralizations, about the meanings they attach to unpleasant marital situations; they may "catastrophize," making exaggerated predictions; or they may "awfulize," magnifying their distress or inability to tolerate frustration. The end result is that when a wife frowns, for instance, her husband may think, *"She doesn't respect me—she never has and never will. It's more than I can take."*

In periods of actual threat, the mobilization of all these mental exercises may legitimately help a person to focus his or her attention on dealing with the threat. But in routine situations—and, particularly, in marriage—these mental processes can cause trouble. The mind is designed to shift into emergency operation in the face of real danger. (Think of a commando behind enemy lines who sees the threat of danger in every movement, every person.) Unfortunately, the mind can also jump into emergency gear when the danger is not real but symbolic. When spouses are embittered, they start to behave as though they are in enemy territory, and their perspective of one another becomes dictated by this shift.

This shift is not a deliberate act of will. Spouses show hypervigilance, combativeness, and the like because of primitive mental operations that are automatically triggered by the perception of danger, whether that threat is real or merely symbolic.

Nonetheless, despite such a profound shift in thinking, spouses can still retune their thoughts and declare a mental truce. That, however, requires that they first identify their automatic thoughts and beliefs, in order to determine how erroneous these beliefs are. The mental apparatus operates to some degree as a thermostat; when corrective experiences occur, it tends to reset itself toward a neutral position. Negative biases and hair-trigger distortions can gradually fade away.

Examples of Typical
Cognitive Distortions

There are so many kinds of mental traps capable of complicating marital relationships that it is difficult to list them all. These cognitive distortions occur automatically, often in a fraction of a second, and the number of distortions that can take place in that short period is considerable. Distressed couples can fall prey to any or all of the following:

1/*Tunnel Vision*. People with tunnel vision see only what fits their attitude or state of mind, and ignore what does not. They may, for example, seize on a single, small detail as the basis for their overall interpretation of an event. Other important details are deleted, censored, or minimized.

For instance, a couple decided to celebrate their fifteenth wedding anniversary together with their twelve-year-old daughter at the lodge where they had spent their honeymoon. En route, they were having a pleasant conversation when a disagreement arose as to which turn to take. The disagreement escalated into an all-out argument, with accusations of total incompetence on the one side and bossiness on the other.

The rest of the trip went smoothly, but several days after they had returned home, they had another squabble. Both spouses then agreed that they could not get along even during a pleasant occasion like their second honeymoon, since they "had fought for the entire trip." To their surprise, the daughter pointed out that the argument on the trip had lasted less than one percent of the time they had been together, and that after the fight was over they had gotten along very well. When they thought back to the trip during a fight a few days later, they had totally blotted out the good part!

Such tunnel vision keeps distressed couples from seeing or recalling the good parts of their marriage; all that they see is the bad. As a result, the memories that come to mind as they think about their relationship are preselected, biased toward the negative. These biased recollections are most likely to occur when couples are fighting.

Similarly, during times when a couple's marriage is distressed, they may find it difficult to recall pleasant moments. As they look back, all they can see is an unbroken chain of unpleasantness. But when the marriage is going more smoothly, they can more easily recall the pleasant times that had been forgotten when they were angry at each other.

In distressed marriages, I sometimes find that the husband, for instance, cannot think of a single, positive act by the wife—even though an impartial observer sees many instances of her support, concern, and warmth. And a complaining wife can recall countless episodes of being criticized, disappointed, affronted, and controlled by her husband while being oblivious to the times he treated her kindly.

For some neurotic people, these distortions are woven into their personality, so that criticizing, blaming, and disparaging others is their stock in trade whether or not they are angry. But a partner in a troubled marriage can become just as caught up in distorted thinking about his or her spouse. At first, such tunnel vision in a marriage may happen only when the spouse is angry, but it then occurs more or less continuously as this attitude becomes entrenched.

2/ *Selective Abstraction.* Related to tunnel vision is the taking of a statement or event out of context to arrive at an erroneous interpretation.

For instance, a wife was recounting to her friends her experience in getting to the hospital for the birth of their fourth child. She told of an amusing incident in which everything seemed to go wrong. It happened to be a very snowy night; the roads were blocked; when they went to get one of the cars, it had a flat tire; when they took a taxi instead, the taxi driver got lost; when they arrived at the hospital, all of the interns and residents were busy, and the attending obstetrician was unable to get to the hospital because of the snowstorm. The wife ended the tale with a laugh, saying, "Despite all this, it was the easiest delivery I ever had."

The husband focused on a single statement in her story and inferred that her account was actually a criticism of him because "he had allowed the car to get a flat tire." By fixating on this single detail, he missed the whole point of the amusing anecdote and arrived at a conclusion that aroused his unjustified resentment toward his wife.

Couples are not inevitably locked into their biased selections or tunnel vision. With a bit of effort, they can shift their focus to a more balanced view that includes the more pleasant events of their marriage. One couple found that they were able to absorb and recall far

more of their enjoyable times together when each partner started to
list them every day. Once a week they would review these positive
events. They were both surprised to "discover" that they had so many
pleasant times with each other.

3/*Arbitrary Inference.* Sometimes a person's bias is so strong that he
or she will make an unfavorable judgment even though there is no
basis for it. A wife, for instance, overheard her husband singing in
another room. Her thought was *"He's doing this just to irritate me."*
Actually, he was singing because he was happy.

In another incident, she was quiet at the dinner table. Her husband
thought, *"She's not saying anything because she's mad at me."* In
fact, the wife—who was always quite free about letting her husband
know when she was angry—just happened to be lost in thought.

4/*Overgeneralization.* One of the most troublesome distortions—and
one of the most difficult to change—is overgeneralization: *"He never
gives me credit for having a brain." "She always puts me down."*
Even though these absolute statements strike an observer as farfetched, they seem very plausible to an irate spouse who moves from
a single incident or only a few to conclude that the behavior is typical
or general. (Of course, overgeneralizations can be glowing, too, as
they are during the infatuation period.) Negative judgments lead into
unfavorable overgeneralizations. Thus, a husband who only occasionally came home late from the office was, in his wife's eyes, *always*
late. Conversely, his wife, who was delayed occasionally in getting
dinner ready, was accused by her husband of "never having dinner
ready on time."

Overgeneralization is particularly common in depressed spouses,
who may have thoughts such as *"You've never loved me," "You never
care about how I feel,"* or *"You're always going to treat me misera-
bly."* Sometimes negative thinking leads to nihilistic conclusions
about the marriage: *"Things will never improve." "The marriage is
dead." "We don't have anything in common." "I've always been unhappy."* At other times negative thinking is directed against oneself:
"I'm a failure as a parent [husband, wife]." Among the key terms that
suggest overgeneralization are all-or-nothing words like *never, always, all, every,* and *none,* as the preceding examples have illustrated.

The impact of overgeneralized, absolutist statements in distressed
marriages can be powerful. For instance, a husband who had been
trying hard to please his wife slipped up and forgot to do something
she had asked. She then scolded him, "You *never* do anything for
me." Her husband, feeling unjustly accused, thought, *"Nothing I do
is good enough for her. I can never satisfy her."*

5/*Polarized Thinking.* Polarized, all-or-nothing thinking is very common, even among couples who are happily married. As with most distortions, polarized thoughts, though credible at the time, usually fade away after a while, with no lasting bad effects. In distressed couples, however, the notion of having only two extreme choices takes hold and dictates not only how the partners feel toward each other but also how they act.

For instance, in the anecdote at the start of this chapter, Frances started with the idea that she could not say anything to her husband about the obligations he had imposed on her, then jumped to the conclusion that she was doomed to be the slave of her husband and his family: "I can't stand my husband. I just have to get divorced. . . . I have to do everything he wants. Right now, his brother and wife are visiting. I have to wait on them hand and foot."

The resulting either-or choice in Frances's mind was *"Either I submit completely or I get divorced."* Having to decide between such unpleasant alternatives could only lead her to frustration, anger, and unhappiness: on the one hand, submission would cause depression and anger; on the other, a blowup would lead to divorce.

Why didn't Frances consider a third option—saying no—as her friend suggested? Under stress, people's thinking about complex problems slides into familiar, pre-formed grooves. The "solutions" represented by these grooves are simplistic: give in or get out; fight or flee, shout or shut up. Frances was also limited to these extreme choices for another reason: she had never learned to assert herself with her husband, so she was unable to perceive refusing him as a viable option. In her marriage counseling, she would need help with self-assertion.

The simplistic, grooved thinking behind these choices divides problems into two categories; things are either good or bad, black or white, possible or impossible, desirable or undesirable. To this way of thinking, if a person cannot be classified as good, he or she is bad; if not happy, then unhappy; if not competent, then incompetent. Perfectionism involves this same type of thinking in opposites. For example, if a performance is not perfect, then it is totally flawed. There are no intermediate points—no shades of gray—in this black-or-white thinking.

Polarized thinking is, in part, a carry-over from the kind of categorical thinking typical of childhood. Such thinking seems to be embedded in a mental plan akin to a computer program. When this program is activated during conflict, it tends to dominate the way one partner thinks about the other. Although the troubled spouses still think clearly about issues *outside* their marriage, when it comes to marital problems, they slip into black-or-white thinking. The rigidity imposed by their polarized thinking explains why conflicted couples find it difficult to compromise: there is no middle ground.

6/*Magnification.* Magnification is the tendency to exaggerate the qualities of another person, whether good or bad, and to "catastrophize" by inflating the severity of a particular event's consequences.

Such catastrophic thinking is often triggered when a threatening situation no longer seems controllable. A husband, for example, was very upset when his wife spent more than they had budgeted for Christmas presents. Envisioning a continuing series of spending sprees that would eventually bankrupt them, he told his wife, in all seriousness, "We will end up on welfare." A spouse's expression of intense, out-of-control emotions often generates catastrophic thinking in the partner. Melanie said, "When Mark has one of his temper tantrums, I get so frightened—I'm afraid he might attack me or the children." Afterward, when she reflected on this fear, she realized how farfetched it was: he had never struck anyone in his life. But when she was growing up, Melanie observed that when her father would become angry, he would be prone to hit her mother or one of her siblings. Thus, she associated the *verbal* expression of anger with actual physical violence.

Catastrophic thinking, often subtle, is frequently embedded in the hidden fears that lead to anger. In a typical sequence, a spouse experiences a catastrophic fear about the marriage, then quickly diverts attention by mentally attacking the mate. A husband, for instance, was troubled that his wife had lied to him. He had a fleeting thought, *"Now I can never trust her again,"* and a spurt of anxiety. The next step in the sequence was preoccupation with the idea that she was a terrible person for having lied to him. He felt surges of anger and had repetitive thoughts of the different ways in which he could condemn her.

Associated with "catastrophizing" is what Albert Ellis has labeled "awfulizing." Some event is categorized as awful or terrible, although in reality its implications are only mild or moderate. Thus, a husband might think, *"It's awful if my wife finds fault with me."* A wife might think, *"It's terrible that my husband disagrees with me."* Another person might think, *"It's awful that my spouse gets angry at me."*

People often "awfulize" about their own emotions. They might think, *"I can't tolerate all this anger"* or *"I can't stand being frustrated all the time"* or *"I can't bear feeling humiliated all the time."* Ellis describes these reactions as the syndrome of "low frustration tolerance."

7/*Biased Explanations*. Negative attributions—finding an unfavorable explanation for what a spouse does—constitute one of the more common thinking problems in marriage. Automatically assuming that there are unworthy motives behind a spouse's actions reflects a more general pattern of assigning causes for events, good or bad; understanding the causes of events makes them seem more predictable and controllable for us. And this sense of predictability and controllability gives us a greater feeling of security. If we know what to expect, we can prepare ourselves in advance, we can handle events better and, if need be, we may even be able to prevent them in the future.

In unhappy marriages, when the distressed couple search for causes underlying their disappointments and frustrations, they inevitably conjure up some negative—even malicious—motive or nasty personality trait to explain their spouse's "offensive" actions. A troubled wife, for instance, blames her husband when he forgets to attend to some detail and attributes his lapse to negligence. A distressed husband blames marital difficulties on his wife, attributing them to a deep flaw in her personality. *"It's all due to his negligence,"* she thinks; *"It's because of her defective character,"* he tells himself.

In identical circumstances, distressed couples are more likely to make negative attributions toward their mate than they would toward someone else, according to several research studies. The attribution of negative intent is a marital barometer. When spouses consistently ascribe negative motives, especially malice, to one another, their relationship is troubled. This is not to say that insidious motives do not occur but that the partners in troubled marriages generally ascribe them far more frequently and indiscriminately than is justified.

8/*Negative Labeling*. This process stems from biased attributions. For example, when a wife finds a negative explanation for her husband's actions, she is likely to attach a critical label. Thus, a particular act becomes "irresponsible," the offending spouse a "louse" or a "bully." The offended wife then reacts to the *labels* she has attributed to her husband as though they were the real thing—as though calling him a bully means that he *is* a bully. Carried to an extreme, this process leads to what Ellis has termed, "devilizing." The husband, in the wife's eyes, almost seems to grow horns.

9/*Personalization*. Many people habitually believe that the actions of others are directed at them. A man whom I treated, for instance, always thought that other drivers were playing games with him—speeding up, slowing down, passing him—just to annoy him. He reacted similarly to his wife. If she came home from work before he did, she was trying to show him up, to demonstrate that she was more dedicated to the children than he was. If she came home from work after he did, she was trying to show that she was a harder worker. He did not take into account that there were reasons for people's actions other than the need to compete with him. He seemed to operate under the principle *"All life is a struggle between me and other people. Whatever happens is directed at me in some way."*

10/*Mind Reading.* The belief that one can tell what the other spouse is thinking has been described several times in previous chapters. As a result of having this belief, spouses fall into the trap of erroneously ascribing unworthy thoughts and motives to their mates. Although at times they may be correct in their readings, they are prone to make errors that damage the relationship.

A related thinking error, also described earlier, is the expectation of clairvoyance on the part of the mate: *"My wife should know that I don't like shellfish"* or *"My husband should know that I want him to visit my parents."*

11/*Subjective Reasoning.* This process is the belief that since one feels an emotion strongly, it must be justified. "Emotional reasoning," a related concept described by Dr. David Burns, states that if a person has a negative emotion, somebody else is responsible for it. For example, *"If I feel anxious, it is because my mate has been mean to me. If I am sad, it means my spouse doesn't like me."* A variant of several of these errors in thinking arises from *over-responsibility.* The wife who assumes total responsibility for her family's welfare may be saturated with a sense of outrage and may silently accuse her husband of not conforming to her expectation that *he* shoulder the burdens.

Mental Distortions in Action

Take, for example, a husband whose hostile frame of mind offers fertile ground for the variety of thinking errors previously described. From the time he awakens in the morning, he is braced for "things to go wrong," for "people to goof up" (negative expectations). He is wary of the breakfast his wife serves him. He checks the temperature of his coffee to see if it is too hot or too cold; he questions the taste of his cereal or the texture of his eggs, looking for signs of "improper" preparation. When his wife's performance falls short of his standards (perfectionism), he is critical. He searches for her faults, weaknesses, and mistakes (hypervigilance). If some difficulty arises, he blames her for it (negative attribution). He has thoughts like *"She never does anything right"* (overgeneralization) and thinks *"This is awful"* (magnification) or *"The whole marriage will go down the drain"* ("catastrophizing"). If his wife makes a critical statement about somebody else, he thinks, *"She is actually referring to me"* (personalization).

When the husband returns home at night, he can repeat only the day's frustrations, mishaps, and disappointments, but nothing positive (selective recall). Again, he pays attention only to irritating events at home—the noise level, the children's ungrammatical speech or unruly behavior, and his wife's "imperfect" housekeeping—and he is oblivious to the friendliness and warmth his wife provides (tunnel vision).

When the children are boisterous, he thinks, *"They never know when to stop"* (overgeneralization), and he readily holds his wife responsible. He thinks, *"She doesn't know how to handle them"* (negative attribution). He explains any and all problems on the basis of his wife's personality: *"She is just weak and incompetent"* (negative labeling).

This problem-ridden husband is a catalogue of the kind of thinking distortions that afflict mates with a hostile perspective. We are all victims, at one time or another, of many of these kinds of distorted thinking, but distressed couples are particularly prone to experiencing these problems. Their vulnerability is due in part to the cumulative impact of prolonged tensions, in part to the entanglements of their personalities, and in part to the unavoidable conflicts fostered by the frictions and the countless negotiations of day-to-day life.

Mental distortions can be regarded as a misapplication of basic survival strategies. Thus, overvigilance and tunnel vision may be useful in an emergency but may cripple ordinary operations of a marriage. The tendency to find a cause for a disturbing event is useful in cases of real damage, but it is easily twisted into faultfinding, blaming, and reacting to imagined injuries. And the compulsive drive to hold a spouse responsible for every frustration and disappointment rather than to help remedy them weakens the marital bond.

Take the real case of an embattled couple. Ruth, who is acutely unhappy with Jerry, is overvigilant, continually watching him to see if he is doing—or even just thinking—something that irritates her. She seizes on anything he says or does that could represent a misdeed (selective abstraction). She interprets this behavior as an affront (arbitrary inference), as directed against her (personalization), and as indicating *"He is deliberately trying to provoke me"* (mind reading). She also thinks, *"He never does anything properly"* (overgeneralization) and *"He is totally inconsiderate—a louse"* (negative attribution). As she ponders the long-range results, she thinks, *"Things will get worse and worse"* ("catastrophizing") and *"It's so bad I can't stand it."* ("awfulizing").

Even though these tricks of the mind are very powerful when we are in their grip, they are not immutable. With the right techniques and some effort, couples can change them and rid the marriage of their spell. Chapter 13 describes in detail some of these techniques couples can use to liberate their minds—and their marriage—from the tyranny of distorted thinking.

9

IN MORTAL
COMBAT

Imagine a pair of buck deer squared off for a fight, stamping their feet, frothing at the mouth, growling at each other, eyes bulging, and then attacking head-on. Now compare this scene with a couple engaged in a shouting match. Their fists are clenched, teeth bared, spittles of saliva on the corners of their mouths, bodies poised for attack. All systems are "go." Although they are not clutching at each other's throats, it is easy to see from the tension in their muscles that their bodies are mobilized as though for a struggle to the death.

Though these adversaries exchange no blows, they attack each other with their eyes, facial expressions, and tone of voice, as well as with their angry words. Stony glares, curled lips, and snarls of contempt—these are all weapons in their arsenal, ready for deployment. In the heat of battle, spouses may hiss like snakes, roar like lions, and scream like birds.

Barbed Messages

Stares, growls, and snorts are signals of attack even when the antagonists exchange apparently innocuous words—or no words at all. As in the case of animals, these signals are designed to warn the opponent to back off or compel him to capitulate.

The "sharp edge"—the threatening tone of voice, the speed and volume of speech—can be more provocative or hurtful than the literal meaning of the words spoken. It is no surprise that people often respond more strongly to the tone of voice than they do to the words themselves. Nonverbal messages expressed through the eyes, face, and body represent a more primitive—and usually a more persuasive

—form of communication than words. Consider the following conversation between a couple:

TOM: Dear, will you remember to call the electrician?

SALLY: I will if you ask me in a nice tone of voice.

TOM: I did ask you in a nice way!

SALLY: You always whine when you want me to do something.

TOM: If you don't want to do it, why don't you say so!

Tom had *intended* to make the request in a polite way, but he had some resentment over Sally's past intransigence, so his request was tinged with the tone of reprimand. Although his words were civil, they were fused with a decidedly negative message transmitted by his tone of voice. When there is a double message such as this, the recipient is likely to respond to the *nonverbal* signals as the significant message and to ignore the words, just as Sally responded to Tom's tone of voice with a reprimand. Not realizing that his tone was provocative, Tom then interpreted her reproach as a refusal of his request, and he retaliated. Sally would probably have agreed to make the call if Tom had not edged his words with a reprimand. But they both got caught up in scolding and retaliating, and so they never got around to addressing the practical problem, namely, calling the electrician.

When one partner attempts to control the other by arming his or her requests with the hint of a threat or reproach, the attempt is likely to provoke rather than persuade. Thus, Sally became annoyed at Tom for his implied scolding, and Tom misinterpreted her reaction as a sign of recalcitrance, prompting his retaliation. The *content* of what they wanted to communicate became lost as they got drawn into punishing each other for their mutual hostility. Using hostile messages to goad each other into complying with the simple requirements of living together made their relationship into a nightmare at times.

If Tom had realized that his fleeting thoughts (prior to asking Sally to call the electrician) were self-defeating, he might have been able to neutralize them sufficiently to make the request in a pleasant way. His automatic thoughts, however, set the stage for a confrontation: *"She never attends to things . . . she'll probably give me a hard time and tell me to do it—even though I don't have the time."* Anticipating a refusal, he delivered his request in such a way as to produce the refusal he feared.

Spouses often put their requests or questions in a way that serves to blame, attack, or deflate their partner (for example, "Why didn't you call the electrician?"). As the dialogue progresses, the words themselves become increasingly abusive. At the peak of the angry exchange, battling couples use all their weapons, including insults, and some resort to the ultimate weapon—physical abuse. If couples want to maintain a pleasant working relationship, they have to be able to separate their reproaches and threats from their genuine requests. Above all, they have to be aware of the provocative nature of the style in which they speak.

Preemptive Strikes

We may attack someone as a kind of preemptive strike when we fear that if we don't stop his or her aggression—whether psychological or physical—we will be injured. In such cases, when we anticipate that somebody is winding up to attack us, we become angry and attack first, before we run the risk of being hurt.

Shelly, for example, wanted to discuss a sensitive topic with her husband—a report that the children were having trouble in school. When she said, "Dear, I'm worried about how the kids are doing," Robert became angry and responded, "You're always worried about the kids. Why don't you leave them alone? If you keep on this way, you'll make them nervous wrecks, like you." Sally responded, tearfully, "You're making me a nervous wreck, yelling at me all the time."

Robert's primary automatic thinking, however, was quite different from his reproach. He had thought, *"Perhaps they are doing badly. She's going to tell me I'm not doing my job as a father and that will make me feel guilty."* These initial thoughts produced a pain which he deflected by finding fault with Shelly.

By yelling at Shelly—a preemptive strike—he avoided the pain of exposing his own shortcomings. As in previous exchanges like this, the injection of emotional issues interfered with addressing, let alone solving, the practical problems.

To prevent such preemptive strikes, it is important to recognize your automatic thoughts, especially those that make you feel sad, guilty, or anxious, and to hold back the impulse to counterattack. While it is true that the preemptive strike may temporarily spare you some pain, it will ultimately cause more pain as a result of the continued, unpleasant encounters with your spouse and the ill effects of the unsolved problem. Putting the brakes on these attacks may require patience and tolerance, but it will pay off in better relations and more successful problem solving.

Many people counterattack the instant they think that they are being criticized, without examining whether the criticism is valid. In this way, they circumvent the pain of the criticism. If a husband, for example, tells his wife that she is neglecting the children, she might accept the truth of his charge, reproach herself, and feel bad. But, by automatically fighting back and counterattacking before the criticism can "sink in," she discredits him and, consequently, the validity of his criticism. The cost, however, is that meaningful communication and problem solving are cut off: if there is some truth to what her husband says, she will never take the time to reflect on it; if he is wrong, she will fail to set him straight.

Using criticism to change what a spouse does may create more problems than it solves. As we shall see in the remaining chapters, partners can learn a variety of methods to prevent or solve problems —without being critical, demanding, or resorting to preemptive strikes.

Overkill

When some expression of hostility is justified, we may become so angry that we actually could fight to the death—even though we limit ourselves to scolding or name calling. Such total mobilization in a marital fight so far exceeds what is called for that it prompts the calmer partner to discredit the other as "hysterical" or "irrational," or to retreat in fear.

A more serious problem is that total mobilization for attack, appropriate perhaps in an earlier age of our species in the wild, can break through inhibitions and lead to physical abuse. Several years ago I was consulted by a couple who complained that although they loved each other, they were always fighting. On several occasions the husband was so physically abusive that the wife had called the police. They described the following incident:

Two days previously, as Gary was leaving the house, Beverly said, "By the way, I called Bob's [a private trash collector], and they will remove all the trash from the garage." Gary did not say anything but became increasingly angry as he thought about her statement. He ended up punching her in the mouth. Beverly ran to the phone and started to call the police until Gary restrained her. After much struggling, followed by a heated discussion, they agreed to see me in consultation.

Gary's reaction seemed inexplicable on the basis of the story that they first told me. As the story unraveled, however, the incident became more understandable. When asked why he had struck her, Gary said, "Beverly really made me mad"—as though the provocation were self-evident. As far as he was concerned, *she was at fault for his hitting her,* because she had angered him by talking the way she did. If Beverly made him angry, Gary believed, he was justified in striking her. His unstated assumption was that, despite her apparently innocent statement, she was in effect saying she couldn't count on him to get the trash out of the garage, that he was irresponsible, and that she was morally superior.

Beverly, on the other hand, maintained that she was "merely giving him information," not accusing him. She had been asking him to clean out the garage for some time and, since he had not attended to it, she had decided to take care of it herself by calling the trash collectors.

In order to obtain hard data about what really had gone on, I decided to have the couple re-create the incident in my office. I asked Beverly to give the background and then to repeat her statement to Gary. As he heard her words, his face flushed, he began to breathe heavily, and he clenched his fists. He looked as though he would hit her again. At this point, I intervened and asked him the fundamental question of cognitive therapy: "What is going through your mind, *right now?*" Still shaking with fury, he responded, "She's always needling me. She's trying to show me up. She knows she drives me up the wall. Why doesn't she just come out and say what she's thinking—that she's such a saint and I'm no good?"

I suspected that his very first reaction (primary automatic thought) to her statement—which he clearly took as a put-down—was the thought that he was a failure as a husband, as he believed she was implying. He had quickly wiped out this painful thought, however, by focusing on her "offensive statement." Although she had repeated this to him in a measured way during the role-play in the office, I suspected that in real life she may have spoken in a cavalier or slightly sarcastic tone.

In my office she acknowledged that when she spoke, she had indeed been having a demeaning thought on the order of *"See, I can't count on you for anything—I have to do everything myself."* Although she did not express this thought at the time, evidently either it came through in her tone of voice, or else he was so sensitized to this message from past experience that he read it into her statement. Thus, a provocation can be concealed in an apparently innocent message. But how can we understand the *intensity* of Gary's reaction? The explanation lies in facets of his personality as well as in the couple's marital history of accusations and retaliations.

Before marrying, Gary had been self-sufficient and considered himself successful. Raised in a poor family, he had worked his way through college and become an engineer. He opened his own consulting firm and prospered from the very beginning. He had a high regard for himself as a successful, rugged individualist.

Beverly was attracted to Gary because of his good looks and his uninhibited, independent manner. She had been raised in a "proper household," in which the emphasis was on good manners and fitting in socially. Somewhat inhibited herself, she was attracted to a man who did not seem bound by social conventions, who was an independent thinker and, above all, who appeared *strong*. She admired him for his successful career and saw in him the fantasy of a knight in shining armor who would always take care of her. Indeed, during their courtship he assumed responsibility for making all the plans for their time spent together, and because she regarded him as superior, she felt very comfortable with this arrangement. Gary was attracted to Beverly because she was pretty, dependent on him, and admired him. She was also submissive, accommodating her own wishes to his.

After they were married, Beverly was initially intimidated by Gary, but she gradually discovered his feet of clay: he procrastinated over household chores; he could not relate to the children. With the passage of time, she became more mature and self-confident, and no longer regarded herself as inferior to him. In fact, from time to time she got satisfaction out of demonstrating that—far from being a "perfect doll"—she was more mature than he in many ways. She attended to details better, was a more conscientious parent, and managed their social life more deftly than he could.

At the same time, Gary had brief episodes of mild depression during which he thought that he was an inadequate father and husband. On these occasions, he would accept Beverly's implied criticisms as valid. He would feel hurt by them, but would not fight back. However, when Gary was no longer depressed, he refused to "tolerate her criticisms" and would lash out at her.

Why did Gary resort to physical abuse instead of limiting his retaliation to verbal attacks? First of all, he had been raised in a "rough" neighborhood, where conflicts were frequently settled by physical fights. Moreover, Gary described his father as a violent man. When angered, his father would hit Gary's mother as well as Gary and his siblings. Apparently, Gary learned early in life that "When you're angry, you should let the other person have it."

Gary never had a model from whom to learn nonviolent ways of settling problems. It developed that he did not have much control in dealing with any of the people in his life, including his employees and clients. If he felt provoked by employees, he would fire them— and then try to hire them back later. If he was in conflict with a client over plans or fees, he would break off negotiations.

This lack of control gave him the reputation of being tyrannical; but, oddly, instead of deterring clients, it attracted them. He conveyed the image of the ultimate authority: superbly self-confident, decisive, and intolerant of opposition—in short, a strong man.

Although his authoritarian style was successful in his line of business, it was ill-suited to marriage. At first, when Beverly would attempt to stand up to him, he would yell at her, but as she began to fight back, he gradually became physically abusive. Eventually, whenever Gary detected a tone of derision or deprecation in her voice, he was moved to react with a physical attack.

During my work with this couple, it emerged that issues of self-esteem were paramount. Beverly was continuously trying to protect her self-esteem by not yielding to Gary when he tried to tell her what to do. To Gary, her opposition meant, symbolically, that she had little regard for him. After all, he *knew* the correct course of action—his employees and clients listened to him and did what he told them to. Thus, her resistance had a deeper meaning for him—that perhaps he was not really as competent as he liked to believe. This notion was painful; his angry attacks served, in part, to dispel the idea.

Further counseling revealed that while Gary was growing up, his older brother used to tease and torment him by calling him a secret specially coined name—"weakness." Despite his successful career, he was never able to shed completely this image of himself as a weakling. He was only rarely haunted by the feeling of being a "push-over," however, because in most of his dealings with people, he had the upper hand.

With Beverly, though, things were different. Gary felt vulnerable. By attacking her, he tried to stave off the pain of having his "weak" side exposed. If she were to get the upper hand, this would offer painful confirmation, in his mind, that he was indeed a "weakness." In fact, at times when she was critical of him, he would painfully think, *"If she really respected me, she would not talk to me that way —she thinks I'm weak."*

Thus, both partners were in a sense trying to equalize the relationship by putting each other down. Gary wanted to maintain his self-esteem, which was based on his exercising control over other people. His polarized thinking—*"If I'm not on top, I'm a flop"*—reflected his hidden fear of being shown to be weak. Beverly's self-esteem, on the other hand, was injured by his assumption of authority, and her attempt to knock him off the pedestal was a way of restoring her own self-esteem. Her hidden fear was of being dominated because of her uncertainties and inhibitions.

Thus, what seemed on the surface to be a dispute over distribution of domestic responsibilities turned out to be a struggle over self-esteem. The who-does-what-and-when question had become a battle-ground where the spouses fought to maintain favorable self-concepts. When one won, the other lost; when one felt good, the other felt bad. Their mutual combativeness and competition for control were generated by the real issue—their need to protect their pride.

I used a two-pronged approach to the therapy. First, we established ground rules for communication. Beverly and Gary were both to refrain from discussing sensitive issues, which we listed, when they got angry. Second, they were to have a weekly troubleshooting discussion (initially in my office but eventually at home) during which they would take turns bringing up problems. If either moved into the "hot zone"—if they felt angry and began to criticize or attack—both were to change to a different, more neutral subject. (See Chapter 17 for a discussion of the "zones.") If that did not work, they were to withdraw physically from each other. If Gary did not cool off promptly, he was to "work it off" by taking a walk.

Once the couple had instituted this new system, which took about four or five visits, I began to see them individually. They were both instructed in the technique of identifying automatic thoughts and countering them with rational responses (see Chapter 13). Gary, for example, learned to deal with his automatic thoughts as shown below. On one occasion, Beverly said in an apparently strained voice, "You didn't pay the cable TV bill last month. They'll probably discontinue the service." Gary was angered, but he managed to take out his notebook and pencil, and write the following:

Automatic Thought	*Rational Responses*
She's trying to put me down.	1 / I don't know that for a fact. She may simply be trying to tell me something.
	2 / What she says could be valid. I can concentrate on that and ignore her tone of voice or what she may be thinking.
	3 / She has her own problems. I don't have to get sucked into them by getting mad.

After a few weeks, Gary was trained to catch the very first (primary) thoughts that preceded his anger-inducing thoughts and impulse to hit her.

Situation	*Immediate Thought*
She scolded me for coming home late. She said, "Why did you come home late?"	1 / She doesn't think very much of me if she thinks she can talk to me that way. [Hurt]
	2 / She must regard me as weak. [Hurt]
	3 / I probably am weak or she wouldn't talk to me that way. [Feeling of pain]
	4 / I can't let her get away with this. [Anger: desire to hit her]

The thought of being demeaned by her triggered the chain reaction that had been set in place decades earlier, during childhood squabbles with his brother. Feeling demeaned by Beverly, Gary then had the thought *"I can't let her get away with this"* and felt the impulse to strike her. Fortunately, he followed my instructions: he tried to ignore any negative overtones in her question; he set aside the meanings expressed in his automatic thoughts; he controlled his impulse to lash back at her; and he focused only on the content of her question. In this way, he managed to take Beverly's questions at their face value. Whatever else a spouse's questions may be, they are also genuine requests for information. It is not necessary to respond to the hidden message. When Beverly asked, "Why did you come home late?" Gary replied, "I was detained at the office."

With the marriage stabilized, at least temporarily, we were able to focus on each spouse's deep sense of vulnerability. Gary was able to explore this vulnerability through living out his childhood fears of feeling weak and inferior. Beverly explored her own sense of powerlessness, stemming from the inhibitions of her childhood. With training, she learned that she could assert herself without being hostile; she could speak directly and firmly and even kindly to Gary, and she did not have to needle him or put him down.

Behind the Fights: Basic Beliefs

To understand more fully why people behave as they do, we have to look deep beneath their actions, beyond their automatic thoughts, and ferret out their basic beliefs. A basic belief, once operative, influences the way a person interprets a situation and how he or she will act. Some of these beliefs are near the surface and can be readily observed; some are buried in a jumble of other thoughts. But with some introspection, people can learn to discern them.

Gary had the following set of basic beliefs, reflecting his tendency to see other people as adversaries:

▷ I have to stay on top so other people won't discover my weakness.

▷ If people knew of my weakness, they would run all over me.

▷ I have to control other people in every situation.

▷ If my wife gets the best of me once, she'll never stop.

▷ My wife enjoys putting me down.

▷ The only way to make her understand that she can't get away with it is to hit her.

Beverly had the following beliefs:

▷ I am much too inhibited.

▷ If I don't express myself, I am powerless.

▷ If I am powerless, I am nothing.

▷ I have to keep Gary in check or he'll run all over me.

▷ The only way I can get him to cooperate at home is to demonstrate that he is falling down on the job.

When we compare the attitudes of each spouse, we can see how their clashes were inevitable. The basic conflict is expressed in their anger and hostility—a seriously disruptive element requiring further modification.

Controlling Anger

Beverly and Gary's case closely resembles countless others in disturbed or broken relationships in which the partners do *not* seek professional help. Even if couples do not have such serious problems, there are a number of principles they can keep in mind to minimize the damage from heated arguments.

1/Partners can be unnecessarily provocative in the way that they talk about management of the home, child rearing, and other issues. They often use techniques such as needling, sarcasm, and criticism when they would do better simply to state what they want.

2/Partners may often use these ways of talking because they feel right. Quite frequently, these were the very techniques used in their families of origin. Surprisingly, even though such methods are counterproductive, partners persist in using them either because they don't even consider other approaches or because they are simply convinced of their effectiveness. They are oblivious to the fact that these tactics are usually counterproductive—producing resentment, opposition, and retaliation.

3/While possibly adaptive in the wild, the emotions of primitive anger and hostility are out of place in domestic life, where "kill or be killed" is not the issue. Partners need to learn how to *control* or reduce their excessive hostility, rather than to express it.

4/Techniques of control consist of such commonsense methods as refraining from acting on anger, trying to move from the hot zone into the temperate zone (Chapter 17), and calling time-out periods when arguments become too hot.

5/When partners learn to identify their automatic thoughts and the basic beliefs that underlie their hostility, they can clear the way for constructive solutions to the real problems at hand, in place of the continual rehash of disguised psychological issues.

Many people subscribe to the notion that expressing anger is a good thing, but they think only in terms of the *immediate relief* and *satisfaction* they get: *"Now that I've gotten this off my chest, I feel much better."* What they fail to take into account is the effect on their spouse. When Gary and Beverly lashed out at each other, they inflicted real pain, and the chain reaction accelerated until it culminated in physical violence.

Your hostility cannot be expressed in a vacuum. It is aimed at someone—your partner—who is bound to react. Further, in order for hostility to be "successful," for the angry words and acts to "work," you have to know that your partner experiences pain. Consequently, you may keep attacking him or her until you see a pained reaction.

If your hostility works and your partner does what you want, you are likely to continue to use this "strategy" in the future to punish or control your spouse. But at times, your hostility may get out of control and you may inflict far more damage than you intended. Just as it is difficult for nations to have a limited war, it is hard for couples to have limited hostility.

Although expressing anger has become something of a shibboleth in marriage, I have found that it usually seems to do more harm than good. The accumulated hurts from being scolded, vilified, and cursed lead the victim to see the attacking spouse not only as an adversary but also as an enemy.

The compelling fact is that there are more efficient ways for partners to settle problems in a marriage than by screaming at each other. For instance, inhibited people like Beverly can practice simply stating their wishes in a straightforward way, and use finesse and explanations rather than attacks. The current trend toward self-assertion and liberation, in the worst sense of the words, has freed many people of their inhibitions but has cost them a great deal in their intimate relationships. They do not realize that it is possible to use self-assertion without depending on anger to fuel their assertiveness.

Inhibition, Anger, and Self-Assertion

There seems little question that much frustration, and consequently anger, stems from the difficulty many people experience in effectively expressing themselves to their partners. Part of the problem appears to be a fear of the spouse's retaliation and a concern about hurting the spouse's feelings. Another part of the problem is the spouse's inability to pinpoint the precise source of the frustration. A major part of the difficulty, however, is the spouse's lack of skill in presenting the problem and in providing a forum for discussing conflicts with his or her mate. Ways of dealing with the problem of self-assertion have been discussed in a number of books (see References at the end of the book). The specific ways in which you can resolve conflict with your partner are presented in Chapters 15, 16, and 17.

Sometimes, the problem of inhibition and difficulty with self-assertion is so subtle that the person is unaware of its existence—and is only conscious of a low-grade depression, irritability, fatigue, and vague physical symptoms. On occasion, as in the following case, the accurate probing of the difficulty can rapidly lead to its resolution.

THE CASE OF THE INHIBITED WIFE

Several years ago, I had an informal conversation with Susan, a friend who complained that she was totally lacking in energy and was unable to get herself motivated to engage in an art project that was quite important to her. She thought she might have some kind of "artist's block" that was getting in her way.

We talked about various aspects of her life. I then started to question Susan about her relations with her husband, and she initially described them as good. Speaking about him in glowing terms, she added that they got on very well together, had common interests, and never had any disagreements.

Although it is theoretically possible for a couple to be so identical in interests and beliefs that they would never have any disagreements, it would probably be rare. A more likely explanation is that one partner (or possibly both) is so compliant to the other's wishes that he or she remains unaware of personal desires, or that one partner is so intent on preserving the idealized notion of a friction-free relationship that he or she dismisses any feelings of disagreement and accedes to the other's wishes.

In this instance I suspected that Susan might fit into the pattern, and in order to test this notion out, I questioned her more closely:

ATB: When was the most recent time when you began to feel an increase in your fatigue?

SUSAN: Phil and I were going out for a drive, and when we came home, I felt as though all the starch was out of me—I felt limp, like a rag.

ATB: When you were out riding, what happened?

SUSAN: Nothing unusual.

ATB: Who was driving the car?

SUSAN: [beginning to appear nervous] Phil was driving.

ATB: What do you recall happening during the trip?

SUSAN: Oh, something happened, but it was really nothing. I was feeling chilly from the draft—the top of the convertible was down—and I asked Phil to close the top, but he said, "I'm really enjoying this. Besides, the cold air is good for you."

ATB: What did you feel at that time?

SUSAN: [appearing more tense] I guess he was right.

ATB: Did you have any other thoughts then?

SUSAN: [now with a somewhat irritated tone in her voice] I thought that he never listens to what I have to say. He always wants to have things his own way.

Susan was somewhat surprised at what she had just said. She hadn't been aware of feeling irritated at Phil. After having made this statement—which she had never articulated to anybody else, including her husband—she started to smile and appeared more animated. She then said, "You know, I feel better already." We then discussed her whole ideal of marriage: of wanting to smooth over any differences and subordinate herself in order to preserve the ideal of a problem-free relationship. This ideal, incidentally, fitted in with the adolescent fantasy of maintaining a carefree life—a fantasy she was working hard to preserve.

When Susan became aware of her submissive tendencies, she agreed it would be a good idea for her to try being more assertive with Phil whenever there was the slightest hint that she disagreed with him. We then enacted a role-play in which I became her husband, forcefully asserting my point of view in a number of areas, and she practiced speaking up to me—sticking to her guns. During the role-play she felt considerable anger toward Phil, but she also recognized that he would probably cooperate if she stood up to him, and especially if she shared her particular problem with him.

Over the course of time, Susan became quite successful at asserting herself with Phil. She began to feel real anger toward him when he imposed his wishes on her—and she told him about it! Her fatigue disappeared during her talk with me, and she found when she got home that her "artist's block" started to go away, disappearing altogether within a few days.

The Anatomy of Anger

A more detailed understanding of the nature of anger and the role it plays in our adapting to threats can help demonstrate why we need not give in to hostile impulses in most situations.

The feeling of anger includes a sense of pressure to *do something,* somewhat analogous to the internal pressures we experience when sexually aroused. And, as with sexual arousal, the tension tends to persist until after the "consummatory act" that relieves it. In the case of both hostility and sex, the consummation brings not just a feeling of relief from tension but an overall satisfaction and dissipation of the original urge. In a sense, anger and sexual excitation serve as catalysts that prompt specific actions. But the feelings are a prelude to—not a constituent part of—these behaviors, just as hunger may drive us to eat although it is not a part of eating.

The term *anger* is often used very loosely to apply to the entire process of negative feelings, mobilization to fight, and fighting. The expression "He expressed his anger," for example, can be used to describe a scenario in which an offended person strikes the offender. But for our purposes, this concept of anger is misleading. The word *anger* is best reserved for a specific *emotion* rather than for the violent acts associated with it.

A better term for the impulse to attack, as well as for the actual attack itself, is *hostility.* A person can attack without feeling angry, and can be angry without attacking. We can, for instance, attack a punching bag with our fists or toss a dart at a target—with no feeling other than the pleasure in using our muscles. Further, we can be mean, even cruel, to another person not out of anger but for the sadistic pleasure it gives us. *Anger,* as we will use the term here, is a feeling that alerts us to the possible need for aggressive action or prepares us to defend ourselves.

When couples get into a fight, a progression is established: first, they perceive having been wronged in some way; next, they become angry; then, they feel impelled to attack; and, finally, they attack. This sequence can be disrupted at any stage: thoughts of being abused may be corrected; feelings of anger can be dispelled; and the impulse to attack can be suppressed.

The *concept* people have of anger has direct consequences for how they deal with it. For instance, the notion of anger as a kind of substance that gradually builds up in a reservoir has spawned a number of prescriptions for dealing with it. George Bach, for example, has advocated that couples "express their anger" and has offered techniques for doing so. Many other writers have justified their advocacy of hostile behavior using similar metaphors, such as likening anger to water boiling in a pot: unless you let the steam out, the pressure will blow off the lid.

These prescriptions have been criticized by authors like psychologists Albert Ellis and Carol Tavris, who propose searching for the cognitive basis of hostility rather than expressing it in action. I also believe that anger is, for the most part, best dealt with by understanding it rather than by acting on it. On occasion, however, acting on anger may be essential to survival. A wife subjected to abuse by her husband could use her experience of anger to initiate effective self-protective action.

How does anger act? The emotion itself consists of feelings of discomfort and tension. The sensations that come from the mobilization of the muscular system and autonomic nervous system (jump in blood pressure, accelerated pulse, tightened muscles) mix with the feelings of anger per se, and may be difficult to distinguish from them. The physical mobilization adds a feeling of being revved up. But this same feeling occurs whenever a person is mobilized—whether to compete, exercise, or attack—and is not necessarily associated with anger.

As a survival strategy in evolution, anger is comparable to pain. Indeed, the word *anger* derives from roots denoting "trouble, affliction, or pain." As with pain, anger seems designed to disturb our state of equilibrium and alert us to trouble. We believe that both serve a purpose in activating us to deal with threats or damage. This disturbance—or signal—prods us to stop what we are doing and shift our attention to the problem that triggers the anger.

As we focus on whatever seems to be responsible for the anger, we are spurred to attack its cause. Thus, anger may be regarded as a sort of irritant, alerting us to threat. Just as we can relieve pain by removing the offending object (a thorn, a speck in the eye), we similarly alleviate anger by eliminating its source. Once the noxious agent is driven off or destroyed, anger subsides and normal equilibrium is restored.

As part of the primitive fight-flight response, hostility is rooted in the most fundamental survival mechanisms. But in modern life, and particularly in modern marriage, acting on that primitive urge can be destructive to relationships. Despite the imperative nature of anger and the pressure to relieve it by carrying out a hostile act against the offender, we need not yield to the urge to attack. Over the course of time, anger dies down, and with it the desire to strike out.

HOW WE INFLICT PSYCHOLOGICAL PAIN

Our hostility aims to inflict physical or psychological pain. Though the sensation of a physical hurt is far different from the experience of a psychological hurt, they are roughly parallel. Physical pain initially arises from stimulation of the peripheral nerve endings and is localized in the area of this stimulation. When we have psychological pain (for example, sadness or anxiety), we cannot point to a specific area where we feel it, but this pain is just as real as—and often more unpleasant than—physical pain.

Despite their differences, physical and psychological pain have some similar effects. An insult, for example, can evoke the same pained expression, the same splinting of the facial muscles, as a slap on the face. Receiving bad news can produce the same kind of physical reaction as can a physical shock—a sudden drop in blood pressure, even a fainting spell.

When Sybil told Max she was thinking of leaving him, his whole body stiffened, just as it would have if she had struck him. We often use bodily similes or metaphors to express psychological trauma ("it was a slap in the face" or "it was like a kick in the stomach"). Both a figurative and a literal slap in the face convey a similar message and evoke a similar response. What is crucial is the specific *meaning* the recipients attach to a physical or psychological trauma.

SENSITIVITY TO HURTS

When we stop to consider how sensitive we are to criticisms, reprimands, and belittling remarks, it almost seems that we have receptors fashioned to ferret out the disparaging message from all others. Perhaps we have a specialized circuit in the brain attuned to picking up psychological threats, just as pain receptors are attuned to perceiving physical pain. This apparatus could alert us to threats to our well-being or safety, which—in cases like an insult or reproach—may be a forerunner of a physical attack. By a prompt reaction to the psychological pain, we avoid bodily damage. Thus, when somebody injures us with a sneer or words of abuse, we demonstrate good adaptive skills by becoming angry and preparing ourselves to ward off a possible physical attack.

When we want people to do as we say, inflicting physical pain on them can be more effective than simply blaming and criticizing them. Animals push, scratch, or growl at their offspring to shape their behavior. But the human equivalents of these primitive acts—a slap or insult, for instance—are counterproductive in a relationship and, indeed, often backfire. That kind of "persuasion" is dangerous, considering that our capacity for physical mobilization is more appropriate to jungle warfare than it is to modern life. And there is always the possibility that a verbal attack may unexpectedly escalate to all-out physical war.

Whether a threat is physical or psychological, the classical mode of reaction, as described by physiologist J. B. Cannon, consists of a fight or flight response in which the threatened animal either counterattacks or flees. Ordinarily, we human beings have a variety of additional options: we can acquiesce to the threat and submit to the demands of the other person, we can withdraw, or we can defend ourselves. If the threat is immediate and overwhelming, we may "freeze" or faint.

Each of these responses seems to derive from a primitive pattern originating in the wild. Whether an attack is physical or psychological, intentional or unintentional, our defensive reaction includes a physical mobilization or collapse (as in fainting). And, whether we exchange physical blows or insults, we experience the same defensive stiffening of our muscles.

Even more important for understanding conflicts is the awareness of what happens in our mind during a confrontation. Not only does our body stiffen but so does our mind—a condition referred to earlier as "cognitive rigidity." In a marital battle, for instance, our view of our opponent hardens; we form a negative image while screening out any legitimate message that our mate wants to convey. Further, we attribute malice to the mate, regarding him or her as mean. Such attributions of malicious intentions and bad character inevitably creep into personal disputes, and a mate who believes the other is malicious reacts by feeling defensive and angry.

But even though the partner may indeed have malevolent intentions during a fight, it does not follow that he or she is a malicious person. Nonetheless, whether a fight occurs between partners or foes, we must recognize that the same mental and physical apparatus is mobilized. At the peak of hostilities, each partner may appear to the other as a mortal enemy: their features and expressions may appear distorted by rage, and they in effect seethe with malevolence.

A couple wishing to reduce their defensiveness and anger can try to identify, evaluate, and modify the negative images they hold of each other. They will find that as their unpleasant image changes, so their anger will change. (Techniques for achieving this will be discussed in Chapters 13 and 17.)

While fighting may be adaptive in the wild, in contemporary life our survival is almost never at stake. Moreover, we are perfectly able to adopt a civilized veneer in public, even when angry. Unfortunately, however, domestic violence is more common than any other kind in our society. We are often unable—or unwilling—to exercise control with our spouse. When our internal brakes fail because they cannot withstand the increased pressure, the rage may progress to the point where it becomes expressed by physical attack. Curiously, our "adversary" is somebody whom we love—or have loved.

RETALIATION AND PUNISHMENT

Once a marital fight leaves a partner feeling rejected or insulted, he or she automatically mobilizes to right the wrong. Although we usually think of punishment and retaliation as voluntary, the mobilization to strike back is as automatic a response to a threat as is the blink of an eye when a foreign body intrudes.

Of course, the mobilization for retaliation does not necessarily culminate in overt action—it simply *prepares* us to act. An intricate system of inner controls acts as a brake, so that while the preparation for action is automatic, the control of action is, to a large degree, voluntary. When we realize that the threat has subsided—for example, if we discover the error in our belief that we were being criticized by our spouse—then the mobilization dissipates.

Such mobilization to retaliate is frequently triggered by a person's perception of a disruption or injustice in the relationship. Thus, a spouse who feels rejected by the mate may retaliate, believing that the punishment will prevent future rejections. But retaliation is usually self-defeating in a relationship. Ted, for instance, "punished" Karen for being late by yelling at her. Instead of apologizing as he had expected, Karen retaliated by withdrawing—an act that stirred up an even greater fear of abandonment in Ted—and he reacted to this painful rejection by threatening divorce. Karen responded by saying, "That's a good idea"—a statement that made Ted feel desolate. Thus, his attempt to punish her backfired, and Karen's retaliation made things even worse.

Partners typically react to a perceived slight with a retaliatory put-down, reminiscent of young boys who believe that one insult calls for another. Retaliation frequently goes beyond the initial hurt. In the personal idiom of crime and punishment, vengeance requires more than just restitution of the status quo; since restitution simply means that the offending individual has not lost anything, vengeance demands more. The victim goes beyond exacting restitution and imposes an additional penalty.

The logic that leads us to inflict more pain than we have received is responsible for the escalation of fights. The expression "violence breeds violence," which is often applied to relations between groups and nations, holds equally well for interpersonal relations. The expression of hostility by one person is, in itself, a very powerful, almost inevitable, activator of hostility in the other. Since each expression of hostility is likely to provoke an even greater degree of retaliation, what starts as a simple exchange of criticisms can eventually grow into an exchange of blows—even in a loving couple. It is, of course, possible to control this combative reaction, but it takes even more effort, since the internal pressure to retaliate gets stronger as the fight goes on.

A reaction that is so reflexive and close to primordial survival responses is bound, at times, to exceed a person's capacity to contain it. Still, people do acquire techniques to control their hostility—by forcing themselves to be silent for a period of time, by distracting themselves, changing the subject, and/or leaving the room. Although these ad hoc techniques are useful preventives against *acting* on hostile feelings, they do not in themselves block the initial activation of the hostile pattern.

Cognitive therapy, as we shall see, offers techniques for nipping that pattern in the bud. One of the earliest signs that hostility has been triggered is anger. By priming ourselves to recognize the early onset of anger and to act at once to control it, we can perform an instant replay—focusing immediately on the automatic thoughts, cognitive distortions, and basic beliefs that underlie the anger. By catching and correcting these distortions on the spot, we can reduce our hostility, as Beverly and Gary learned to do. In Chapter 17, we will discuss in detail how to head off marital hostilities by pinpointing the roots of anger and taking the necessary steps at the earliest stages— before a minor resentment escalates into all-out warfare between partners.

~ 10 ~

CAN YOUR RELATIONSHIP
IMPROVE?

One problem in distressed marriages is the strong belief that things cannot get better. Such a belief thwarts change because it robs you of the motivation to try anything constructive, to modify your own thinking and behavior. On the other hand, I have observed that if one spouse starts to make constructive changes, this not only helps the relationship but generally leads to positive changes in the other spouse.

The order of the rest of the chapters in this book reflects the progression of changes couples can make. The next chapter considers the foundations of a sturdy relationship: commitment, trust, and loyalty. You should first address these elements of your marriage to see whether they need shoring up. If so, you can concentrate on the weaknesses in these pillars—try to foster cooperation, devotion, and trust—and see what attitudes or actions may be undermining them. For instance, even if you are mistrustful of your spouse, it would be helpful—for now, at least—to try to behave "as if" you can rely on his or her cooperation and loyalty until you have had the opportunity to put into practice some of the techniques I will be describing.

Having adopted for the time being a constructive, cooperative attitude, you can start to do things to tune up the relationship. For example, you can begin to focus on your spouse's pleasing actions and acknowledge them. Also, you can think of things to do that would give your spouse a greater sense of satisfaction and, indirectly, increase your own—an approach I will detail in Chapter 12.

Once you have created a favorable atmosphere, you may be ready to tackle your own unproductive thinking. Chapter 13 will tell you how. While this may take more effort than the other assignments I have suggested, it can have a large pay-off in reducing your suffering and helping you deal more effectively with your spouse. You then should be ready to try to improve communication and collaboration with your spouse—the focus of Chapters 14, 15, and 16. It would help, of course, if your spouse agreed to participate in the effort, but even on your own you can raise the level of discourse by improving your clarity, by active listening, and so on, even if your spouse does not help out.

As you eliminate some of the static from your conversations, you can try the methods for coping with anger described in Chapter 17. The approach involves trying to de-escalate hostility to the point where it is no longer damaging. This goal can be attained through on-the-spot techniques of "anger control" and by scheduling special sessions for you and your partner, in which you both express what bothers you and, if needed, vent your pent-up anger. Another approach, which explores the roots of your anger, seeks to reduce it by modifying your tendencies to magnify, "awfulize," and distort.

Finally, you will find it helpful to try some special arrangements for solving the practical problems of marriage and eliminating "undesirable" habits and patterns. In Chapter 18 I will offer hints about how to arrive at creative solutions to special problems, such as those associated with stress, sex, and dual careers.

Resistances
to Making Changes

As you consider making changes, you may run up against some attitudes or beliefs that weaken your motivation. These attitudes may be expressed in the form of automatic thoughts, as described in Chapters 7 and 8. After recognizing these resistances to change, you can begin to override them with reason, by providing explanations that show why they are incorrect and exaggerated.

Read through the list below and check any of these beliefs you or your spouse hold:

Beliefs about Change

Defeatist Beliefs

_____ My partner is incapable of change.

_____ Nothing can improve our relationship.

_____ Things will only get worse.

_____ People are set in their ways and can't change.

_____ My partner won't cooperate and nothing can be done without his [her] cooperation.

_____ I've suffered enough. I don't have the energy to try more.

_____ If we need to work at it, there's something seriously wrong with the relationship.

_____ Working at the relationship will make it worse.

_____ It only postpones the inevitable.

_____ Too much damage has been done.

_____ My marriage is dead.

_____ I don't feel I'm able to change.

_____ If we haven't gotten along up till now, how can I expect that we can get along any better in the future?

_____ It doesn't matter if my partner starts to act more positively, it's my partner's *attitude* that is the problem.

Self-Justifying Beliefs

_____ It's normal to behave the way I do.

_____ It feels right to think the way I do.

_____ Anybody else in my position would react the way I do.

_____ He [she] hurt me. He [she] deserves to be hurt.

Reciprocity Arguments

_____ I won't make an effort unless my partner does.

_____ It takes two to tango—I don't see why I should be the one to change.

_____ It's not fair for me to have to do all the work.

_____ After all the effort that I've made, it's my partner's turn to do the work.

_____ What do I get out of it?

_____ My partner hurt me badly in the past, so now he [she] must do a lot to make up for it.

_____ How do I know my partner is committed?

The Problem Is My Partner

_____ If we start to explore the relationship, my partner will get worse.

_____ There's nothing wrong with me. If my partner would shape up, everything would be fine.

_____ My partner doesn't care about improving our relationship.

_____ My partner is impossible.

_____ My partner is crazy.

_____ My partner doesn't know how to be any other way than he [she] is.

_____ My partner is just filled with hate—that's the problem.

_____ I had no problems in my life until we were married.

If you entertain some of these beliefs, it is worth examining just how valid they are. Such beliefs may pop up as automatic thoughts at the moment you contemplate change. If so, you can try using a number of counter-arguments, discussed shortly, to address these automatic thoughts.

I have found that defeatist beliefs are rarely totally valid. Of course, it may be true in certain cases that a spouse is unwilling to change— if she is in love with somebody else, for instance, or if he is absolutely set on getting a divorce. Then it may be difficult, if not impossible, to salvage the relationship. But couples already committed to divorce are not looking for ways to improve the marriage.

However, those who would like to revive their relationship, as well as those who would like to see their marriage become more fulfilling, can begin by attempting to rebut any defeatist beliefs they might have. I will describe several typical defeatist attitudes to give you an idea of how to evaluate and deal with them.

DEFEATIST BELIEFS

"My partner is incapable of change." This statement is virtually always wrong. Even the heaviest psychological armor may be penetrated in counseling. People who seem utterly impermeable to helpful suggestions may, to everybody's surprise (including their own), suddenly take them to heart and change for the better. Whether your spouse is *willing* to change is another matter. But if *you* make some changes, this in itself may prompt changes in your partner—it very often does. Further, you may find your partner does not have to change greatly to become more congenial and easier for you to get along with.

It is important to recognize that people *do* change, constantly, throughout their lives. Our central nervous system is organized to encourage our learning new and better outlooks and strategies. New patterns of thinking or behaving that increase pleasure on the one hand or reduce pain on the other are reinforced and so persist. Consequently, if you and your mate develop ways of viewing and acting toward each other that are more rewarding than the old patterns, they can work their way into your repertoire of habits. I will describe examples of such improvements in the following chapters.

"Nothing can improve our relationship." This belief can be tested. One way is to define specific problems in your relationship, then select the one problem that seems most amenable to change, and apply the appropriate remedies. This does not necessarily require "work." It may be as simple as planning to have dinner out once a

week alone together or agreeing to share an interesting, personal anecdote each day. These activities can introduce a small, new element of satisfaction that starts to shift the balance toward happiness.

The remaining chapters concentrate on strategies that have helped many troubled couples enhance their relationship. You will be able to test the validity of your pessimistic attitude that "nothing can improve our relationship" by trying these techniques. You can conduct a kind of experiment to see which methods are the most successful for you. Even if the methods I describe don't produce dramatic enough results for you, additional help from a marriage counselor may very well make the difference in improving your marriage.

"Things will only get worse." Some partners have suffered so much from painful conflicts that they feel numb. They may be reluctant to get more involved in the relationship for fear of being hurt again.

Wendy said, "I expect zero from Hal right now. I tried so many times, and he always let me down. I ended up in a depression. I don't want to go through that again. If I get my hopes up, I'll only get hurt. I'd sooner expect nothing—I won't enjoy things, but at least I won't get depressed."

Wendy and Hal, high school sweethearts who had married straight out of college, had stuck together through seven years of escalating bitterness and conflict. At first glance, the fear of feeling worse would seem to be a valid reason for Wendy to refrain from getting help for her marriage. There are, however, compelling reasons why Wendy would benefit from becoming involved again, despite her fears.

I told Wendy, "In the past you made your several attempts to improve things and, as you say, you got shot down each time. But now you have some tools for dealing with your upsets." I then pointed out the following to Wendy:

▷ By her own admission, Hal was "nice" to her most of the time.

▷ After an angry outburst, he generally said he was sorry, and meant it.

▷ During his calm periods, he was willing to discuss problems.

Next, I helped her see the kind of exaggerated thinking she went through after a blowup and how she could deal with her negative automatic thoughts (see Chapters 8 and 13). For instance, she recalled the following thoughts from a previous conflict: *"There he goes again. This is awful. I can't stand it. He is always beating on me."*

After examining her automatic thoughts, Wendy realized that they represented a gross distortion of the actual "combat situation." She realized that she *could* stand it, that she had a tendency to "awfulize" —and that the blowups were not really as bad as they seemed at the time. And she was overgeneralizing. Hal's angry outbursts happened only occasionally—about once or twice a month. She then arrived at the conclusion that while her emotional withdrawal was understandable, it was unnecessary. If she countered her "awfulizing" and overgeneralizing with rational responses, she could endure his occasional flare-ups *until he made progress in curtailing them.*

Wendy decided to give it another chance. Although history repeated itself, in that Hal did blow up again, Wendy was able to handle her negative automatic thoughts. Ultimately, they agreed on a policy for managing Hal's outbursts (described in Chapter 17), and their marriage started to improve. The couple used techniques that consisted of postponing hot discussions, recognizing when Hal was ready to flare up, and determining when to bring up touchy subjects and when to back off.

Judy, a talented artist married to a very harried sales manager, also was reluctant to engage in a program to help her marriage for fear of being painfully disappointed. She said, "Cliff never pays any attention to my needs. He is just totally preoccupied with his own needs and is incapable of paying attention to mine." As with Wendy, she also had a blind spot to what was positive, to the times when her husband *did* fulfill her needs. Once Judy realized this, she found that when she got upset at Cliff's self-centeredness, she could identify her overgeneralizations and so ease her feelings of pain. Judy was encouraged to overcome her resistance to trying a marital-help program and, finally, found that her marriage—far from getting worse, as she had feared—actually got better.

"My partner won't cooperate and nothing can be done without his [her] cooperation." Even if your partner is skeptical or passive, you can initiate the process of change. More often than not, once the reluctant or passive spouse sees the possibility of improvement, he or she can be stirred from this state of inertia. Further, the tangible demonstration of your good will may very well prod your partner into reciprocating.

"I've suffered enough." While it may be true that you have suffered a great deal, the tasks that I am proposing are designed to *relieve* that suffering. And at the beginning, at least, they require little effort. In fact, many husbands and wives find the idea of discovering new ways to get out of the rut intriguing. The methods I will be proposing can be viewed as a challenge, an opportunity to take steps to lessen your pain and improve your satisfaction. You will find that by applying these methods, you will get control over your life.

"If we need to work at it, there's something seriously wrong with the relationship." Despite some similarities in taste and personality, most people enter marriage with major differences in style, habits,

and attitudes. Few couples know how to reconcile those differences. They usually have not observed their parents engaged in solving problems, and they never received any formal education in marital skills, analogous to the training they had in preparation for their careers.

Thus, you can't regard your relationship as flawed if you have yet to develop those skills for adapting better to each other. On the contrary, problems should have been expected. Making some effort to eliminate the rough spots and enhance the satisfaction makes sense when you consider that no couple—no matter how loving and devoted they are—meshes in all respects. By regarding difficulties in a marriage as a sign that it is "sick" or "defective," couples foreclose on the opportunity to help their relationship grow.

This belief keeps many couples from changing, or even trying. It's easy to fall in love. But it takes thought and diligence for a relationship to develop and thrive. As marriage partners mature, many of the needed changes come more naturally, but the process can be speeded along by the application of certain principles.

"Too much damage has been done." The pessimistic view that a marriage is beyond repair should be addressed realistically. It certainly is true that many partners have drifted beyond the point of no return by the time they consider doing something to save their marriage. Nonetheless, you cannot know for certain that your marriage is doomed until you have tried some basic remedies. I have often been surprised at how an apparently bad relationship can be helped when partners work together to correct deficits and reinforce the strong points of their marriage.

"My marriage is dead." Many couples arrive at this belief after years of wrangling or drifting apart. They may have tried reading marriage manuals, receiving counseling, talking to their clergy— without any improvement. As they look ahead, they can see only a continuation of the empty relationship. Such couples should focus their attention on a natural phenomenon in operation. A normal, negative bias seems to develop over the years, causing partners to screen out the good parts of their relationship—past and present. This bias makes them recall only the pain, none of the pleasure; all the defeats and none of the victories. As couples are instructed to refocus their attention on the positive aspects of their relationship, they often recognize that they are not as bored as previously thought.

Even though your own efforts to improve your relationship have not succeeded in the past, it may be that you have not used the appropriate methods. Successive chapters in this book will give you a variety of suggestions, and you may very well find that if you press the right buttons, your relationship will come back to life.

"Working at the relationship will make it worse." Some couples have this fear, but I have found it to be groundless—provided they work on their relationship *properly*. It is true that you can make things worse if you engage in counterproductive measures, such as handing your spouse a laundry list of his "faults" or threatening to leave her unless she changes her ways. Accusations, threats, and ultimatums frequently do aggravate a tense situation. On the other hand, if you use the methods outlined in the following chapters, they should make things better, not worse.

The notion that working at the relationship will only postpone an inevitable split is another doomsday prophecy. A more helpful attitude is an empirical one—trying the various techniques I will be describing and testing how well they work for you. Only after you have conducted such an experiment with a variety of methods can you determine whether your relationship can become more satisfactory.

SELF-JUSTIFYING BELIEFS

Self-justifying beliefs pose a real obstacle in that they confer an aura of reasonableness and self-righteousness to continuing your ways without trying to change. It may be true, of course, that other people might react as you do with your spouse. But you have to do what is best for *you* and not be guided by what others do.

If your reactions contribute to an impasse in your marriage, they are self-defeating, even if they "feel" justified. The fact that others might react the same way is not a valid reason to perpetuate what only hurts you—particularly when you can change it. Even if you firmly believe that you are right and your partner is wrong, there are ways to change your partner's attitude.

The idea that you are justified in pursuing a counterproductive mode of action because you have been hurt only ensures that you will continue to be hurt. The cycle of hurt and retaliation never ends. Somebody has to take the initiative to break the cycle—and it might as well be you.

RECIPROCITY ARGUMENTS

You may have automatic thoughts at this point, such as, *"Why should I be the one to change?"* To help you respond to them, I have provided some tentative answers that you can use to counter such ideas:

"I won't make an effort unless my partner does." The answer to this thought is that both partners need not start at the same time. One of you needs to take the initiative to inject new life into the relationship or to arrest its downhill slide. Once the momentum is in the right direction, there is a reasonable chance that your partner will join in. Even if your partner does not actively participate, you may find that as you make changes, they will have a positive effect on your mate.

"It's not fair for me to have to do all the work." By bringing the doctrine of fairness into consideration, you may be operating on an unrealistic or irrelevant premise. The most likely reason you may not be pulling together is that you differ in motivation, awareness of the problems, and ability to make changes. For example, you may be better qualified than your mate to take the initiative simply because you are more optimistic. Or you may be experiencing more pain, which motivates you more than your mate. In either case, you will certainly benefit from any improvement your efforts bring. The hope would be that as the relationship improves, your partner, too, will assume a more active role.

It is not absolutely necessary for both partners to work simultaneously on the relationship. I counseled several people whose spouses were unable or unwilling to try marital therapy, and these individuals were able to induce favorable changes in their partners by virtue of the benefit they had received from their own therapy. This was particularly true in those cases where the spouses in treatment were initially inhibited in asserting themselves. After my coaching in self-assertion, the inhibited spouses were able to get their partners to change significantly.

In essence, the "it's-not-fair" argument is counterproductive because it ignores the reality of differences between mates. One mate is almost always better prepared to initiate changes than is the other. If the prepared mate waited until the other was equally ready, the opportune moment might never arrive. It is far better to accept the "inequality" and get something accomplished than to cling to abstract doctrines of fairness and see the marriage continue to sputter.

THE PROBLEM IS MY PARTNER

"There's nothing wrong with me. If my partner would shape up, everything would be fine." Focusing on the faults of your partner may in itself be a symptom of a disturbed relationship. Research indicates that when partners continually and unrealistically blame each other, their marriage is distressed. The better approach is not to determine

fault—who is right and who is wrong—but to develop new strategies that will help the relationship.

Even if you believe that your partner is largely to blame for your problems, by working on the relationship you can compensate for—if not reverse—some of his or her undesirable qualities. For example, if there is a lot of friction because of poor communication, your partner may be reacting in a surly or explosive manner, which is painful for you. However, if you take measures to improve the communication, your partner's unpleasant ways may be replaced by more agreeable ones.

"My partner is crazy." Pejorative thoughts such as *"My spouse is impossible"* or *"My spouse is sick"* may reflect your *perception* more than an objective appraisal. While it is true that when people are anguished or enraged they sometimes seem irrational, this does not mean that they are "crazy." Any irrationality that you see may be the outgrowth of their distress, a sign of the disturbance. The spouse who rants and raves during a domestic argument usually can be completely rational with other people. Thus, the best approach is to ignore the irrationality—at least initially—and focus on what you can do to reduce the disturbance: concentrate on the cause, not the effect. Changing the causes can, in turn, move your spouse to become more rational.

Another fact to keep in mind is that your vision of what seems to be your spouse's obnoxious ways may be greatly magnified or distorted, as described in Chapter 8. What an impartial observer might label simply as odd or excessive may appear to you as grotesque or bizarre.

"My partner is impossible." Your belief that your partner is impossible may simply reflect the struggle that is going on between you. When people are locked in combat, when neither will give an inch, they each seem impossible to the other. But when you resolve the impasse, you are likely to find your partner far more flexible and reasonable.

Of course, I have seen some husbands and wives whose internal conflicts or personalities are such that they *are* difficult to live with. Such people often benefit from psychotherapy. However, the judgment as to whether your partner is such a person should be made by a professional—not by you. In any event, making an effort to change the marriage will establish whether your perception that your partner cannot change is correct.

What Should Be Changed?

Once you decide to try to change, you might wonder *what* should be changed first: thinking patterns or behavior? When I see a couple in therapy, I concentrate on their behavior first. It is much easier to change concrete actions, or to introduce new ones, than it is to change patterns of thinking. And when actions change, there is frequently an immediate reward, such as a spouse's appreciation for his or her partner's ability to do something pleasing or to stop something that is upsetting.

The rewards may be slower in coming when you start to work on your thinking patterns. You may, for instance, feel less angry or sad and be less likely to retaliate, but you don't feel as much in control of the relationship as when your partner acknowledges a positive act on your part with a smile or a kiss. In the long run, however, reducing your own degree of upset lowers the temperature of your spouse's outbursts, and he or she will be more likely to respond in a friendly, sympathetic way when you are upset.

Another pertinent question arises: is it more important to enhance the positives or to eliminate the negatives? Although negative actions in a marriage are usually less frequent than positive ones, they have a far greater effect on the level of happiness. Sometimes it seems that one negative act (a scolding, for example) can outweigh a dozen friendly or kind actions.

It would seem, then, that eliminating the negative should take precedence over emphasizing the positive. In actual practice, however, if you begin by focusing on your spouse's abrasive habits, you may seem to be blaming or criticizing, thus making things worse. At the onset, it is best to work on making things more positive. Later, when you are both working as a team, you can deal with what you would like to see changed (see Chapter 16).

Creating Problems Instead of Solving Them

> ▷ "He's a louse."
> ▷ "She's a nag."
> ▷ "He never does anything to help me."
> ▷ "She's always on my back about something."

One obstacle to change in a marriage occurs when the problems are not defined as problems but rather as broad characterizations or caricatures of the spouse. Problems in the relationship are seen as the fault of the spouse. If you see your mate as *the problem,* you may conclude that there is nothing you can do. To make things worse, you may magnify the problem so much and make it seem so impossible that it appears futile even to attempt a solution.

In the complaints previously listed ("He's a louse," "She's a nag"), it seems the partner is already framed in a negative way (Chapter 3). While the initial difficulty might have been that the spouse was inattentive or withdrawn or complained a great deal, these negative aspects are blown out of proportion so much that—if true—they *would* be insoluble. The fact is that these alleged traits of the spouse result from the *interplay* between husband and wife. Say your spouse behaves in a particularly bothersome manner. You then react in a way that annoys your spouse, who promptly reacts to you in a negative way. Thus, the problem resides not in either spouse but in the relationship itself.

In distressed marriages, a major hindrance to change is the partners' inclination to attribute all unpleasantness to each other's negative personality traits (for example, selfishness, arrogance, and cruelty) and to discredit each other's positive actions. The tendency to make sweeping generalizations is discussed in some books on intimate relations. As described by these books, the problems are built into the personalities of each sex—"men who hate women" or "women who love too much." Such notions are misleading and discourage husbands and wives from even trying to improve their relationship.

A more realistic view is that some people have certain habits and sensitivities that make them vulnerable or lead them to hurt other people. At a deeper level, they have attitudes that are expressed in self-defeating ways. The stereotypical clinging wife—who has strong doubts about how acceptable, worthy, or competent she is—attaches herself too closely because of her *unrealistic attitudes.* The "hateful" husband, who unrealistically fears being dominated or trapped, lashes out as protection against being controlled or manipulated.

Further, how the spouses' personalities mesh can determine whether their traits are seen in a positive or negative light. If you pair a woman who craves intimacy with a nurturing man, there is usually no problem. Or, match an autonomous husband with an easygoing, self-sufficient wife, and they can get along well together. Problems arise when the match between two mates is not good. However, even in this case, they can be traced to the *relationship,* the interaction between the partners, rather than to any individual shortcomings.

If you can change one side of the equation, transformation can be effected on the other side, too. Take the case of Hal and Wendy, the former high school sweethearts already introduced. Hal had a way of talking to Wendy that made her "feel put down." This slightly patronizing manner of speaking mimicked that which his father used with his mother, and his older brothers with their wives. But Hal was not aware that he was talking down to Wendy or that this bothered her. When I raised this issue with him, he could not believe it at first, and he asked Wendy to point it out when it occurred. After Hal learned to recognize his patronizing tone of voice, he was able to catch himself whenever it crept into his speech.

Hal's tone would not have bothered most people, but because of her sensitivity, it upset Wendy. As she put it, "He drives me out of my mind!" Although his brothers adopted the same tone of voice, their wives were not troubled by it, as Wendy was surprised to discover when she questioned them.

Likewise, Wendy wasn't aware that she had a habit—a reproachful tone of questioning—which made Hal feel guilty. For example, if he arrived home a bit late from the airport, she would demand, "Why didn't you call?" instead of just saying she was happy to see him again. Hal and Wendy used a tit-for-tat approach to make changes: Hal dropped his patronizing tone and Wendy softened the edge of reproach that she had injected into questions.

Redefining the Problem

When a problem is expressed only vaguely, or through name calling, or as an immutable trait of the spouse, any attempt to change a seemingly hopeless situation will appear pointless. To make things worse, attacks on one's character stir counterattacks and antagonism that initiate more opposition.

For instance, when Wendy says, "He's a total slob" or Hal says, "She's a world-class pushover for the children—they run wild," the problems seem insurmountable at the time. But by translating such complaints into solvable problems, you can take specific, concrete actions to resolve them. A starting point for Hal was to put his soiled clothes in the hamper instead of leaving them on the chair or the floor. The route for Wendy was to be firm in setting a bedtime for the children.

Such simple acts can have an appreciable effect on the other spouse. It may change a hopeless attitude into a more moderate one: *"He can change if he wants to"* or *"She's not a complete pushover."* Thus, if you can define your marital problems in as concrete terms as possible, even small changes can provide the impetus for improving your relationship. This approach is discussed fully in Chapter 16.

How Do People Change?

How does change occur? Granted that partners are *willing* to change, what assurance is there that they *can*? To answer these questions, we have to delve a bit into theory. There are many marital techniques that are relatively easy to learn. Others, particularly those that require unlearning well-entrenched ways of interpreting a mate's behavior, are more difficult. For example, it is easier to adopt a new habit of speech, such as giving more complete answers to a mate's questions, than it is to cease interpreting his or her suggestions as an attempt at control.

As we grow up, we acquire habits of interpreting and dealing with other people, and relating to them—how to respond to a friendly gesture, how to ignore an implied slight, how to handle a demand. These habits become refined over the course of time, and they comprise what we call a "repertoire of social skills." People who are well endowed with these skills are generally regarded as smooth, socially masterful, and so on.

But for most of us, our social skills may not be so flexible or attuned. If we reach wrong conclusions about people—exaggerate their good qualities or magnify their faults, for example—we may be too trusting or too cynical. Similarly, if we are too abrupt or overstep our bounds, we may hurt or alienate others, or we may be too inhibited or subservient and so not get our due.

As described in Chapter 1, our coding systems automatically decode a particular event—a grimace, smile, or blank face, for example. Just as we learn certain ways of interpreting events, we also learn how to misinterpret them. When we are growing up, our parents, siblings, and others around us are prone to make grossly exaggerated statements and attach inaccurate labels to others—or to us. As children, we pick up those exaggerated descriptions and work them into our coding systems.

Our interpretation of a given event involves a delicate matching between the event and our code for it. If our code is peculiar, our interpretation will be peculiar. A man who believes that women are rejecting is prone to interpret his wife's moodiness as a sign that she doesn't love him. A woman who believes that men are manipulative may conclude that her husband is using her when he wants sex.

These methods of interpretation or relating to others are eventually built into habitual patterns. Their derivation is too complex to discuss in detail here, but suffice it to say that these patterns are acquired from observations of significant figures, such as our parents or older siblings, and from passive experiences, such as reading or viewing television and movies. Finally, specific experiences involving anyone in our "social environment"—members of our family, peer group, teachers, and so on—may implant certain beliefs and attitudes that will be carried into our adult life.

Specific experiences in our past can lead us to develop attitudes and patterns of thought that differ, at least in degree, from the reactions of most other people. Thus, a boy who was ridiculed and teased a great deal by his older sisters tended, as an adult, to be overly cautious and inhibited with his dates and ultimately with his wife—for fear of being ridiculed. He adopted the code *"Women are prone to be contemptuous and hypercritical."*

A women who reacted with rebellion to her authoritarian father, a military man, tended to view all of the men she dated as domineering. She ultimately married a man several years older than she and found that she was continually rejecting his suggestions, as though they were all direct orders or non-negotiable demands. After some counseling, she recognized that she was projecting her image of her father onto her husband, who was benign.

While these habitual patterns of reaction *feel* natural, they are very likely to cause marital difficulty. Derived from painful events experienced during the early, vulnerable years, they make a particularly lasting impression on a person. And someone who has a specific sensitivity to being rejected, controlled, or frustrated builds up protective habits to guard against being hurt.

Such protective patterns—overvigilance and inhibition in the case of the young man afraid of being demeaned; rebelliousness in the case of the woman afraid of being dominated—are far stronger than patterns based only on imitation of the parents. The strongest patterns are those that combine the attitudes of significant people from childhood with the painful experiences of childhood. For instance, Gary (who physically abused his wife, as described in Chapter 9) reacted to his brother's bullying by assuming the role of the other men in his family—and became a bully himself.

Such sensitivities are not easy to unlearn completely, but you can keep them under control by recognizing them and correcting their expression in the form of misinterpretations or exaggerated conclusions. In Chapter 13, we will discuss the way in which to catch and modify automatic thoughts, which should help dilute their force. If your patterns are particularly strong or intractable, however, it may be necessary to consult a psychotherapist in addition to doing your own self-help work.

To return to the question of whether people can change—they *can*, or at the very least modulate their reactions, if they are sufficiently motivated and use the proper techniques. Some changes are relatively easy, like remembering to call your spouse if you are going to be late, helping with your spouse's chores at home, or taking time out when your spouse wants to talk to you. Other changes are more time-consuming and difficult, such as not flaring up when your mate tries to correct you, or not being jealous when your spouse speaks to other people.

Given the appropriate techniques, you can bring about basic changes in a variety of ways. For example, if you recognize that your spouse is sensitive to criticism, you can tone down your critical comments or even suggestions that might be taken as criticism. Knowing that special days (birthdays, anniversaries) are important to your mate, you can be sure to acknowledge these days with a token of some kind. If you practice techniques such as these, they become habits.

It takes much more practice, however, to change your built-in sensitivities, attitudes, and patterns of reaction. Part of the change takes place from corrective experiences that contradict an underlying belief. For example, suppose you are tight-lipped with your spouse out of fear of being demeaned for revealing a fault. If you should open up to your spouse and your spouse is pleased with your openness, this experience can lead to a new attitude, such as *"My spouse accepts me with my faults."* The new attitude can compete with the existing belief *"She would look down on me if she knew the real me."* Similarly, as you learn to catch your misinterpretations or exaggerated interpretations (as described in Chapter 13), you will begin to adjust your coding system.

A Program for Change

In considering what improvements you would like to see in your relationship, you need to make a practical decision about which changes you should attempt first. If you are reading this book on your own and your spouse is not involved at this point, you will want to continue in sequence through the remaining chapters, and start to change your own misunderstandings and patterns of reaction (Chapter 13). If your spouse is collaborating with you, you both might want to start with making changes in communication (Chapters 14 and 15), reducing anger (Chapter 17), and introducing new methods of solving problems (Chapter 16). If you are able to cooperate to determine more precisely what your spouse legitimately wants or doesn't want, likes or dislikes, you are in a better position to make those changes (Chapters 12 and 16).

The kind of program I am advocating is not designed to produce change just for the sake of change, but to introduce more satisfaction and pleasure into your marital life and to alleviate much of the unnecessary pain and unpleasantness. Achieving this requires certain steps.

First, you need the proper mental state, one that means you are open to learning what these chapters have to offer. If your mind is prepared in this way, you will be able to benefit from experiences with your mate—even distressing ones—by observing more objectively what seems to go wrong and by pinpointing the probable cause. Further, you will be better prepared to see the pleasing side of your mate and thus provide the foundation for future change.

Second, you need the motivation to *apply* the principles in this book. This does not require that you be tremendously optimistic or feel driven to change yourself or the nature of the relationship. It is enough that you be willing to try some of these techniques and see how they work. As you start to see tangible results from the work, you will naturally become more optimistic and so desire to work harder. As you receive increasing pay-offs from your efforts, you should move well along.

11

REINFORCING
THE FOUNDATIONS

Love, affection, and tenderness, which give pleasure, ecstasy, and enrichment to relationships, can fluctuate over the course of time. Even though a couple may pledge undying devotion during the period of infatuation—in the belief that their love will last forever—love can begin to diminish and their devotion slip away.

Passion, of course, draws partners together and creates the climate for a lasting, stable relationship. Further, love and affection can soothe many of the tensions that arise in couples and can override the natural self-centeredess that crops up periodically. Nonetheless, love alone is not enough to provide the connective tissue of a relationship. The other basic qualities that strengthen the marital bond and ensure the durability of a relationship arise gradually and spontaneously. If they fail to develop, couples need to make an effort to build them into the relationship.

Once developed, the forces for stability—commitment, loyalty, trust—protect the closeness, intimacy, and security of the loving bond. Knowing that your mate will never desert you, for instance, gives you a sense of security and confidence in the relationship.

While infatuation is a powerful magnet drawing people together, it also contains the nucleus of forces that can drive them apart. While under the spell of infatuation, many couples exaggerate qualities in each other or see potentials that are not there—hence, the disillusionment when partners later discover their error.

At first, couples expect that they will ride a wave of euphoria right through the marriage and that their mate will always be devoted and self-sacrificing. A series of large and small shocks awaits them as they later discover that these expectations are unfounded. For example, sensitivities, moodiness, and differing rhythms for love making can lead to a cycle of frustration and blame.

Many couples find there are innumerable demands that require joint solutions, yet they have little experience in solving such problems jointly. The process of attending to pragmatic details can lead to psychological problems. For instance, when they are making decisions, one mate may take over the dominant role and the other the submissive. The dominant one may complain about having to take responsibility for everything, while the submissive one protests always being in the "one-down" position.

Love and affection in themselves do not dissolve such difficulties, but they can offer powerful incentives for partners to find ways of overcoming them. Listed below are a number of ingredients that make up the foundations of marriage. As you review them, you might evaluate how effectively they are built into your relationship. You may be surprised to find that these important values are stronger than you realized. On the other hand, you may find areas that you will need to shore up.

Cooperation: Working to fulfill your joint objectives as a couple and a family. Basic attitudes: *"We will work together in making important decisions." "We will coordinate what we do in activities that are best conducted jointly." "Each of us will fulfill his or her own area of responsibility."*

Commitment: An expectation that you will stay in the marriage no matter what the difficulties. You do not question the permanence of the marital relationship any more than you would question the permanence of your relationship with your child or parents or siblings. Attitudes: *"If we have troubles, I will work on them with my spouse." "I will not withdraw from my spouse when things get difficult."*

Basic Trust: The assumption of dependability and availability on the part of one's spouse. Basic trust consists of the following attitudes: *"I can depend on my spouse to guard my best interests." "I know that my spouse would not intentionally hurt me." "I know that I can depend on my spouse for help in ordinary situations or in an emergency." "I know that my spouse will be available when I need him or her." "I can assume good will on the part of my spouse."*

Loyalty: A dedication to the spouse's interests. You will stand by your spouse in times of duress. Basic attitudes: *"I place my spouse's best interests first." "I will support my spouse as an ally." "I will stick up for my spouse."*

Fidelity: Sexual loyalty and faithfulness. *"I will not have sexual relationships outside of the marriage."*

Cooperation

How can we expect any improvement in a relationship in which the partners are enmeshed in conflict, have fixed negative images of each other, and are filled with hostility? When their marriage is truly on the rocks, distressed couples will require the services of a skilled marriage counselor. But they, as well as those with less severe problems, can benefit from applying the insights they gain from reading these chapters to their marital problems.

First, consider the obstacles to true cooperation. Given the power of self-serving bias, egocentricity, and hostility, how can we expect fundamental change? Fortunately, we are born not simply with the tendency toward being self-centered but also with capacities for cooperation and sacrifice. We see empathy clearly in parent-child relations; with a few notable exceptions, parents automatically respond with loving care to the needs of their infants. Further, in its early stages most couples show enthusiastic cooperation in building their relationship. The sense of gratification from unity is a strong binding force in human affairs, whether an organization is composed of only two people—as in a marriage—or of many, as in a team or social club.

Cooperation in a mature marriage differs from that in a romantic infatuation, where self-denial and fusion of interests are prominent. In a mature marriage, the partners' interests and goals may diverge, but they can negotiate or submerge their own special interests—for instance, to solve problems like the division of household labor or different attitudes toward child rearing—for the sake of their long-term goal: an enjoyable, stable relationship.

Of course, there are also immediate rewards. The spirit of cooperation, of pleasing the spouse, and of settling problems is inherently satisfying. Many spouses identify themselves with each other—so that the pleasures of one are shared by the other; the pains of one are felt by the other. These positive forces must be pressed into action if a couple are to override the divisiveness produced by a conflict of interests, a clash of perspectives, and accumulated hostility.

Commitment

As passions subside after the initial infatuation, dedication to each other's welfare and happiness emerges as the major binding force in a relationship. These feelings more or less coincide with the marital, and later the parental, roles. The partners assume responsibility for each other "for better, for worse; for richer, for poorer; in sickness and in health . . ." Responsibility, the hallmark of commitment, offers a standard by which spouses measure themselves and their partner.

Although some partners may believe, at first, that they are committed to the relationship, their commitment may not be robust enough to withstand marriage's inevitable storms. Others may consider their commitment strong but hold still stronger reservations, which may persist for many decades—even throughout the marriage.

These "holdouts" on total commitment lose something of great value. They may, for example, be on the alert for flaws in the marriage because of a nagging fear of being permanently trapped, or they may insulate themselves from emotional closeness because they fear their spouse may reject them. Still other holdouts might want the benefits of an intimate relationship without making a wholehearted effort to ensure its continuation and growth.

The unhappiness that incomplete commitment may bring is illustrated in the case of Marjorie (see the Introduction), who came to see me after several years of marriage. She had experienced an unpleasant childhood, largely because of constant battles between her parents. Her father tended to be domineering, critical, and explosive. Her mother, who was mildly critical of the father, was the victim of his attacks. Marjorie identified herself with her mother and developed the fear that if she got married she would be subject to the same abuse as was her mother. After an impetuous romance, Marjorie married Ken, a former college athlete. Despite Ken's obvious devotion to her, she was always concerned that he might someday start to act like her father.

Prior to their marriage, Marjorie had exacted a pledge from Ken that he would agree to a divorce if she ever wanted one. To "humor" her, he agreed. Ken fully expected that Marjorie would be happy and that she was simply nervous about making a major change in her life. Marjorie, however, had never fully committed herself to the marriage. By always providing herself with an "out," she could never be totally "in" the relationship. Marjorie held back, and over the years she was watchful for Ken's flaws.

Because of her fear that a minor flaw in Ken would turn into a major deficiency, Marjorie examined the smallest of his faults microscopically, and so magnified them. As a result, she was ever-vigilant for, and silently critical of, the defects that she detected. Ken interpreted her critical silence as a sign of her lack of affection and reproached her—an act that she, in turn, interpreted as confirmation of his basic hostility.

When the couple came for counseling, it was apparent that one pressing problem was Marjorie's faultfinding. I was able to discern the fear underlying her wavering commitment, and set up for Marjorie a kind of balance sheet, listing in a double column the pros and cons of not making a total commitment:

In Favor of Incomplete Commitment	Against Incomplete Commitment
I would be less likely to get hurt if my husband "misbehaves."	I would more likely be critical of Ken.
I will be able to get out of the marriage more easily.	I would more likely be threatened by his "misdemeanors."
I can be more independent.	I would experience less intimacy and therefore less satisfaction.
	I would always be on edge for fear that Ken would leave me.

Of course, it was difficult for Marjorie to state the actual advantages of making a total commitment since she had never taken this step. As an incentive, however, we listed some of the *potential* advantages, such as her increased security and participation in a more giving relationship. It was not until the advantages and disadvantages of her incomplete commitment were brought out into the open that Marjorie realized how much she was losing by holding back.

Marjorie reviewed with me all of the past evidence of the relationship's durability: the many crises they had weathered together, how they had worked as a team in raising the children. Taking a hard look at the facts and at Ken's performance persuaded her of the sturdiness of the marriage. Marjorie also realized that although he got angry at times, Ken did not share her father's explosive nature. She found that by simply repeating to herself, *"This relationship is going to last,"* she was relieved of some of her insecurity.

In order to bolster this belief, however, Marjorie had to change her habit of focusing on her husband's flaws. He was, after all, human. Ken occasionally criticized, sometimes neglected to follow through on his promises, and often procrastinated. But instead of dwelling on these faults, Marjorie made herself concentrate on each of the signs that they could have a stable, happy marriage: his expression of devotion to her, his concern about her well-being, and his eagerness to improve their relationship.

It was only gradually that Marjorie could allow herself to let go of her nit-picking and trust Ken, but the rewards emerged almost immediately. She found herself feeling more spontaneous and able to give more—as well as receive more—from the relationship. And as she relaxed, Ken became more loving and attentive.

In analyzing the profound change that occurred, I observed that Marjorie's ability to concentrate on the positive features in her marriage, instead of on its defects, gave her a more balanced perspective of herself and her husband. This change in perspective neutralized her fear that Ken would someday resemble her father. As her perspective changed—and her fears subsided—she was able to commit herself to making the relationship work, to plan on *staying in* the marriage rather than *getting out* of the marriage.

An important rule can be extracted from this case: fears can prevent people from making a commitment, but holding back can keep the fears alive. A corollary accompanies this rule: by taking a chance and allowing themselves to trust and be dependent on the spouse, partners may at first increase their sense of vulnerability, but ultimately they can learn that it was worth the risk.

Marjorie had seen her aloofness as a way to keep Ken in line and also to protect herself. Part of my counseling involved working through her fears of risk taking:

ATB: Why don't you want to make the commitment?

MARJORIE: I'm not sure I can trust him.

ATB: Suppose you find out that he can't be trusted, then what?

MARJORIE: He might hurt me.

ATB: Then what happens?

MARJORIE: If he hurts me, I'll really feel miserable.

ATB: Then what will you do?

MARJORIE: I'll think of getting out of the marriage.

ATB: But you've been thinking of getting out since the day you got married. What would you actually lose if you made your commitment that things will work out, instead of that they might not work out?

MARJORIE: I guess I could find out that I can't trust him.

ATB: So you'll find out once and for all that he is untrustworthy. But suppose you go all out and he passes the test?

MARJORIE: I suppose I'll discover that he's okay after all . . . and I guess I'll feel more secure.

I set up a three-month experiment with Marjorie in order for her to test the following hypothesis: *"If I totally commit myself to the relationship, look for the positive instead of the negative, I will feel more secure."* After three months, she discovered that indeed she was more secure and had fewer and fewer thoughts about getting out of the relationship.

This case illustrates the importance of questioning one's most deeply held assumptions, for example, that one should never allow oneself to be vulnerable. By trying to avoid an indefinite risk—of being trapped in an unpleasant marriage—Marjorie had paid a definite price, of never being totally happy or secure. She had gotten herself into a vicious cycle: to "protect" herself by always looking for an escape route, she had created an unstable relationship; the uncertainty led her to further insecurity, increasing her need for self-protection. The cost of eternal vigilance was continuous insecurity.

Similarly, Marjorie was leery of making a firm commitment to her job or friends because of her fear of getting hurt by a rejection. Her sense of vulnerability and need to protect herself from risk was also expressed by her insistence on maintaining a large reserve in her bank balance—even though the money would have gotten a better return had it been otherwise invested—and by her taking out large amounts of disability insurance. In a sense, Marjorie's marital policy illustrates the value of making a more substantial investment in the marriage rather than holding a large emotional reserve.

COMMITMENT TO FIDELITY

Often a person is unwilling to make a total commitment to one thing because it requires giving up something else. Some people, for instance, enjoy marriage but are unwilling to make any sacrifice for it. They want to have the best of both worlds—for example, the security and continuing love offered by a marriage, but also the freedom and lack of responsibility that go with being single.

Terry and Ruth, a couple who seemingly had everything going for them, came to see me because of Ruth's suspicions that Terry was being unfaithful. A very busy professional (he was a systems analyst for factories undergoing automation), Terry traveled frequently, and Ruth was tormented by the fear that her husband was seeing other women during these trips.

When I interviewed Terry alone, I discovered that, indeed, he had had a number of intimate relationships with other women while away from home. As he put it, "I want to have my cake and eat it, too." He was very self-indulgent and failed to see why he should deprive himself of any satisfaction, even though this lack of restraint would hurt his wife and damage their relationship.

As I had done with Marjorie, I used the double-column technique of assessing pros and cons with Terry. Initially, he protested that he wanted to maintain his relationship with his wife "more than anything in the world." But when he weighed the advantages and potential dangers of wanting to have everything his own way, he then felt that he was being robbed of his "due." I pointed out to him that to ensure a lasting relationship, one has to limit satisfactions to those things that are compatible with marriage and to relinquish those that threaten the partnership. In such cases, the uncommitted spouse has to look seriously at how much he or she is actually losing by not making sacrifices. Terry and I once had the following exchange:

ATB: You seem to be pursuing the dream that by grasping for everything, you'll be able to have everything.

TERRY: That's right. What's wrong with that?

ATB: But are you actually having everything? I gather that Ruth is threatening to leave you.

TERRY: I don't think she will.

ATB: But suppose she does, what will you have?

TERRY: I guess I'll have to get another wife.

ATB: Is that what you really want?

TERRY: No-o-o.

ATB: In order of importance, which means more to you—your flings or your marriage?

TERRY: My marriage, of course.

ATB: If you had to choose, which would you take?

TERRY: I already told you.

ATB: So what will be subtracted if you give up running around?

TERRY: I won't have as much fun on the trips.

ATB: And what will you gain?

TERRY: I guess my wife will get off my back.

It was essential to point out to Terry the obvious: he would have to give up something to preserve the marriage, but he would lose much more if he continued his attempt to get everything he wanted. Terry had never really faced the fact that he had to make a choice. Indeed, for most of his life, he had been able to get what he wanted, and to get away with it. For the first time, he was confronted with the fact that this "have-it-all" attitude toward life was no longer tenable. After much consideration, Terry came to see that despite the lure of other pleasures, the vitality of his relationship was paramount.

Of course, eliminating a single problem does not in itself foster a commitment. A true commitment requires more: the spouse has to become immersed in the marriage and learn from *experience* the satisfaction of living more as a unit, a couple, and less as two people sharing the same house.

A major aspect of commitment—one that many observers believe has become rarer in recent decades—is the determination to maintain the relationship even after difficulties, disappointments, and disillusionment. It is a truism that many more marriages could be saved and improved if couples would put their energies into solving their problems instead of running away from them. Future chapters provide guidelines for finding these solutions.

Basic Trust

Even when committed to their marriage, partners can fail to develop a solid sense of trust. A wife's trust, for example, encompasses the firm belief that her husband has her best interests at heart, would not intentionally hurt her, and will be available when she needs him. A durable and lasting trust is difficult to develop and easy to shake.

According to many authors, the roots of basic trust are established long before marriage. Erik Erikson has noted that this attitude starts to develop out of a child's experiences with major figures in the family. This trust goes beyond the blind dependency of infancy, springing from a child's feelings about parents and siblings. A child's basic trust includes the following themes:

▷ I can count on my family when I need them—no matter what.

▷ Outsiders may hurt me, but my family respects me and will protect me.

▷ The important people in my life will not overstep their bounds, take advantage of me, or knowingly injure me.

This early trust may not carry over into peer relations. A trusting child may find out that other children can be cruel, deceitful, and unreliable. With maturity, he or she may acquire the notion that members of the opposite sex are manipulative, exploitative, and untrustworthy. Such underlying attitudes of mistrust may be carried into marriage, though masked by the love relationship. Although a mate may be reliable and trustworthy, this undercurrent of mistrust may continue to exist, waiting for an incident to force it to the surface.

Many spouses trust their partners part of the time but not all of the time. In certain areas—for instance, in spending money, relations with in-laws, or time spent away from the house—they may feel distrust. One spouse may sense the other's lack of trust and feel hurt. Or the mistrust may lead him or her to rebel and act on impulse, in keeping with the maxim "I might as well be hung for a sheep as a lamb."

Partners may get a better understanding of mistrust by recognizing that in the areas at the heart of their relationship, they tend to think in absolutes. Thus, if a wife is untruthful on one occasion, her husband may think, *"I can never trust her."* If a husband breaks a promise, his wife may conclude, *"He is unreliable."* It is, of course, far better for mates to view traits such as truthfulness and dependability on a continuum rather than as an absolute, as points on a scale rather than as a fixed category. Thus, an injured wife may reframe her husband's fib as a sign that he is imperfect: not a totally honest man, but not a chronic liar either. And a husband with a penchant for statistics might rate his wife as only 75 percent dependable rather than as consistently unreliable.

As it happens, no one can be totally honest all the time. For one thing, there is no absolute truth. There are so many facets to a situation that of necessity one has to select some and exclude others in giving an honest answer to a question. In attempting to provide an honest appraisal of our motives, for example, we have to recognize that they are often mixed, and it is impossible to separate them with full objectivity. Moreover, our feelings and attitudes may change from one minute to the next, and something we believe strongly when we are angry may not hold a few minutes later when we have calmed down. Further, tact and sensitivity often require some shading of unpleasant facts.

Assuming Good Will

Even in marriages where both partners have good intentions, where they want to be helpful and kind, faulty communications and erroneous readings of signs can cause these good intentions to be discounted, allowing one mate to infer that the other has ulterior motives. And once a husband, for example, assumes his wife is motivated only by narrow self-interest, his observations of her will be shaded by this assumption.

Suppose an offended wife, however, is able to say to herself, *"Even though my husband's actions may be misguided and hurt me, I assume that he means well, that he doesn't want to hurt me."* This acknowledgment in itself may help her view her husband's actions from a different perspective, and by contrasting this perspective with her negative judgments of her husband, the wife may be able to arrive at more benign explanations for his seeming meanness.

Of course, the assumption of good intentions cannot be taken for granted, and not all intentions are good. In fact, a wife may be able to report valid examples of her husband's self-serving or hostile acts. But by reviewing *all* his past behavior—the "good" (concern and selflessness) as well as the "bad" (indifference and selfishness)—she can obtain a more balanced overview.

If the couple is caught in a cycle of attack and counterattack, of struggling for dominance, then their hostility needs to be addressed first. Strategies such as those outlined in Chapter 17 may be useful initially. And once the hostility has subsided somewhat, the partners may then agree on at least one assumption: that they *do* have a basic good will toward each other and that they will get along much better if they attribute such good will to each other. This working assumption will help neutralize the hostility that arises from the mutual attribution of malicious intent, which occurs so often in distressed marriages.

The Benefit of the Doubt

Each mate in a marriage comes to learn the other's specific sensitivities and recognizes that respecting them prevents unnecessary upsets. However, what if your spouse acts suspiciously? Suppose that, quite out of character, a wife comes home much later than she told her husband. When she arrives, her explanation—that she had to stop at the bank to cash a check—has a hollow ring. The explanation might be true, but to her husband it is implausible. He suspects that she stopped off to visit her mother, a point of conflict in the past.

The husband has two choices: he can give her the benefit of the doubt or he can confront her with his suspicions. Which should he do? In general, he would be better off accepting his wife's explanation and dropping the matter. If her explanation is true, then doubting it can only deplete the store of good will between them and make her feel unjustly accused. If the truth is that she did stop to see her mother, then he would still do best to let her keep her secret—she very likely is telling a white lie to avoid a potentially destructive confrontation. Thus, he should accept her explanation—even on the chance that he is letting her get away with something.

The expectation of total honesty is counterproductive in a marriage between two fallible human beings, beset by sensitivities, pride, and defensiveness. Of course, people often have mixed motives for what they do—some less benign than others. But partners' motives do tend to be more harmless than they may appear. And by adopting the more benign explanation for his wife's tardiness, the husband is more likely to feel warmth toward her.

Giving one's spouse the benefit of the doubt applies to a wide variety of instances in which he or she may or may not be culpable. A husband may have forgotten to run an errand because he was preoccupied with a business problem—not because he didn't care. His wife might have invited some new friends to their house without checking with him first, out of the feeling that he would like them—not out of "thoughtlessness."

Having said all this, I must acknowledge that in ideal marriages, the mates would feel free to voice all their doubts and even question each other's motives. However, such an ideal is difficult to attain and should not be used to devalue an otherwise rewarding relationship.

Loyalty and Fidelity

Loyalty and fidelity differ from commitment in that a partner may be dedicated to maintaining a marriage—and may in fact commit a good deal of enthusiasm and resources to the marriage—and still be disloyal. Loyalty, in this sense, refers to the partner's placing the spouse's interests above the interests of others. For example, when a husband is criticized, he expects that his wife will stick up for him. Similarly, loyalty involves not taking sides with others against the spouse.

At times, a mate's expectations of loyalty may become extreme; nonetheless, it is important for one spouse to recognize the other's definition of loyalty, and to take that into account. A woman, for example, was very upset by her dealings with her husband's sister. She had made some arrangements with his sister about getting household help, and a misunderstanding led to a fight. The wife believed that her husband should take her side, and when he attempted to be impartial, she accused him of disloyalty. As she put it, "I need an ally, and you put yourself up as my judge."

In marriage, the sense of *alliance* has great symbolic meaning. *"My wife [or husband] . . . right or wrong"* means that one spouse can always count on the other for protection and support. And the support and protection do not depend on the spouse's judgment of which party is right or wrong. In intimate relationships, neutrality is often perceived as disloyalty. All things being equal, it is generally better to err on the side of loyalty than impartial justice.

The issue of loyalty often arises in public situations. For example, a husband may accept criticism from his wife in private, but be devastated if she criticizes him in front of other people. The greater meaning of such public criticism is *"She is not my supporter."*

The husband feels *vulnerable* because of his wife's "disloyalty." According to some kind of primitive logic, if his supposed ally sees fit to criticize him publicly, this gives others license to do so. Also, he is likely to interpret his wife's public criticism as an open acknowledgment of their inability to get along with each other. Thus, all of his fears of public exposure—the embarrassment, shame, and humiliation—are brought to the fore.

Being publicly challenged by one's mate is often interpreted as a kind of betrayal. Sometimes a husband will be a stickler for accuracy and contradict his wife's every minor inaccuracy. Because she in turn is trying to make a good impression, she can easily consider herself "stabbed in the back."

For example, Ted and Karen got into a conversation with another couple at a beach resort. When questioned by them, Karen replied, "We love to come here. We have such a good time that we come here all the time." Ted, viewing this statement as inaccurate, interrupted to say that this was only their second visit. Karen went on to tell the other couple that another thing they liked about coming to this resort was its inclusion in a good package deal with the airline. Ted again corrected her by saying, "That's not really the reason we came. We wanted to come anyhow and would have been willing to pay the full price. It just happened that my travel agent was able to get us a good deal." Karen felt that Ted's corrections were a blow to her credibility in the eyes of the other couple.

Ted was a stickler for accuracy and did not want other people to catch him making inaccurate statements. His dread of having an error exposed was what prompted him to correct Karen's "errors." Karen, on the other hand, liked to be spontaneous and weave her own stories without having to be precise about every detail. Further, she wanted to preserve a united front when talking to others—to create the impression that she and Ted got along well together. To her, Ted's open disagreement undermined her credibility, and she perceived him as disloyal.

INFIDELITY

In some marriages, spouses may be willing to accept infidelity by their mate; in other marriages, infidelity is quietly tolerated, though still a source of distress; but in most marriages, infidelity is regarded as the peak of disloyalty, and not only is unacceptable but leads to a permanent cleavage, justifying divorce. If the marriage survives the infidelity, the hurts may persist indefinitely. I have often found that even when an infidelity occurred many years previously, an injured spouse will continue to make needling allusions to the event decades later.

Why is infidelity so destructive in marriage? To understand the enormous impact of even an isolated extramarital affair, we must return to the topic of symbolic meanings. Whereas for the offending spouse being unfaithful may simply mean enjoying the "variety" experienced prior to marriage, to the offended spouse the infidelity is a direct attack on the relationship itself, a mockery of the supposed mutual commitment.

Terry, for example, wanted to continue having extramarital affairs. His contention was that these affairs in no way had any bearing on his relationship with his wife. He said, "I love her just as much whether I am having an affair or I'm not having an affair." But he did believe that since his affairs would be upsetting to Ruth, it was better that she not know about them. He followed the old dictum "What she doesn't know won't hurt her." Since he knew that these other relationships were transient and did not involve any commitment on his part, he could see neither the merit in giving them up nor the threat they were posing to his marriage.

What he did not realize was that crucial issues of basic trust were involved. His wife interpreted his behavior as a sign that he was untrustworthy, not truly committed to her, and that he did not really love her.

Aside from the moral implications of infidelity, the act of being unfaithful cuts so deeply into the fabric of a relationship, into the partner's own self-image and trust, that it can be destructive even to a relationship that is otherwise solidly based. In a relationship that is already shaky, infidelity may sound the death knell. The ways of dealing with a partner's infidelity are so complex that they will be described in a special section (see Chapter 18).

12

TUNING UP
THE RELATIONSHIP

You may recall that Karen was a romantic who loved to do things impulsively, in contrast to her husband, Ted, who was systematic and "rational." One of my early projects in therapy was to encourage them to look at the pleasing aspects of their relationship—to try to recapture what they had once found endearing in each other. I also suggested that they try to sense each other's needs and meet them, if possible. Part of the reasoning behind this program is that couples become oblivious to what they like about each other when they are going through a troubled period.

As it turned out, Ted was better at implementing my suggestion about pleasing his spouse than was Karen; being assigned a plan to follow complemented his general approach to life's demands. In the next session, Karen reported, "Ted was such a dear this past week. He called my mother several times and had long talks with her . . . it made me feel soft and tender toward him."

Karen found it hard to call her mother, who had a serious, progressive illness. When Karen called, she would sometimes break down and cry. When she choked up, her mother would begin to feel bad, too, and the conversation would become very trying for them. So, when Ted took the initiative and offered to call her mother, Karen felt grateful.

This episode was crucial. Ted's gesture unlocked warm feelings that Karen had felt for him earlier. She said, "I forgot what it felt like to love Ted," and she began to see him once again as a steady, reliable person whom she could count on for help and support. She told me, "I know that I'm flighty and I'm really weak at times—but Ted is like a rock. I know I can reach for him when I need him." This trait of Ted's had been lost from her view during their stormy times.

What may be obvious in this episode is that Ted's phone calls had enormous symbolic meaning for Karen. She said, "He did this for *me*" and considered the gesture an enormous favor—especially since she had not specifically asked it of him. Karen realized that Ted was able to sense her need and respond to it without being asked, and that he really cared. For Ted, it was no great task. He liked Karen's mother and was pleased to do this favor for Karen.

The important principle is that if you sense your partner's needs and meet them in some way, you can provide a tremendous boost to the relationship. Meeting your partner's needs often requires only a minimal effort on your part—although *sensing* the needs may be harder. One reason for this is that many people have not developed ways of letting their partner know specifically what their needs are, or they prefer to have their partner perceive their needs without having to be prompted.

Karen's reactions to his efforts gratified Ted. He was happy that he could do something to please her and that she appreciated him for it. But even more important for Ted was Karen's tenderness and affectionate touching afterward.

Even though Ted was aware of his extra effort to show Karen he could be sensitive to her feelings, his motive in doing so was genuine. Before the period of their quarreling, he had often done things to please Karen, and it was not out of character for him to resume the initiative once he perceived a signal telling him what she wanted.

Of course, the relationship did not turn around overnight, but this episode was pivotal in starting them in the right direction. Still, for a while they were both wary and fearful of being hurt; they did not trust each other completely. Karen continued feeling afraid of being controlled by Ted, and Ted continued being sensitive to the least sign of rejection by Karen.

As part of therapy, I asked them to tell what they had enjoyed about each other early in their relationship. Karen described the pleasures of doing things with Ted on the spur of the moment. Ted told of enjoying wide-ranging discussions with Karen.

At the next visit, they reported progress. Karen related how much she had enjoyed taking a long walk with Ted that week, something they had not done for several years. During their walk, Karen asked Ted about what he had been reading. He spoke with enthusiasm, analyzing the political and economic situation in his reading matter. Karen admired Ted's mind and enjoyed listening to him. Her admiration pleased him.

Many distressed couples develop blind spots for what is good in their relationship. By looking only at what they do not like, they fail to see how to improve what they *do* like. If you are having marital difficulties, it would be helpful for you to use the list at the end of this chapter to analyze your relationship. Keep in mind that if your relationship is rocky, you might underestimate some positive aspects because of an existing negative bias. This may blind you to what *is* working well in your marriage or what it is that you like about your mate. (Even without such a negative bias, it is easy to get so bogged down with the seriousness of life—balancing the budget, taking care of the children, managing the household—that you miss the enjoyment and fun of marriage.) To counter any negative bias, you might try the exercise of looking for the positives and making a daily list of them for a week or two.

Some people have a strong tendency to disqualify all that is good in their marriage and in their mate on the basis of a few negatives. One husband, for example, complained, "I can do ten things right . . . and then I forget to do one thing and—bam!—she's on my back. It wipes out everything good that's happened." The power of a single, unpleasant event to erase many positive ones is an important principle contributing to the problems of misinterpretation, miscommunication, and anger. It will be further discussed in later chapters.

Loving
and Being Loved

Since many couples seem to lose sight of just what the building blocks of a strong marriage are, it is important to spell them out. Having more precise information, for instance, can guide a husband who complains, "I'm at my wits' end to know what my wife wants. She says I should be more caring and understanding—but I *am* those things. What else does she want? What is she bugging me about?"

The emotions of infatuation can ripen into mature love in long-standing marriage. The wife feels a glow in saying, "I love you," and the husband feels a thrill in hearing it, because affection and mutual attraction get woven into the fabric of loyalty, trust, and fidelity—creating a stronger, deeper love.

There are several basic ingredients in mature love:

Feelings of warmth replace the intensity of infatuation (the obsessive thinking about the loved one, the idealization, the overpowering desire to be together, the highs and lows, peaks and valleys, the exaltation when together and the despair when apart) as time goes on. But unless disrupted, the loving bond persists. Couples married for over forty years have told me they get turned on emotionally when they see each other, just as they had decades earlier.

Caring means believing in and letting your mate know that "You are important to me. I am concerned about what happens to you. I will look after you." Two major facets of caring are being concerned about your mate's welfare and being ready to act to help or protect your mate. Unlike a hired companion or housekeeper, who has a job to do, you help your mate out of a sense of commitment and feeling. Thus, concern and affection are crucial to caring.

Expressions of affection are such an obvious way to stir warm feelings in your mate that discussing them might seem superfluous. Yet, as marriages progress, the affectionate gestures such as putting your arm around your mate, hugging, and whispering words of love become increasingly confined to the bedroom. And, in distressed marriages, they may disappear altogether.

Ted and Karen were both very loving with each other during their courtship and most of the first year of their marriage. But as strains developed, their touching, loving, smiling, and whispering words of affection became rare. After a few sessions of counseling, though, they realized that a tender word or a pleasant smile could break the tension between them, and they started once again to express their affection whenever they genuinely felt it.

Acceptance tends to be unconditional in a mature love relationship. You can acknowledge differences in your ideas about religion, politics, and people without being critical of each other; you can accept your mate's ineptness or weaknesses without being judgmental. Such acceptance is deeply reassuring. It gives partners a sense of accepting themselves. If their mate can accept them totally—blemishes, warts, and all—they can relax and let down their guard.

As Ted and Karen improved their relationship, Ted described the feeling of acceptance: "I can be myself with Karen. I don't have to impress her. She takes me as I am." Karen's attitude of acceptance contrasted with that of Ted's parents, who praised him for intellectual feats and criticized any lapses.

Of course, acceptance does not mean blindness to your partner's shortcomings, but in an atmosphere of acceptance, you can work with your mate against whatever interferes with your being close. Note that if your love is conditional on "good behavior," you can *never* achieve the closeness that is possible when your love is a given and the good behavior is a goal you work toward together.

Empathy is the ability to tune in to your partner's feelings—to experience, to some degree, his or her pain or pleasure, suffering or joy. When people are preoccupied by worries or swept by emotion, whether sadness or euphoria, they may temporarily lose the capacity for empathy. In the anecdote at the beginning of this book, Ted was so concerned about his business problems that he was oblivious to

Karen's high spirits over getting a new client. But Karen, in her happiness, was equally insensitive, unaware of Ted's pain and need for reassurance.

After counseling, Karen became more acutely aware of Ted's worries—particularly his fears of rejection and abandonment. As a result, she was able to make a special effort not to keep Ted waiting, or to call him if she was going to be late. Ted, on the other hand, became more conscious of Karen's desire to be a free spirit, and he consequently restrained his impulse to organize their life together. He tried to loosen up so that he could respond more spontaneously to Karen's impromptu suggestions.

Sensitivity to your mate's concerns and vulnerable spots—such as Ted's fear of abandonment, Karen's fear of being controlled—is essential if you are to reduce his or her needless pain and suffering. While some people naturally have more sensitivity than others, this is a quality that can be cultivated. If your mate overreacts to certain things you do, for example, instead of being critical or defensive, you can stop to consider what the underlying problem might be. Gently explore with your mate his or her secret fears or concerns. Resist the temptation to attribute any overreaction by your mate to some undesirable trait, such as compulsiveness or the need to control. Realize that such overreactions are signs of hidden vulnerabilities.

Karen, for example, learned that Ted's insistence on promptness was due to his fear that something bad might happen to her. And Ted discovered that Karen's anger over his attempts to organize her life sprang from a fear of being controlled.

Recognizing your "hang-ups" does not mean that they cannot be modified. Indeed, in the course of counseling, Ted largely overcame his fears of Karen's rejecting or abandoning him. And Karen was able to shake off her belief that adapting herself to some of the limitations Ted sought would lead to a loss of her freedom and spontaneity.

Understanding is akin to sensitivity but carries this quality further. When your mate tells you of a problem, he or she can feel understood without having to spell out every detail. Further, understanding means being able to see events through your mate's eyes. When Karen was upset over the obnoxious ways of her clients, Ted was able to bring himself to view the difficulty as Karen saw it—not necessarily as he would.

Mutual understanding is one of the first victims of a marital fight, its demise often signaled by the lament "I just don't understand why he [or she] acts that way." Part of the difficulty is that distressed couples act in ways out of character with their more loving side: they take hard positions, for instance, or they try to outwit or deceive each other. A more serious problem is that as the conflict heats up, partners become more prone to misinterpret the meaning of each other's actions. Soon the accumulated misinterpretations swamp whatever understanding the partners had or could have had of each other's true motives.

There are several ways to ward off such misunderstandings. One is to examine your automatic thoughts about your spouse to see whether they are reasonable, logical, and valid (see Chapter 13). Another method is to check out your mind reading of your spouse's intentions, as described in Chapter 8.

Companionship is treasured early in a relationship but seems to fade in many marriages with the passage of time. As a husband and wife become more preoccupied with concerns like providing the family income, taking care of the children, or running the household, they tend to spend less time together, and the quality of that time suffers. In Chapter 14, you will read about Cliff and Judy, whose sense of companionship was weakened by Cliff's involvement with his job. By evaluating the toll that involvement was exacting on his marriage, Cliff was able to reignite the spark that had died in their relationship.

Companionship is one asset of a good marriage that you can improve simply through planning. It takes thinking of activities that you both enjoy—a trip together, decorating the house, going to the theater—and setting time aside to do them. There is also comradeship in the satisfaction of just being together during the day-to-day moments of life. Sitting together watching television, talking walks, or attending to household routines such as washing dishes and cleaning the house together can foster a sense of togetherness.

Intimacy can range from discussing everyday details of your life, to confiding the most private feelings that you would not share with anybody else, to your sexual relationship.

In a way, intimacy is a by-product of caring, acceptance, sensitivity, and understanding. By the same token, it is undermined by misunderstandings, indiscriminate criticism and blaming, and insensitivity. When couples indulge in criticizing, punishing, or controlling each other, they have to consider what they lose in intimacy. When intimacy is lost because of conflicts and battles, a major binding force in marriage goes with it.

Friendliness refers to the genuine interest you take in your mate as a person. This quality seems to become either one-sided or else muted in many, if not most, marriages. Some polls have shown that women do not regard their husband as their best friend, but rather see some other woman in this role. Most husbands, by contrast, regard their wife as their best friend.

You can cultivate friendship by focusing on your mate as a person. Try to elicit what matters to him or her. Often, forming this bridge demands finesse. In Chapter 14, for example, I describe the "follow-up questions method," a way to get your mate to discuss his or her experiences.

Pleasing your spouse is, of course, crucial to a happy marriage. But the pleasure should be mutual; not only can you give your spouse satisfaction from what you do, but you can also share in his or her satisfaction. Sometimes, you have to extricate yourself from overly traveled ruts by doing something special. For example, Ted pleased Karen enormously by talking to her mother on the phone, and Karen then wanted to please him in return. While in a bookstore, she bought a copy of Garry Wills's *Cincinnatus: George Washington and the Enlightenment*, which she knew would fascinate Ted.

Later in the chapter, I will describe how couples can set up a regular program of doing things to please each other. Such consideration can go a long way toward revitalizing a flagging relationship.

Support for your spouse conveys a sense that you are dependable, a Rock of Gibraltar that your spouse can lean on during difficult times. You may underestimate the symbolic significance of cheering up your partner when he or she is discouraged, or helping to sort out problems when they become overwhelming. Coming to your partner's aid at such moments of need can have enormous meaning, conveying to your spouse that you stand ready as a supporter or rescuer.

Some mates, for instance, are too neutral when their spouse wants to embark on a new venture or assume a new responsibility. Their hesitation in taking a positive stance can undermine their spouse's sense of initiative and capability. Take the hypothetical case of a husband trying to be objective, who comes across to his wife as indifferent:

WIFE: I've been given a chance to move up to be an account manager. What do you think I should do?

HUSBAND: Well, what do you want to do?

WIFE: I don't know. That's why I'm asking you.

HUSBAND: Well, you have to decide what you want to do. I can't decide for you.

The wife perceives her husband as uncaring. But in a similar, actual situation, Ken (who had had counseling with me following the interchanges described in earlier chapters) responded to Marjorie in a more supportive way.

MARJORIE: I've been given a chance to move up to be an account manager. What do you think I should do?

KEN: Well, that is certainly a compliment. You must be pleased that Helen [the boss] has that much confidence in you.

MARJORIE: Well, she may have, but I don't have the same confidence.

KEN: Is that why you're not sure what to do?

MARJORIE: Yes, if I had more confidence, I would take the job.

KEN: With every job in the past, didn't you always lack confidence at first, but then feel it later—once you got into it?

MARJORIE: You're right . . . so you think my lack of confidence is just an emotional thing, and I should take the job if that's the only thing holding me back?

KEN: That's right.

Ken was able to identify Marjorie's problem—a lack of confidence. Through judicious questioning, he guided her to the underlying "emotional" problem and indirectly gave her support by implying that he thought she could do the job.

Ken might have jumped in with enthusiasm and tried to talk her into taking the job, but this approach would have been premature and ineffective until she could confront the real problem, her lack of confidence. The technique he did use—first exploration and then reassurance—can be highly effective in supporting a spouse through both understanding and encouragement.

How one mate gives support to another varies enormously from couple to couple. What may be supportive for one can be a turn-off for another. While we all can use a cheering section at times, just what form the cheer should take depends on the individual's personality and state of mind. Usually, asking your mate questions will help to bring the problem into focus. Then, watching for feedback, signs of acceptance or rejection, will help. In general, gauging the best way to be supportive takes a certain amount of trial and error.

Closeness, of course, means much more than simple physical proximity—although many couples complain that they don't even see each other enough. To make this point, one wife called her husband's secretary to make an appointment to see him.

Even when spouses spend much time together, the *quality* of that time can be unrewarding. Judy, for instance, complained that even when her husband, Cliff, was home, "he wasn't really there" but was thinking of other things, instead. Preoccupation with problems on the job, financial difficulties, or troubles with the children can cause an artificial distance between partners. And the greatest repellent of all is hostility, which can drive a strong wedge between them.

Feelings of closeness, however, need not drift away permanently but can be recaptured with a bit of forethought. For example, partners' time together spent discussing matters of import on the job or at home, sharing plans and goals, or reflecting on the day's triumphs and tragedies builds a spontaneous closeness. In addition, loving acts that show affection, acceptance, and support can combine to make partners feel closer.

Keeping Track
of Positive Behavior

It is important for couples to be aware of what their mates do and to respond accordingly. Your reading of Chapter 11 probably brought to mind the kinds of things your spouse might do that would be meaningful to you. Remember that your mate may already be doing some of these things, but you may not be totally aware of them. For a start, try to notice methodically what your mate already does that pleases you. Later, when you begin to have "sessions" with each other, you can apprise him or her of these, and also drop some hints as to the other kinds of things that would mean a great deal to you (see Chapter 14). It often helps to write down each instance of your mate's doing something that pleases you.

After I proposed to Karen and Ted that each take notes of what the other did that was pleasing during the previous week, Karen reported the following:

1 / Ted was great. I was really upset by some of my clients. They are a real pain. They all have opinions about what they should have in their homes, and they don't know the first thing about decorating. They really gave me a hard time, and a couple of them canceled their orders—after all the work I put in, they had the nerve to change their minds! Anyhow, I told Ted about it. He was very sympathetic. He didn't try to tell me what to do. He said that if he was in my position, he would probably feel frustrated, too. He said that my clients are tough to deal with. I felt a lot better.

2 / When he came home, the house was a mess. I didn't have time to fix things up. Instead of complaining about what a mess it was, he pitched in and started to straighten things out without saying anything.

3 / Ted talked to me while I was folding the laundry, so it wasn't such a chore.

4 / He offered to go for a walk, which I enjoyed.

Each of Ted's actions pleased Karen, who remarked, "They were like presents." Although Ted had done similar things for Karen in the past, they had been erased from her memory because of her negative view of Ted.

Just listening to Karen's complaints and sympathizing with her was a major accomplishment for Ted—his natural tendency was to do the opposite. In the past, instead of really listening to Karen, he would have dismissed her concerns by telling her that she did not need to be upset, that clients always acted that way, and that she should try to roll with it.

The time that he came home and saw the mess, his sense of order was offended and he wanted to reproach Karen. However, as a result of the counseling, he suppressed his tendency to complain. Instead, he asked himself, *"What is the mature thing to do?"* He quickly decided to start cleaning things up—without even asking Karen whether he should do this. What was so important was not that he relieved Karen of a physical burden but that his actions had symbolic meaning for her: he was sensitive to her situation (of being swamped with work), he was cooperative and caring, and he was uncritical.

Ted gave the following report:

1 / On Tuesday night I came home really exhausted. I felt strained from all the problems at the office. Karen said, "We're going out tonight." We had a quick dinner at a restaurant and then took in a movie, which really got my mind off the problems at work.

2 / Karen was loving several times during the week.

3 / Karen took my suit to the cleaners.

These incidents meant a great deal to Ted. They demonstrated to him that Karen was devoted and eager to please.

Len and Harriet also had conflicts in a number of areas (Len: not talking at meals and unromantic in love making; Harriet: preoccupied with her classes). I asked them to start doing things that would please each other and to list them. The results follow:

Harriet

1 / He asked me about how I spent the day.

2 / He gave me a back rub.

3 / He told me I looked nice when we went to the theater.

4 / He acted romantic before we had sex together.

5 / He put down the newspaper and sat next to me while I was watching TV.

Len

1 / She asked me what friends I would like to have over. She prepared a gourmet meal for our dinner party.

2 / She got tickets for a play that I wanted to see.

3 / We had sex this week.

4 / She was home in time for dinner every night.

Harriet and Len felt much more accepting of each other after a week of such "good deeds." Such small gestures pay off because they have a large symbolic meaning.

Lifting the Blinders

Mark Kane Goldstein, a psychologist at the University of Florida, has used a simple method to help husbands and wives keep track of their partner's pleasant actions. Each spouse is given several sheets of graph paper on which to record whatever his or her partner does that is pleasing. The spouse rates these acts on a ten-point scale, indicating degree of satisfaction. Dr. Goldstein found that 70 percent of the couples who tried this simple method reported an improvement in their relationship.

Simply keeping track of the small pleasures of their married life makes a couple more aware of the actual degree of satisfaction. Prior to making these systematic observations, the couples had rated their marital satisfaction lower than they did after they kept a systematic score. All that had changed was their *awareness* of what was going on. Before keeping track, they had underestimated the pleasures of their marriage.

You can try Dr. Goldstein's method as a way to determine whether you may be underestimating the satisfaction in your marriage. You may discover, as did many of his clients, that you have more satisfying moments together than you had realized. And, as your relationship begins to change for the better, keeping track of pleasant experiences gives you a baseline for later comparisons.

Dr. Goldstein showed me another technique which I subsequently found very helpful for many couples. The technique aims to open up the blinders that prevent many angry partners from seeing, or at least appreciating, their spouse's pleasing acts. With this method, both husband and wife (or either one) are asked to place several sticky labels somewhere on the other mate's clothing, such as on the lapel of the jacket or on the collar. Each time the husband, for example, does something that pleases his wife, she removes one of the labels. The couples keep track of the number of labels removed each day. Usually, most or all of the labels have been removed by bedtime.

Although this technique may seem simplistic to some, it yields powerful results. In order to note pleasing actions, spouses begin to really *look at* each other. (When they were angry, they had tended to look away from each other.) This method forces spouses to break through the barriers that obstruct their vision of their partner's good deeds. The assignment prompts them to be on the lookout for their mate's pleasing actions, and then to do something that shows they have seen these acts. This, in turn, helps both to reinforce the acts, so they will be repeated, and to highlight them in their minds. Finally, the technique of applying and removing labels brings a distressed couple into closer physical contact.

After you have observed your spouse's spontaneous good behavior for a while, you should start to tell him or her what else you would find pleasing. This should be stated in a straightforward manner, without sarcasm, accusations, or innuendos. For example, avoid making conditional requests—veiled attacks, really—such as "I'd like you to help me with the dishes, but take that pained expression off your face" or "I'd like you to talk to me when you come home from the office instead of dashing in to watch the six o'clock news." The simple request is much more likely to get you what you want.

You might make such requests during "marital meetings"—if you can get your spouse to agree to them. (These sessions will be further described in Chapter 16.) In either case, the main strategy at this point is to *emphasize the positives* in your marriage. Eliminating the negatives, while extremely important, is best carried out after a more positive atmosphere has been created. Applying the principles in this chapter will help.

If you are reluctant to have a marital meeting, or if it is premature but you still want your spouse to do certain chores or other things that will please you, you should prepare written lists. One woman, for example, complained to me, "I'm sick and tired of asking my husband to attend to things." At my suggestion, she made a list of the things she wanted him to do and attached it to the refrigerator. Within a short period of time, he had checked off all the items on the list! Another woman wrote out one or two requests each day on adhesive note paper and stuck it on the bathroom mirror, where her husband would see it when he shaved.

But just asking is not enough. Whenever your spouse does something that pleases you, it should be followed up with a reward of some kind—an appreciative note, or a kiss, for example. Rewards are a far better way than punishment to change how your spouse acts.

The checklist below can be helpful in identifying the ways in which you and your spouse show each other your affection and caring. The scale is useful as a guide for evaluating your present status and determining possible areas for improvement. There are no absolute scores for rating your relationship.

Expressions of Love

Read each question. Determine how frequently you could answer yes for each one, and write down the appropriate number in the space provided:

(0) *never*　　(1) *rarely*　　(2) *sometimes*　　(3) *often*
(4) *almost always*　　(5) *always.*

If a particular question does not apply, just skip it and go on to the next.

Feelings of Warmth

_____ 1 / Do you feel a warm glow when you see or think about your partner?

_____ 2 / Do you have tender feelings when you are together?

_____ 3 / Do you miss your partner when you are apart?

Expressions of Affection

_____ 1 / Do you use terms of endearment with your partner?

_____ 2 / Do you express affection in your tone of voice?

_____ 3 / Do you show affection through physical contact—touching, holding hands, and so on?

Caring

_____ 1 / Are you concerned about your partner's

_____　　a / welfare?

_____　　b / pleasure?

_____　　c / pain?

_____ 2 / Do you try to show your partner that you care?

_____ 3 / Do you avoid saying or doing things that will hurt your partner?

Acceptance and Tolerance

_____ 1 / Do you accept differences of opinion, tastes, and style?

_____ 2 / Do you accept your partner in totality, as someone with weak points as well as strong ones?

_____ 3 / Do you avoid being judgmental or punishing your partner for his or her mistakes?

Empathy and Sensitivity

_____ 1 / When your partner is feeling down, do you find you can share some of that feeling?

_____ 2 / Are you able to sense that your partner is feeling bad without being told?

_____ 3 / Are you able to determine and respect your partner's sensitive areas?

Understanding

_____1 / Do you find you can understand why your partner may be upset?

_____2 / Can you see things through your partner's eyes even when you disagree?

_____3 / Can you tell what your partner is upset about when he or she complains?

Companionship

_____1 / Do you enjoy doing exciting things with your partner?

_____2 / Do you like your partner's company when doing routine things?

_____3 / Do you enjoy just having your partner around when you are not doing anything in particular?

Intimacy

_____1 / Do you share your private thoughts and wishes?

_____2 / Do you feel free to tell your partner things that you would not tell anybody else?

_____3 / Do you like your partner to confide in you?

Friendliness

_____1 / Do you feel an interest in your partner as a person?

_____2 / Do you like to know what your partner is thinking or how he or she is doing?

_____3 / Do you like to solicit your partner's opinions about your problems?

Pleasing

_____1 / Do you try to think of things the two of you can do that will make your partner happy?

_____2 / Do you try to make yourself more attractive?

_____3 / Do you say or do things that please your partner?

Support

_____1 / Do you try to bolster your partner when he or she is discouraged?

_____2 / Do you help out when your partner is overwhelmed?

_____3 / Do you encourage your partner when he or she wants to engage in a new venture?

Closeness

_____1 / Do you feel emotionally close to your partner?

_____2 / Do you have a feeling of closeness to your partner even when you are apart?

_____3 / Do you enjoy being physically close to your partner?

CHANGING
YOUR OWN DISTORTIONS

We have seen in the previous chapters how faulty interpretations lead to misunderstandings, which in turn contribute to the decline of a relationship. But the misinterpretations and exaggerated meanings that underlie marital strife can be corrected through the application of several cognitive therapy techniques. As I mentioned earlier, these techniques are skills that can be learned, and as you practice them, you can expect to acquire increasing proficiency.

Some techniques can be used by each partner separately; others work best when both partners apply them. The following are the ones you can use on your own: recognizing and correcting your automatic thoughts, testing your predictions, and reframing your perspective of your mate. After reviewing the overall strategy that you can use individually, I will outline the specific nine steps in applying the techniques. In subsequent chapters, I will describe how you and your partner can work together to resolve your marital problems and increase your mutual satisfaction.

General Guidelines

As a starting point, try to identify troublesome situations and the meanings you attach to them. For example, suppose your spouse speaks to you in a gruff way. Your automatic thought may be *"My spouse is displeased with me."* You have to be particularly vigilant to pick up the *hidden fear* or self-doubt, such as *"Have I done something wrong?"* or *"Is he [she] going to scold me?"* Next, tune in to the entire chain reaction:

Have I done something wrong? (anxiety)

▽

My spouse has no right to be mad at me. (anger)

▽

My spouse always acts unfriendly.

▽

My spouse is a hostile, hateful person.

▽

My spouse will make life miserable for me.

▽

I can't stand this.

▽

Our marriage is a failure.

▽

I will never be happy again.

Resist the natural tendency to accept these thoughts as true simply because they "feel right" or seem reasonable. Examine them and look for supporting evidence, contradictory evidence, alternative explanations, and more logical inferences.

Oppose the temptation to slip into your well-worked, self-defeating reactions, such as retaliation, defensiveness, or withdrawal. By yielding to your temptation to react in one of these ways, you validate your negative interpretation. By counterattacking, for instance, you are acting on the assumption that your spouse *is* wrong or bad, an assumption that justifies your punitive reaction. Your negative interpretation is more likely to become a fixed conviction if you act on this assumption. Then, the next time a similar event occurs, you will be more likely to reach the same negative conclusion, which will be less susceptible to correction—even though it is wrong.

Of course, it is not always feasible, or even desirable, to keep from expressing your hostility toward your mate. Some people experience so much anger that they feel a great pressure to relieve it. In these circumstances, specific techniques such as seeking a special time to express hostility, preparing an agenda, setting time limits, and providing time outs might be helpful (see "Choice 5: Schedule Ventilation Sessions" in Chapter 17).

The Nine Steps

Below are detailed guidelines for evaluating whether your interpretations and the elaborations you build on them are correct. You will also find rules for deciding whether your interpretations represent problems in thinking (such as overgeneralization, all-or-nothing thinking, or mind reading).

There are a number of steps in applying the principles of cognitive therapy to improve your marriage. Each step involves practices that couples who have consulted me have found very helpful in dealing with their misleading, self-defeating beliefs.

STEP 1: LINK EMOTIONAL REACTIONS WITH AUTOMATIC THOUGHTS

The main strategy here is to identify an unpleasant emotional reaction, relate it to the relevant situation or event, and determine the hidden connecting link—the automatic thought—that joins the two.

Consider the following incidents, reported by Wendy and Hal:

▷ Wendy looks at the clock and feels angry.
▷ Hal is driving home and suddenly feels anxious.
▷ Hal later is talking to Wendy and suddenly feels sad.

These emotions—anxiety, anger, and sadness—do not come out of the blue, although at times they may appear to. They occur in a specific context. For example, Wendy feels angry when she reads the clock because she realizes that her tardy husband has kept her waiting. To show the context for Wendy's emotional reaction, we can note the following:

Relevant Situation or Event	*Emotional Reaction*
Wendy observes that her husband is late.	Anger

Although it seems plausible that a wife might be angry or anxious if her husband isn't home on time, it is *how she interprets the situation* rather than the situation itself that will determine what she feels. In this situation, she might experience any of a variety of emotions, depending on the personal meaning of the event. Another wife, for instance, might experience relief at her husband's lateness because it would give her more time to attend to personal affairs.

Take the next scenario: Hal is driving home, realizes that he is late, and feels anxious.

Relevant Situation or Event	*Emotional Reaction*
Hal observes he is late coming home.	Anxiety

As we shall see, Hal's observation leads to a specific thought, which then leads to his anxiety.

In the third scene, Hal, after driving home, suddenly feels sad when talking to Wendy. The relevant event is that Wendy suggests that they go out for dinner instead of eating at home.

Relevant Situation or Event	*Emotional Reaction*
Hal realizes that Wendy does not want to make dinner.	Sadness

If you were filling out this form yourself, it might be relatively easy to complete so far, by simply determining your emotional reaction and its relevant situation or event. The more difficult part is next: identifying the missing link—your *interpretation* of the relevant situation (automatic thought)—and the symbolic meaning you give it. For practice, try to guess the automatic thoughts of each partner in these scenarios that I have just described. Now check below to see whether you guessed them correctly.

Relevant Situation or Event	*Automatic Thought*	*Emotional Reaction*
Wendy notices Hal is late.	He doesn't want to come home.	Anger
Hal notices he is late.	My wife will be angry.	Anxiety
Wendy decides not to make dinner.	She doesn't care about me.	Sadness

Although each of these thoughts could be correct, they are actually only guesses or hypotheses. Since such interpretations have a crucial bearing on your relationship, as well as on the appropriateness of your reaction, they need to be authenticated, as outlined in Step 5.

STEP 2: USE IMAGINATION TO IDENTIFY THOUGHTS

You can experience these emotions and automatic thoughts not just when a troubling event occurs but also when you *imagine* such an event. For example, imagine the following scene as vividly as you can. As you picture the scene, write down what you feel and the thoughts going through your mind about it. It may help to concentrate on the thoughts and feelings if you close your eyes after you have read the scene.

You have been busy all day in town and your spouse has arranged to pick you up at a specified intersection at 5:00 P.M. You arrive promptly, but your spouse is nowhere to be seen. The seconds and then the minutes tick off and still your spouse has not arrived. You keep checking your watch as it gets later: 5:10, 5:15, 5:20.

When you have fully imagined the scene, write down your emotional reactions and automatic thoughts on a separate sheet of paper.

Automatic Thought (Interpretation)	Emotional Reaction
1 /	1 /
2 /	2 /
3 /	3 /

People visualizing this scenario have very different thoughts and feelings. One man felt very anxious and was able to identify the thought *"Perhaps something happened to her."* By contrast, a woman felt sad when doing this exercise. Her thoughts were *"I'm here all alone. It's the story of my life. Everybody abandons me."* Another man reported that he felt angry, thinking, *"It's typical of her. She never gets to appointments on time!"*

Let's continue with the scenario:

You look at your watch again. It's 5:25. Then you notice a familiar car pulling up at the corner. You recognize your spouse, who says cheerily, "You know, I forgot that I was supposed to pick you up . . . I just remembered when I was on my way to get my hair cut."

Now, write down your emotional reactions and automatic thoughts on a separate sheet of paper.

Automatic Thought	Emotional Reaction
1 /	1 /
2 /	2 /
3 /	3 /

You probably did not have much difficulty in pinning down your feelings and thoughts about the situation. Many spouses performing this exercise feel angry and indignant at this point, and have thoughts like *"He's got a lot of nerve"* or *"She has no right to treat me this way."*

It is relatively easy to identify your reactions when you are focusing on them, with no distractions. In a real-life situation, you might have the same thoughts, but since they occur so quickly—often overshadowed by your anger—you might not notice them in the heat of the moment.

STEP 3: PRACTICE IDENTIFYING AUTOMATIC THOUGHTS

If you observe your thinking, you can identify automatic thoughts as they flash across the horizon of your awareness. These internal messages trigger emotional reactions, such as anger or sadness, and wishes, such as a desire to scold the spouse—and then fade, while the emotion or wish persists. But most people believe that their emotions stem directly from the situation; they pay no attention to the fleeting thoughts that connect the situation to the emotions and wishes.

Learning to recognize your automatic thoughts is a skill that can be mastered, though proficiency requires practice and persistence. A big pay-off will be the reward for your efforts, however, because by acquiring this skill, you can get a grasp of the inner workings of your mind, gaining insight into what makes you tick. And with this insight you can become more the master of your emotions and less the slave. You can gain some control over the circumstances of your marriage rather than be controlled by them.

Some of the more common automatic thoughts in marriage are listed below. Either spouse could have any of these thoughts. See how many you have had at one time or another.

▷ She's hopeless.
▷ He's completely self-centered.
▷ She's inadequate.
▷ He's weak.
▷ She'll never let me alone.
▷ He never does what he promises.
▷ She's lazy.
▷ He's irresponsible.
▷ Nothing I do pleases her.
▷ He never does anything right.

Of course, simply recognizing your automatic thoughts does not clear the road to utopia. But this recognition gives you a tool to modulate your emotions, and so deal more effectively with the real problem. It is important to practice recognizing automatic thoughts. For this purpose, keep a pad handy, and when you have an unpleasant experience with your spouse—or with anyone, for that matter—just jot down a brief description of the relevant situation or event, your emotional reaction, and your automatic thought, using the column format in this chapter.

After a brief period of instruction, Tom and Sally, whom I will describe more fully in Chapter 16, compiled a list as follows:

Relevant Situation or Event	Automatic Thought	Emotional Reaction
Tom was driving too fast.	What if we get into an accident.	Nervousness
	▽	▽
	He's doing this to upset me. He doesn't care how I feel.	Annoyance
Sally wasn't home when I arrived.	I'll be all alone in this empty house.	Sadness and loneliness
	▽	▽
	Damn her! She's always off to some meeting or another. One hell of a wife!	Anger

STEP 4: USE REPLAY TECHNIQUE

If you had trouble pinpointing your automatic thoughts in an upsetting situation, as described in Step 3, try to relive mentally the event that once upset you. Imagine it as vividly as you can. Now try to capture the automatic thought by asking the key question: *"What is going through my mind* right now?"

Many people who do not recognize their automatic thoughts in the heat of a troubling exchange are able to identify these thoughts later, when they relive the event in their mind. The imagery, in a sense, re-enacts the scene in slow motion and allows you time to pick up the thoughts that had eluded you in the original situation.

STEP 5: QUESTION YOUR AUTOMATIC THOUGHTS

At this point, you may wonder how the act of merely recognizing negative thoughts in response to your spouse's apparently offensive behavior is going to improve your relationship. The answer is that, as we have seen, our emotional reactions are often way out of proportion to the actual situation—particularly in marriage. To determine whether your automatic thoughts are exaggerations or distortions, you need to put them to a test.

Even though your automatic thoughts may "feel" plausible and correct, they may not stand up to scrutiny. To gauge their validity, ask yourself this series of questions:

▷ What is the evidence in *favor* of my interpretation?

▷ What evidence is there *contrary* to my interpretation?

▷ Does it *logically follow* from my spouse's actions that my spouse has the motive that I assign to him or her?

▷ Is there an *alternative* explanation for his or her behavior?

Take an example in which your spouse spoke gruffly or in some other way that upset you. Ask yourself these questions:

1/ Does it follow that because my spouse spoke sharply he or she was angry at me?

2/ Are there alternative explanations for my spouse's tone of voice (for example, he or she could have a cold or be hoarse)?

3/ Even if my spouse was angry, does it follow that:
   a/ My spouse doesn't love me?
   b/ My spouse is always unfriendly?
   c/ My spouse will make life miserable for me?
   d/ I did something wrong?

4/ What evidence is there on the *other* side? Have there been times, recently, when my spouse has been friendly or loving?

STEP 6: USE RATIONAL RESPONSES

In an earlier example, a conflict between Wendy and Hal was introduced. Hal was feeling anxious because he was late, and called to tell his wife that he was tied up at the office. He thought, *"She'll be mad at me because I'm late, and she'll give me a hard time. This will put a real strain on our relationship."* Wendy thought, *"He's always late. He's inconsiderate. He knows that I work, too, but I'm always home on time."*

When Hal came home, Wendy suggested that since it was too late to prepare dinner, they could either go out or order one in from a restaurant. Hal became annoyed, thinking, *"She's getting back at me for being late,"* and he got angry. Then he thought, *"She really doesn't care about me or our home at all. All she's interested in is her career,"* and he felt even more angry.

Later, each spouse filled out an automatic thought form. They had also learned to respond to their automatic thoughts—to give a rational answer to those thoughts by means of a kind of inner dialogue. Here are some of their thoughts and counteracting, rational responses:

Wendy's Automatic Thought Record

Emotional Reaction	Automatic Thought	Rational Responses
Anger	It's not fair—I have to work, too. If he wanted to be home on time.	His job is different. Many of his customers come in after work.
	▽	▽
	He doesn't really care about me.	He did call to say he'd be late. Being late doesn't necessarily mean he doesn't care. Besides, most of the time he does show real concern and affection.

Hal's Automatic Thought Record

Emotional Reaction	Automatic Thought	Rational Responses
Anger	She's getting back at me. It will spoil the whole evening.	Even if she is annoyed, she always gets over it in a few minutes.
	▽	▽
	She doesn't care about me or the home.	Just because she doesn't want to cook doesn't mean that she doesn't care about me or our home. She is a super housekeeper and takes care of a lot of my needs.
	▽	▽
	All she cares about is her career.	She wants a career, but she says that her relationship with me is very important. Why shouldn't I believe her?

The rational response evaluates the reasonableness of the automatic thought. For example, in evaluating the automatic thought *"It's not fair,"* Wendy countered with the notion that since Hal's job was different from hers, it was more difficult for him to come home early. She thus recognized that the automatic thought was based on faulty evidence. Similarly, she rebutted her thought *"He doesn't really care about me"* with contradictory evidence—*"He did call,"* plus *"Being late doesn't necessarily mean he doesn't care. Besides, most of the time he does show real concern and affection."* Finding the rational response helps you to see your automatic thought in perspective—as a reaction and interpretation, not as "the truth."

EXTRACTING THE MEANING

Wendy became upset because Hal, usually talkative, was silent after he arrived home. She found it hard to pinpoint the reason for her feelings. When Wendy used the instant replay technique, she could get only a vague idea of why she was distressed. I then helped her through the sequence:

1 / What is the meaning of his behavior?
  He's fed up with me.

2 / What does this mean to me?
  That he may want to divorce me.

When we had worked her way through to these hidden meanings, she said, "This really clicks. That is the way I really think about it."

Reviewing the sequence in this way helps you determine the hidden meanings behind your reaction. This gives you an understanding of why your reaction is so heated, and it also helps to train you to catch your automatic thoughts more easily the next time you are upset.

STEP 7: TEST YOUR PREDICTIONS

Wendy was upset by the intrusions of Hal's parents. We had the following discussion:

WENDY: My mother-in-law calls me all the time. She's always checking up on me. I guess she doesn't trust me to take proper care of her dear son and her grandchildren.

ATB: Is there any other explanation for her behavior?

WENDY: Ah, I know what you're getting at. She may just be showing that she's concerned and wants to be helpful. Well, I'd like to say something to Hal about her, but I'm afraid to.

ATB: What are you concerned about?

WENDY: I'm afraid if I say anything to him about his mother, it will cause a rift between him and me. I'm always afraid of getting into a fight with him.

ATB: Let's write down your belief, and then we can test it. Your belief is "Telling my husband about his mother will cause a rift." What is the evidence for this?

WENDY: I guess there isn't any evidence. He always takes my side when I have an argument with my in-laws.

ATB: Suppose we make a prediction and test your belief "If I talk to my husband about his mother, it will cause a rift."

WENDY: He will probably be upset, but I don't think it will be permanent.

Wendy agreed to test this prediction by having a talk with her husband about her mother-in-law. When she considered the prediction of a rift more objectively, her fear of a dire consequence seemed less strong. However, in order for her to be convinced, it was important for Wendy to have an actual corrective experience. Further, to improve her relationship with her husband, it was essential that she feel more free to discuss such touchy subjects with him.

As Wendy had anticipated, Hal was upset by her bringing up the subject of his mother. He said, "I feel as though I'm caught in the middle." But he saw that Wendy's feelings had to be respected, and he offered to talk to his mother about her intrusions. Wendy appreciated this important action on her behalf and, as a result, felt much closer to Hal.

STEP 8: REFRAMING

As described in Chapter 3, when a relationship goes downhill, the partners begin to see each other through a negative frame, which consists of a composite of disagreeable traits (*"He's mean and manipulative"*; *"She's irresponsible"*) that each attributes to the other. These unfavorable attributions color how the offended mate sees the partner: negative actions are exaggerated and neutral actions are seen as negative. Even positive acts may be given a negative coloring.

Reframing consists of reconsidering these negative qualities in a different light. Sometimes, for example, it is the very qualities that have attracted a couple to each other that later in the relationship come to be seen as negative. The attributes that you once enjoyed or admired are still there. The problem is that your negative frame of mind allows you to see only the "down side" of these qualities and not their advantages.

It is important to be aware that when you and your spouse clash, the less desirable aspects of your personality become accentuated, leading to a vicious cycle in which hitherto pleasing qualities come to seen as unpleasant. For example, Sharon was attracted to Paul because he was easygoing, totally accepting, and full of fun. Paul, a free-lance writer always on the verge of "making it," was attracted to Sharon because she was sure of herself as an assertive, competent lawyer and didn't allow her colleagues and clients to boss her. After a few years of marriage, their image of each other changed. Paul became "lazy, irresponsible, and passive"; Sharon was seen as "pushy, critical, and controlling."

What had happened? When Paul failed to live up to some of Sharon's expectations regarding his job, she pressed him to try harder. Paul perceived Sharon's exhortations as nagging and controlling, and he retreated into greater passivity. Sharon interpreted his withdrawal as a sign of laziness and became more critical, which made Paul pull back even more. The interplay of the partners' personalities is crucial in producing such vicious cycles.

In working with each of them, I discovered that their negative frames were the flip side of their original perceptions. By reexamining this positive side, Sharon and Paul were able to recapture some of the good feelings they originally had for each other.

This was Paul's flip-side analysis of Sharon:

Negative View	Flip Side
She's controlling.	She's actually decisive, gets a lot done, contributes to family income.
She's critical.	She's sharp and incisive; she's very successful; she doesn't intend to hurt me.

This was Sharon's flip-side view of Paul:

Negative View	Flip Side
He's lazy.	He's laid-back, easygoing.
He's too passive.	He's completely accepting of me.
He's irresponsible.	He admires me for what I've done.
He makes a joke out of everything. He's not serious enough.	He's got a great sense of humor. He can always make me laugh when I'm feeling down.

When Sharon was able to reframe Paul in this way, the negative qualities lost their sting. She wrote down the following rebuttal of her frame:

I can now accept the fact that he is not as successful as I expected him to be. But I've done very well so we don't need much additional income. I guess that what's important to me now is that he loves me and accepts me. He never nags me the way my mother did and never criticizes me. If I would stop nagging him, we could have a good time, because he is really fun. I know he's not very responsible about money and doing things around the house, but I can make up for that.

You should note: *It is not necessary for you or your mate to change your personalities in order to promote a more harmonious relationship.* Generally, a relatively small change in behavior is enough to reverse the vicious cycle. As Paul became more active in taking on responsibility, Sharon relaxed her pressure on him. Then, Paul could more naturally tune in to Sharon's wishes. Such changes can occur most easily in a climate of friendliness and acceptance. By forming the best possible interpretation of each other's behavior, spouses can foster the process of reframing.

As Sharon's view of Paul became less negative, his view of her started to change, as well. He began to feel grateful that she was able to compensate for his own weaknesses. He felt a greater sense of pride in her career. In addition, when she stopped nagging him, he tended to chores more spontaneously.

Such changes do not occur overnight, but by bringing themselves to view their mate from a different perspective, spouses can regain many of the positive feelings that originally drew them together. Further, the "new look" can foster more friendliness and supportiveness, which in itself reinforces the reemerging positive perspective.

PRACTICE ALTERNATIVE EXPLANATIONS

Marjorie's complaint that Ken "snaps at me all the time" provides the starting point for another example of reframing. At my suggestion, she marked down her interpretations of her husband's behavior in sequence:

> He has no respect for me.
> ▽
> He enjoys putting me down.
> ▽
> He doesn't love me.
> ▽
> He hates women.

Marjorie tried to find a benign explanation for Ken's irritability, but she wasn't able to. She considered the possibility that he was under stress at work, but she dismissed this explanation when his irritability persisted after his job-related stress had abated. She began to think more and more that his peevishness represented his "real self." Then Marjorie read a book called *Men Who Hate Women and the Women*

Who Love Them, and everything crystallized: her husband, whom she loved so much, "hated women."

Fortunately, Marjorie decided to explore her beliefs further by checking them out with Ken. When she told him about this, his eyes grew moist and he said that he had not realized that he had been so irritable, although he admitted to having a "short fuse" lately.

Ken explained that by the time he came home at night, he was filled with a resentment that had grown during his working hours. Although the hostility was actually directed toward his boss and some fellow employees, it persisted when he came home—hence, his low tolerance for any of his wife's actions that displeased him. Certain of Marjorie's habits, which had never bothered Ken in the past, now triggered the hostility. Since he was already charged up—mobilized to attack—any petty frustration like finding dinner slightly late or no beer in the refrigerator was sufficient to set him off. Marjorie thus became the target for a hostility that was engendered by, and meant for, others.

After their talk, in which she checked out her beliefs (see Chapter 12), Marjorie was able to regard Ken in a different—and more realistic —light. She reframed her view of him from being "uncaring and hateful" to being "stressed and upset," which was much easier for her to accept.

STEP 9: LABELING YOUR DISTORTIONS

It often helps couples to label various problems in their thinking, as described in detail in Chapter 8. One of the most common of these distortions is *polarized*, "all-or-nothing," or "either-or" thinking. If your spouse is less loving than usual, for example, you might conclude that he or she no longer loves you. In such polarized thinking, anything less than the most desirable is labeled as undesirable. There is either total love or total rejection, total consideration or total inconsideration—nothing in between.

Overgeneralization refers to the formulation of a sweeping statement based on a small number of events. If your spouse interrupts you, he or she "always" interrupts you. If your spouse shows some disrespect, he or she is "never" respectful.

Tunnel vision, or screening, applies to the selection of a single detail from an experience and the screening out of other data—to interpret the entire event on the basis of that sole detail. Example: "My husband hated the meal I prepared—he complained the soup was too hot."

Personalization occurs when you consider yourself the cause of your spouse's behavior despite the fact that it has nothing to do with you. Example: "She's in a bad mood. It must be because she's angry at me."

Negative (global) labeling occurs when you apply a global negative label to a person, not just to that person's action. Examples: "He is a weakling because he did not ask for a raise." "She is a nag because she wants me to quit drinking." "He's a slob because he doesn't pick up his clothes." People also may use the same type of flawed thinking in evaluating themselves: "I never do anything properly. I always antagonize people. I'm a failure."

A PRACTICAL EXERCISE

To develop the habit of using these labels with your own thoughts, it helps to practice. In each anecdote or statement below, indicate the type of thinking problem at work:*

	Thinking Problem
1 / Ever since she lied to me, I have never trusted her.	1 /
2 / My husband is either for me or for his parents.	2 /
3 / When my spouse is angry, I think that it's because of me.	3 /
4 / When she stares at me, I know she's criticizing me.	4 /
5 / I would have had a good time at the party, but my spouse was late.	5 /
6 / He hasn't been talking much lately. It's a sign that the relationship is falling apart.	6 /
7 / He didn't enjoy the movie the way I did —we have nothing in common.	7 /
8 / He contradicts me. It shows he does not respect me.	8 /
9 / We had another argument. That's terrible.	9 /
10 / She's a louse for keeping me waiting.	10 /

---

*THE CORRECT ANSWERS: (1) overgeneralization, (2) polarized (all-or-nothing) thinking, (3) personalization, (4) mind reading, (5) tunnel vision, (6) "catastrophizing," (7) overgeneralization, (8) mind reading, (9) "awfulizing," (10) negative labeling.

These labels will be useful in filling out your thought records. It is often helpful to add another column to record the names of the specific thinking problems. Once you try applying these terms, you may realize how often you misinterpret or exaggerate your spouse's behavior. And by talking things over to test out the true applicability of these terms, you can gain greater objectivity and straighten out the misconceptions that feed marital strife.

Take the following example from an automatic thought record:

Relevant Situation or Event	Automatic Thought	Thinking Problem
Hal blew up at me while we were making love.	He's crazy. ▽	Negative labeling ▽
	He always gets upset. ▽	Overgeneralization ▽
	We will never get along together.	"Catastrophizing"

After you have had sufficient experience in analyzing your own reactions, you can consider working jointly with your spouse on the relationship. The next two chapters discuss in detail ways the two of you can work together to improve communication and understanding, and to alter self-defeating patterns.

14

THE ART
OF CONVERSATION

Few experiences are more gratifying than saying something vague or difficult to express and knowing that your partner understands exactly what you mean. The ability to converse in a private language—with obscure references, veiled hints, knowing glances, shrugs and winks —represents a very special kind of closeness.

The finely tuned conversation expresses the essence of rapport. Each person knows just what the other is saying, and feels a gradually accumulating pleasure at being able to speak freely, being understood, and having his or her partner concur. The dialogue runs smoothly, with a distinctive rhythm or beat, somewhat like a dance in which each partner alternately leads or follows in harmony.

But in distressed marriages, the pleasures of conversation are lost in a fog of angry complaints, missed cues, and misunderstandings. Instead of knowing winks, witty allusions, and private codes, there are angry glances, critical references, and veiled threats.

How did the smooth dialogue get lost? The rhythm is gradually upset when, over the course of a relationship, differing conversational styles, conflicting interests and perspectives, and misunderstandings accumulate. Even couples who were well tuned in to each other in the early years may later find that their simplest conversations are jarred by misinterpretations leading to the complaint "That's not what I meant."

Whenever Ken and Marjorie started to talk, their conversation seemed to be derailed despite their good intentions. Instead of producing a smooth discussion, their conversational gears would grind against each other. One of them would try to lighten the heavy mood with a joke, and the other would react as though it were a dig. Each

213

attempt to salvage the discussion would only make matters worse. Consequently, they avoided serious discussions.

Couples like Ken and Marjorie lose sight of the fact that aside from their sexual relationship, their most intimate exchanges occur when they are engaged in conversation. Since they spend far more time talking together than making love, their conversations are crucial for the survival and growth of their rapport. Unfortunately, many couples —perhaps most—lack specific skills in marital communications and so unwittingly produce continual abrasions, misunderstandings, and frustrations.

The very meaning of talking can differ for a wife and husband. One partner, for instance, may regard conversations simply as a forum for making joint decisions. The mate, however, may see their conversations as the deepest expression of the relationship itself, offering the chance to share secrets, to show interest in each other's problems and triumphs, and to experience solidarity and intimacy.

Pinpointing Problems
in Communication

The observation that distressed couples "don't communicate" with each other has become a cliché, but there is much truth in it. Since "we don't communicate" is such a global, vague statement, it is essential to translate it into specific problems, which can then be dealt with.

Some obstacles to successful communication, such as interrupting, listening too passively, and talking in circles, have been described in Chapter 5. Other difficulties stem from particular attitudes about the spouse or subject matter of the discussions. Some of these problems will now be discussed.

PROBLEM: *"I can't be honest with my spouse."*

Total honesty is not just difficult in a relationship—it's impossible. This may seem paradoxical, since marriage is just the type of relationship in which one might expect total honesty to be successful. But there are several reasons why this doesn't work. Total honesty, put starkly, can be as stinging as a slap in the face. A direct statement like "I don't feel like talking tonight" can easily be taken as a rejection. For instance, at the peak of his anger, a husband perceives his wife with a highly negative bias; thus, what he says while angry is not an objectively honest statement but a strongly biased honesty.

While he is angry, the husband is in a unique cognitive state: he sees his wife—temporarily, at least—as an adversary. His frame of mind tends to magnify her negative actions and traits, to ignore her positive traits, and to convert her neutral ones into negatives. Such twisted and exaggerated judgments reflect how he sees things right at that moment, not how he usually experiences her when he is not angry.

Such "honest," derogatory remarks can inflict deep wounds in one's spouse. The momentary conviction of honesty is often a self-deception based on the angry person's subjective feeling. But the spouse who is the target of the attack bears the wound long after the anger passes.

One misleading belief about relationships is that people should always be direct and totally honest. But truth has many faces and nuances that one can neither explore nor express easily. And the naked truth can be destructive. While at the height of their anger, people are often quite candid in saying what they think; when they have calmed down, they see things quite differently. However, as the following dialogue shows, the person on the receiving end of the "honest" criticism might continue to accept the negative label as a genuine expression of the partner's true feelings.

TOM: Why are you moping around?

SALLY: You told me I was stupid.

TOM: I really didn't mean it. I was angry at the time.

SALLY: I *know* you really do think I am stupid.

TOM: That just isn't true. I was angry.

SALLY: You always say that when people are angry they express their true thoughts.

This is one of the knottiest problems in "letting it all hang out"— the myth that the feelings expressed in a strong emotional state are somehow more genuine than those expressed at other times. The fact is that at times of high emotion, people are *least* likely to express their true thoughts; what they express are often thoughts generated by a primitive thinking program (described in Chapter 9)—twisted by distortions and overgeneralizations—which is not at all what they think in a more calm state.

It is easy to confuse being *honest* with being *direct*. For instance, you can answer a question directly without revealing all your innermost thoughts and feelings on the matter. Thus, if somebody asks you how your family is, you can truthfully say fine (referring to their health) without adding that your marriage is shaky or that your children are doing poorly at school. Simple, direct answers suffice in most conversations and do not require total disclosure.

For many people, being indirect offers a way to protect themselves. Instead of saying what they mean, they ask a question or make a roundabout or ambiguous statement, leaving it to the listener to decipher what they are really getting at. Since many mates complain that their spouses are too indirect, it is worthwhile understanding the reasons for this approach.

Sometimes the indirectness is due to stylistic differences in how men and women converse, or to ethnic and family backgrounds—the reputation New Englanders have for being taciturn, for example. But apart from conversational style, indirectness is often a strategic move, a way of playing safe. We may want to express ourselves with caution so that if we don't get a positive response, we can easily take it back or suggest that we meant something else.

By being indirect, we can test the waters before we jump in and commit ourselves. Then, depending upon whether our mate is receptive, we can advance or retreat. Rather than just blurt out our ideas, we send out feelers as a way of sensing the reactions, and then we shape the presentation of our ideas accordingly.

Such conversational diplomacy is common in broader social life but often fails in marital relations. Some of the most effective business leaders, for instance, seem to have the knack of knowing when to pursue a given line of action, when to pause, and when to stage a strategic withdrawal. However, when these same managers are dealing with their spouses, their polished techniques and conversational ploys suddenly seem to vanish.

Of course in marriage, one does expect to be free to let one's hair down, to get things off one's chest. And in many relationships this works—much of the time. On the other hand, if the topic is sensitive, when there is a conflict of opinion or interest, or when one or the other mate is fatigued or stressed, the up-front approach can boomerang.

Missing the Message. Sometimes an indirect answer to a direct question is formulated so as not to appear rude. When the questioner presses for a direct reply, the other person may become angry, because he or she wants to keep some things unspoken. Take the following dialogue between Sue and Mike, the couple from disparate backgrounds we met earlier. They often encountered problems when Mike made too blunt a response on an issue that was sensitive for Sue.

SUE: How do you like the paper that I wrote?
MIKE: I think it's very good. But it could use some more work.

SUE: Are you telling me that you don't like it?

MIKE: [irritated] I told you that I thought it was quite good.

SUE: Then why are you acting so disgusted with me?

In this case, Mike wanted to give an upbeat response to Sue's question and was concerned that if he gave a totally frank appraisal, Sue would be hurt. In fact, he was right: she sensed his qualification as a hint that the manuscript was flawed. She could not take what he said at its face value because she was looking for unqualified acceptance. For Sue, anything less than that amounted to a rejection.

There was a mismatch between Sue's expectations and Mike's response. Sue was looking for encouragement, while Mike thought she needed a critique. But he could have responded to her expressed wish by first telling her the truth—"I appreciated it"—and *then telling her what he liked about it.* If she then asked for a critique, he could give it to her—but only then. In this way, Mike could avoid giving Sue the impression that he didn't like her paper.

PROBLEM: *"I can't be spontaneous."*

Many people complain of not being able to be spontaneous in talking with their spouse—of having to be on guard. They fear their spouse will become angry, hurt, or inhibited if they are themselves. A wife says, "I have to watch every word I say to my husband. I can't be myself." A husband remarks, "If I can't be up-front with my wife, what is marriage all about?" A wife complains, "When I tell my husband anything, he reacts like a whipped cur."

Spontaneity depends on certain automatic modes of speech. It is as if we press a button and the mental machinery goes into action. We don't need time to think about what we are saying. The machinery operates effortlessly because certain patterns of speech are so "grooved" that the message simply slides out, as if it were an object riding down a chute.

But suppose we want to change how we talk to our spouse—to become more assertive, for instance, or more diplomatic. It is not really what we say that needs to change so much as the form and the style in which we say it. For example, "When will dinner be ready?" can be asked in a demanding, complaining, or accusatory way.

At first, changing to a more diplomatic or assertive mode may feel forced or unnatural. But developing new habits of speech is akin to learning any skill, such as driving a car. When I was in England several years ago, I vividly remember having to drive on the left side of the road and take wide right turns or sharp left ones—the opposite of the driving patterns in the United States. Once again, just as happened when I first learned to drive, I had to concentrate continuously. After a while, the new habits took over and I was able to drive more or less automatically again. I had changed the mold.

Conversational routines are similar to the automatic driving patterns that relieve us of having to monitor our every move on the road. After these routines have been mastered, conversation flows effortlessly, because we have developed speech habits. But when we were first learning these skills, we had to make mistakes and corrections until we had acquired the final mold.

When your spouse reacts negatively to your conversational style, then you are in the position of a driver who has to retool; you must relearn conversational modes. Retooling your speaking patterns is like learning a new way of driving. At first it may seem an effort, but over the course of time it becomes automatic.

A husband, for instance, may ask his wife for information in a demanding way or make a request in a hostile tone. His way of asking questions can be altered to sound less demanding—if he is motivated. To achieve this, the husband has to "listen to himself." (Recording and listening to your conversations on a tape recorder can be an enormous help.) Then he can gradually correct the pattern until the new way becomes automatic.

Making Civility Spontaneous. Our reactions tend to be "situation-bound"—that is, they are determined by the situations we are in. For example, in business relationships we habitually display courtesy and diplomacy. With our marital partner, we may freely express bluntness or criticism. Our reactions within marriage are caused in part by the surplus meanings we bring to the relationship and in part by the manners we learned from our original family and even from examples on television or in the movies. Many husbands and wives who contend that they would have to make drastic changes in order to be more diplomatic and considerate were the epitome of manners during their courtship. Here again, it is a matter of "situation specificity." The manners that apply specifically during courtship come to be replaced over the course of marriage by a different set of manners, embodying the residual pettiness, complaining, and faultfinding of childhood.

The real challenge is in bringing our outside manners inside the home. To learn how to speak to your spouse in a new way, think of how you would present the same question or request to a host or guest. You would frame your words in a diplomatic fashion and your tone would be pleasant. Or you could reenact the forms and etiquette that you practiced with each other prior to marriage.

There are problems in working these conventional manners into your marital relationship if you now habitually address your mate in a demanding, critical, or complaining way. If so, it will take effort to change these patterns. Habits are not easy to break. But once the new patterns are learned, you can be more civil to your spouse "spontaneously."

PROBLEM: *"My spouse yells at me all the time."*

Some people are intimidated by their spouse's loud voice, which they interpret as a sign of anger and even as a moral lapse. A wife, for instance, was raised in a family that avoided any open expression of hostility. She grew up believing that open expressions of anger were immoral; that it was sinful to hurt another person. When her husband would occasionally express himself in a loud voice, she not only became frightened but felt that what he was doing was immoral.

In such cases, both partners can work together to relieve the static produced by speaking loudly. The injured spouse has to recognize that he or she may be misinterpreting the loudness and reading hostility and anger where there is none. At the same time, the other spouse can attempt to lower his or her voice. A more elegant solution would be for the sensitive spouse to become desensitized to a loud voice or a temporary show of anger so that it no longer upsets her.

PROBLEM: *"My husband is out of contact with his feelings, and he hates to hear me talk about mine."*

        "My wife is always probing for my feelings. She wallows in her own feelings, so she wants me to wallow, too."

It seems, from both routine observations and scientific studies, that men and women usually experience and express feelings differently from each other. Women are much more inclined to emphasize the emotional side of a marital problem, whereas men tend to analyze the situation. Of course, as with most generalizations, we may find the opposite holds for a given couple.

Marjorie came home from work weighed down with disappointment over her boss's failure to acknowledge a memo she had prepared for him. She talked at great length about how bad she felt and what a "bastard" her boss was. Ken tried to reason with her and make her feel better.

MARJORIE: I have every right to feel bad. He's just a bastard.

KEN: He can't be that bad just because he didn't give you a pat on the back.

MARJORIE: You don't understand anything, do you? He has this attitude that nobody's good enough for him. Everybody in the office is upset with him.

KEN: That's no reason for you to get upset. It's probably just his style.

MARJORIE: Why are you so against having feelings? If you'd allow yourself to have some feelings, you'd be a more complete person—and you could understand me better.

KEN: There you go again—turning everything against me.

This exchange illustrates a typical, though not universal, difference between men and women in how they express their feelings. Marjorie wants to get across to Ken how hurt she is over being ignored by her boss. Ken takes a "rational" approach, in the hope of making her feel better. They are sending signals to each other over two different channels. Marjorie is talking about her feelings and her need to be comforted; Ken is talking about facts and the need to be realistic. Each believes the other is completely off-track.

Since Marjorie has introduced the subject and it is so important to her, it would be well for Ken to tune in to her channel. But adopting her perspective may seem silly to him, because he believes that *he* would take the boss's behavior in stride and that his wife is overreacting. To be helpful, however, Ken has to understand that Marjorie's ego is hurt, that she thinks her boss has been unfair.

For example, Ken could say, "I can see why you'd be upset, since you put so much effort into the memo. You expected some kind of response and he didn't pay any attention at all." He could say this without necessarily agreeing with Marjorie's conclusion—just to let her know he understands her feelings. He could resonate with her disappointment without agreeing that the boss is a bastard and unfair.

As an alternative approach, Ken could have asked a question like "Does he generally ignore the staff's memos?" Ken could also help Marjorie explore her feelings further by asking, "What do you think his attitude is to your memo?" This question might lead her to talk more about feeling slighted and, perhaps, reveal that the boss's actions made her question her own competence.

There are other ways in which Ken might react that could *aggravate* Marjorie's distress. If he had said, "Why does that upset you?" she most likely would have retorted, "Who wouldn't have been upset?" Or he might have made a belittling interpretation: "Why do you need to have people's approval all the time?"

Ken needs to realize that when Marjorie is feeling hurt, she wants a champion, a supporter, not an analyst. By using a "realistic" approach, he seemed to be condoning the boss's behavior—which, to Marjorie, meant that she had no right to feel angry. (Of course, sometimes your spouse wants only practical advice and does not want to talk about feelings. Your failure to recognize this preference may also lead to disappointment and frustration.)

Having their husbands talk about their own feelings is very important to many women. Sharing feelings makes many wives feel closer to their husbands—and vice versa. It is also an equalizer, showing that both husband and wife have emotional reactions to life's ups and downs.

A number of authors regard men's reticence about their feelings as an inevitable male shortcoming. This widely held belief is taken up by many wives: "My husband is a block of granite. If he would just let himself *feel*, he would be more of a person." Many husbands, however, resent the notion that they are incomplete if they don't reveal their feelings. Since men in general are less introspective than women, they do not seem to be as aware as women of their feelings. But even a husband who is somewhat unconnected to his own feelings can build a bridge to his wife by discussing hers. And becoming more attuned to her feelings may in turn sensitize him to his own.

PROBLEM: *"The conversation runs smoothly but the relationship is stale."*

Many relationships that seem superficially successful may nonetheless be unsatisfying for both spouses. They may operate well together in handling the family finances, making major household decisions, and bringing up happy, well-adjusted children. They may appear to be living up to the unwritten marital compact—yet they are bored, if not unhappy, with each other.

Since the partners seem to be doing everything right, we have to look beneath the surface to understand their problem. Among the many factors that might account for the absence of former joy, for the marriage's decline, is the richness—or poverty—of their conversation. Each partner no longer brings up topics that interest the other. Further, the lightness and playfulness of their earlier conversations have disappeared. They no longer make an effort to entertain or amuse each other.

What has stripped their conversation of its richness and enjoyments? First, despite the apparent success of their numerous discussions, they may have arrived at the solutions to family problems at a great cost to the relationship. In many relationships, a whole sequence of little kinks gradually adds up to produce stress. These kinks may also be a sign of important differences between the partners in their outlook and values—differences that their surface agreements never resolve. Thus, the free flow of conversation is inhibited by the threat of intrusions of unresolved conflicts. Perfectly tuned conversations are interrupted by signals of possible discord that introduce static into the communications.

Second, although the partners may get along when they are dealing with practical problems, their conversation may be devoid of references to the more pleasurable aspects of the relationship. The partners have not learned to demarcate problem-solving discussions from pleasant conversations. Thus when one partner starts a conversation with a loving comment, the other may decide that this is a good time to bring up some conflict. As a result, there is a dearth of conversation that revolves simply around expressions of caring, sharing, and loving.

Fun, Playfulness, Humor. Some marriages get bogged down in seriousness, losing all sense of playfulness. The combination of "awfulizing," "catastrophizing," and struggles casts a life-or-death pall over the relationship. Such couples, exhausted after wrangles and mutual recriminations, complain that they no longer have any "fun."

Humor is an important ingredient in enjoyable relationships—an important antidote to the grimness caused by periodic wrangles. A "marrying judge" found that when she asked couples what drew them together, a great many replied, "We laugh together." It requires finesse to appear humorous rather than sarcastic or needling. Making yourself the target of a joke works better than aiming one at your spouse.

Spouses in a troubled marriage often forget the kinds of entertainment they enjoyed prior to their conflicts. While it may seem prosaic to advocate vacations—especially trips without children—these sometimes can give a couple the time and space they need to rediscover playfulness and, perhaps, to revive a failing marriage. Other possibilities are suggested in psychiatrist William Betcher's book *Intimate Play.*

Rules of
Conversational
Etiquette

There are guidelines that can make your conversations more enjoyable as well as more effective. By following these suggestions, you will be able to prevent the kinds of glitches that impede many discussions.

Tune In to Your Partner's Channel.

▽

Give Listening Signals.

▽

Don't Interrupt.

▽

Ask Questions Skillfully.

▽

Use Diplomacy and Tact.

RULE 1: TUNE IN TO YOUR PARTNER'S CHANNEL

Having a fruitful talk demands that a husband and wife be tuned in to each other, that they connect with each other. Although they may be talking about the same topic, their approach can be so different that they fail to make meaningful contact.

Sometimes a spouse, in trying to relieve a partner's distress, accomplishes just the opposite. Judy is an artist. One evening she was quite upset by her problems in getting ready for a show, and she started to tell her husband, Cliff, about them. She wanted his support, encouragement, and sympathy. But Cliff instead fired off a barrage of instructions: "One, you've got to get all the people together in the group. Two, you have to call anyone else who is involved. Three, you want to get your accountant in on it—check with the bank to see how much money you still have. Four, you could contact the PR people. Five, call the gallery and see about the time."

Judy felt rejected by Cliff and thought, *"He doesn't care about how I feel. He just wants to get me off his back."* But in his eyes, Cliff thought that he was filling the bill. He had given her his best advice —he thought that he *was* being supportive. To Judy, however, Cliff was being controlling, not supportive. She was seeking sympathy and emotional rapport, while he was tuned in to problem solving.

How can you find the appropriate channel? One point to keep in mind is that the approach that works in impersonal or business relations may backfire in an intimate relationship. If a husband, for example, discovers that his advice only stirs up his wife, he should resist his temptation to instruct her and, instead, try another strategy, such as showing he understands her feelings. Further, the next time his wife tells him her problems, he can keep in mind that he need not plunge in with advice giving unless she clearly wants it—that she may just need to talk over her feelings.

How could Judy have acted differently, and avoided the "He doesn't understand me" trap? For one thing, she could have anticipated his tendency to give pragmatic, didactic advice and said, "I've got a problem. I think I know the answers, but I'd like to talk it out—how I *feel,* not what to do. Is that okay?" Presenting the problem in these terms would help prepare Cliff to explore her feelings rather than to construct a game plan for her.

One advantage of such clarification is that it can give couples a chance to untangle the complex web of meanings attached to a given problem. Judy's problems had many meanings for her: *"I can't handle this . . . I'm really inadequate . . . the stress of this assignment is too great . . . I can't take it."* When Cliff intervened with practical suggestions, she thought, *"He doesn't think I can handle it either . . . he doesn't care about how I* feel.*"*

By putting into words the ideas associated with her feelings, she was able to see for herself that those feelings were exaggerated. If Cliff tried to reassure her right away, she would not have the opportunity to evaluate these automatic thoughts. Through *listening attentively* and then asking questions, he could help her to see for herself that she was exaggerating the problem and minimizing her ability to handle it.

Of course, there are times when your spouse wants practical advice rather than emotional support. You have to be sensitive to the signals so that you can switch to the proper channel.

RULE 2: GIVE LISTENING SIGNALS

Sometimes a wife will complain that her husband never listens to her, while he protests that he has heard every word she says. Studies have shown a real sex-linked difference: while listening, women are much more prone to make sounds like "mhm, uh-huh," and "yeah," which indicate they are following what is being said, whereas men are more prone to silence. Other signals, such as facial expressions and subtle gestures, inform your partner that you are tuned in.

People sometimes forget that conversation means a *mutual* exchange of information and ideas. Speaking without getting feedback is like talking to a wall. If you are the silent type, it may be helpful to get into the habit of giving nonverbal feedback and not leaving your mate wondering whether you are really listening.

RULE 3: DON'T INTERRUPT

Interruptions may feel very natural to the offender but can evoke a number of negative thoughts in the person being cut off: *"He's not listening to me," "She doesn't think much of what I have to say," "He's only interested in hearing himself talk."*

As with other speech habits, interruptions may be part of a person's conversational style rather than an expression of egocentricity or disagreement—although this habit is frequently interpreted as such by the interrupted speaker. Here, too, we have a gender difference. Men tend to interrupt more than women do. They interrupt other men as much as they do women. Hence, the wife who thinks of negative explanations for her husband's interruptions should bear in mind that they may simply represent his conversational style. Nonetheless, an interrupter would do well to refrain from voicing his or her ideas until the conversational partner has finished.

RULE 4: ASK QUESTIONS SKILLFULLY

Asking questions can initiate a conversation and keep it going—or stop it prematurely. Some people are naturally reticent or inhibited, and they need to be nudged in order to be drawn into a conversation. A well-phrased question can sometimes work magic in getting your mate to talk. But a question that is poorly timed, too probing, or irrelevant can stop the flow.

Many people unwittingly stop further conversation because of their style of talking. Len, for example, habitually responded to questions with one- or two-word answers such as "yes," "no," or "nothing much." Until this habit was pointed out to him, he unintentionally thwarted most of his wife's attempts to engage him in conversation. For instance, after he came home one evening, his wife, Harriet, asked about his night out.

HARRIET: How was your poker game?

LEN: Okay.

HARRIET: Who was there?

LEN: The usual.

HARRIET: Did you talk about anything?

LEN: Nothing much.

HARRIET: Did you win or lose?

LEN: Neither.

In a case like this, instead of endlessly—and fruitlessly—plying her husband with questions, Harriet could have made a general but pointed observation, followed by a question: "I'm having trouble starting a conversation with you. Do you prefer not to talk, or is something wrong?"

On another occasion, Harriet used her ingenuity to get Len talking.

HARRIET: What happened at the hospital today?

LEN: The same old thing.

HARRIET: You said you were going to discuss your research project with your chief. How did it turn out?

LEN: Oh, he actually had some good ideas . . . [goes on to discuss this at some length].

Len's first response was a *conversation stopper,* but with some finesse and an artful query, Harriet was able to prod him on. This follow-up question method indicates to a taciturn spouse that you are really interested. An initial question may be regarded as perfunctory, but a sequence of questions shows you have a serious interest. A good *conversation starter* is to ask your partner's opinion on a matter.

HE: I wonder if you have any ideas about what I should do about my assistant? He's always late.

SHE: Have you considered asking him why he's late all the time?

HE: No, but I suppose I could—that's a good idea.

Sometimes the way a question is phrased may choke off conversation. *Why* questions are frequently conversation stoppers because they seem to have an accusatory tone: "Why were you home late yesterday?" "Why are you all dressed up?" It may be difficult to avoid *why* questions at times; if so, it is best to find some other way of phrasing them should they make your spouse defensive (see Chapter 5).

RULE 5: USE DIPLOMACY AND TACT

This rule might seem out of place in intimate relationships, yet practically everybody has sensitive areas—and even a loving, well-intentioned spouse can injure them. For example, some people are sensitive about their appearance, or the way they speak, or certain members of their family. If, for instance, in the course of conversation a wife implies that her husband is overweight, or his sister is immature, or his grammar is incorrect, she may put an end to pleasant conversation. This rule does not mean that you have to walk on egg-shells—it merely calls for awareness and judgment.

Most of the advice in this chapter applies to casual conversations, not to more serious discussions about such issues as resolving conflicts and making decisions. I have found that unless couples make an effort to keep light conversations separate, they drift into more serious discussions that take much of the lightness out of the relationship. In the next chapter, I address the difficulties that arise when couples grapple with the above-mentioned issues of resolving conflicts and making decisions.

❧ 15 ❧

THE ART
OF WORKING
TOGETHER

Explanation of Differences

Sometimes partners work themselves into such opposing positions that they seem incapable of reaching even a compromise. They dig their heels in, sticking stubbornly to their own point of view. They see their own views as eminently reasonable and those of their partner as unreasonable. Above all, they cannot recognize or acknowledge that their partner's wishes or complaints might be legitimate.

Take the following example:

SALLY: Tom and I can't get together on anything. We quarrel about everything. We had a big fight over opening the window at night.

TOM: She opens it and I close it and she opens it again. I just can't stand the cold draft. It makes my asthma worse.

ATB (*to Sally*): Why do you suppose Tom wants it closed?

SALLY: He says it makes his asthma worse. He coddles himself just like a baby.

ATB (*to Tom*): Why does she want the window open?

TOM: She's a fresh-air fiend. She believes in toughening herself. The colder she gets, the better she likes it.

ATB: What's behind your positions? What problem are you trying to solve?

SALLY: I can't stand the stale air. It's so stuffy it makes me nauseated.

TOM: I can't stand the draft.

Once an argument starts, each party tries to score points. No matter who "wins," however, the real issue between them is seldom resolved. Getting your way does not change the underlying conflicts. What solution can you think of to the problem of the window?

In approaching such a conflict it is essential to try to *clarify* the other's position and then be receptive—rather than antagonistic—to suggestions so you can focus on the problem at hand. Don't get sidetracked, for instance, by the needling (being called a coddler or fresh-air fiend). A systematic approach helps to clear the air. Asking specific questions, as I did in the following exchange, gets to the crucial information:

ATB: Now you know we have been through these problem-solving exercises before. First, you have to clarify exactly what it is in the situation that displeases you. Now, Sally, in just two or three words, tell me why you want the room cold.

SALLY: I want it cold—so I won't suffocate.

ATB: Now, Tom, in a nutshell, what is it that you don't like about the cold air?

TOM: It's the draft.

ATB: So we know that it is not so much the temperature that is producing your disagreement but the circulation of air. Sally, you don't like the warm air because it is not circulating. Tom, you don't like the cold air when the window is open because it is circulating too much. In other words, you get a draft. Now, let's generate some possible solutions.

TOM: I guess we could open the window just an inch or so, or we could install a fan to circulate the air, or I guess we could completely turn off the heat in the house and then the room would really be cold.

SALLY: None of those ideas are any good. How about if you just bundled yourself up with a lot of covers?

TOM: That wouldn't work, because I would still be breathing in the cold air.

ATB: There is one other solution that you have not yet come up with . . . and that is to open the window in the adjoining bathroom. In that way, Sally, you can get your cold air—which will circulate faster than warm, stuffy air. And Tom, you can be spared having a draft.

They agreed that this was a feasible solution. I then suggested that in the future—instead of automatically assuming that their partner is wrong, selfish, or obstinate—they make a systematic effort to solve a problem: (1) to define what each wants, (2) to determine the specifics of their differences, (3) to brainstorm until they have generated a variety of possible solutions, and (4) to select the solution that satisfies each of them the most.

LEVELS OF DISAGREEMENT

Why do couples get into arguments that progress into all-out battles? There are two general kinds of marital fights. In the first, there is no genuine disagreement between the mates, but the ways in which they talk to each other and hear each other are so filled with static that their messages become garbled. In the other variety of discord, there is a real conflict that needs to be resolved. Of course, most arguments combine a genuine conflict and poor communication. Fights are aggravated by the fact that as the partners assume contrary positions, their perspectives of each other and of the problem tend to be strongly polarized; thus, mild differences become charged into seemingly polar opposites. To resolve differences, it is helpful to pinpoint what kind of conflict is at work.

DIFFERENCES IN SPECIFIC WISHES

Some disagreements are transient. At a particular time, one partner might like to have Chinese food, the other Mexican. One might like to go out to the movies, the other prefers to stay home and watch television. One might favor conversations, the other reading the paper. When such wishes do not reflect basic disagreements and tastes, but simply momentary differences, they are easily resolved—unless there is already friction in the relationship. When tension already exists, then temporary differences in what each partner wants may be magnified into a real conflict.

DIFFERENCES IN TASTES OR SENSITIVITIES

All couples differ to some degree in the activities they prefer. Many husbands get their greatest enjoyment out of watching sports on weekends, while their wives would prefer spending weekend time together in a more personal way. As a marriage matures, the couple's tastes may become more similar: a wife with little interest in athletics "learns" to enjoy spectator sports, attending sporting events, or playing tennis or golf; a husband with little interest in music or literature develops a taste for symphonies, opera, or reading. Of course, people also differ not only in what they like but in what they dislike—Sally liked the windows wide open in the winter, while Tom could not stand them that way.

DIFFERENCES IN POLICY, ATTITUDE, OR PHILOSOPHY

Some partners have vastly different attitudes about child rearing, budgeting, division of labor, vacations, and the like. One mate may believe in being strict with the children, the other may favor leniency; one may consider spending money a great pleasure, the other may consider it a sin; one may consider vacations without the children as a special treat, the other may regard it as an unnecessary indulgence. When it comes to specific issues, the partners may dig in their heels and defend their points of view, on the one hand, or they may attempt to be flexible, accommodating, and compromising, on the other.

DIFFERENCES IN PERSONALITY

It is ironic that basic personality differences that may have initially attracted people to each other, and been highly valued during the relationship's early years, can become the source of difficulties as time progresses. You may recall such a conflict in the personalities of Karen and Ted. Karen loved doing things on the spur of the moment, whereas Ted's personality called for meticulous planning and organization. Their personality differences were reflected in differences in their perspectives—in the ways that they viewed the same event and, ultimately, themselves. Each saw him- or herself as reasonable, agreeable, and flexible, and the other as disagreeable, unreasonable, and rigid.

DIFFERENCES IN PERSPECTIVE

Sometimes the most mundane differences are blown all out of proportion because of mates' different perspectives. The partners are so blinded by their self-interest that they fail to perceive simple solutions to their differences. For example, Sally and Tom had difficulties with the division of labor around the house. Each was so busy at work that there was little time for household duties. Interestingly, during courtship, they had no problem doing things for each other, even when it meant making a real sacrifice. Tom would wait in a long line to get opening-night tickets to the opera and get dressed up in formal clothes to please Sally, and she would go sailing with him even though it made her feel queasy.

A few years after they were married, however, they had shifted to thinking in terms of self-interest. This shift from altruism to egocentricity was apparent in the different ways they saw the same problem. The difficulty was a "cognitive" one: they could size up a problem from their own personal viewpoints only; neither could see it from the standpoint of the other.

A few days after a counseling appointment, Sally and Tom needed to get some groceries, but both were very busy. They tried to apply my suggestions about problem solving.

TOM: Since you're busy, I'll go to the delicatessen and buy them.

SALLY: Okay, I'll make out the shopping list.

TOM: Good. Call the order in so I won't have to wait, and I'll pick it up in a half-hour.

SALLY: I don't have time to call it in. I'm tired and busy. It wouldn't kill you if you took in the order and waited around the store while they filled it.

TOM: But I'll have to wait in line. You know I hate to wait around. You're being unreasonable.

SALLY: You're the unreasonable one.

Sally and Tom got into an argument over who was unreasonable and completely forgot their assignment to try to clarify differences and then brainstorm for solutions. Neither paid attention to the discomfort imposed on the other by the plans they had suggested: Tom was painfully restless when he had to wait, and Sally felt so strained at that moment by household responsibilities that phoning in the list herself made her burden seem overwhelming.

Since they forgot about generating possible solutions, neither thought of the most reasonable one—for Tom to phone in the order! That would have relieved Sally of the burden of phoning in the list and spared Tom a wait in line. Since Sally was the partner who customarily made the phone calls when something was needed, it had not occurred to them to shift roles in this instance.

Couples can slip easily into seeing disagreements only from their own perspective, not recognizing that their mate might have a reasonable point. That leads them to believe that their mates are being bullheaded, bossy, or unreasonable. But when they can see things from the mate's perspective, it may then appear that both are "right" —at least from their own frame of reference. Both Sally and Tom had a valid point, but they failed to see the other's perspective because they were locked into their own.

Use of Questioning

Many couples who are devoted and wish to accommodate to each other's wishes or needs have failed to develop habits of communication that will help them avoid misunderstandings. For example, few couples whom I have interviewed use questioning in a skillful manner.

Though questions are a prime way to get information, they also *give* information. Thus, the partner who is asked may confuse information requesting and information giving. Let's examine a conversation between Sally and Tom, each of whom is trying to be accommodating to the other. Sally notices that Tom is tired. To display her concern and cheer him up, she initiates the following dialogue (note that the conversation starts with a question):

SALLY: Do you want to visit the Bakers tonight?

TOM: Okay.

SALLY: Do you really want to go?

TOM: [in a loud, irritated-sounding voice] I said okay.

SALLY: [hurt] If you really don't want to go, we can stay home.

TOM: Why are you giving me a hard time?

SALLY: [indignant] I was just trying to be considerate, and you make it into a fight.

Sally saw that Tom was tired and thought he would like to visit some friends. Because she wasn't certain that this was what he wanted to do, however, she had reservations about the suggestion and asked him in a somewhat tentative manner.

Tom took the tentative-sounding question as a hint that *she* really wanted to go. He felt he was being controlled or manipulated but decided that it would be a good idea to oblige Sally. In his mind, the question wasn't really whether he wanted to go but whether he would be a sport and accommodate her. Consequently, in the spirit of cooperation, he said yes.

Sally, noting the hesitation in his response, thought she may have inadvertently pushed him and thus wanted to give him the chance to back out. Tom felt cornered, though. Here he was trying to be accommodating, and Sally was pressing him and going to make him look like a "heavy" if he said that he didn't really want to go. He knew that she liked to do things with other people more than he did. He wanted to satisfy her and did not want to be "exposed" as antisocial. Thus, her questioning put him on the spot.

Tom's reaction seemed illogical to Sally. Why was he getting angry when she was trying to find out what his wishes were? She wondered what was wrong with him. He always seemed so illogical to her when they talked about social arrangements. His hostility outraged her because it seemed not just illogical but unfair.

Because of their history of misunderstandings, Sally and Tom have to pay more attention to the art of questioning than one might expect. While Sally's question certainly seems legitimate, the fact that it contains a suggestion ("visit the Bakers") connotes to Tom that she is being self-serving and manipulative in this situation, and not asking him a mere question. While further counseling would address Tom's hypersensitivity, Sally could have avoided even this conflict and granted his wishes priority had she used a different style of questioning. Instead of the narrow, yes-or-no question, she could have used one of the following approaches:

Open-ended question: "What would you like to do tonight?" If this works, it is fine. But it might simply evoke an indefinite "I don't know."

Multiple-choice question: Start with two choices: "Would you like to go out or stay home?" If Tom elected to go out, Sally could have said, "Would you like to visit anybody, or should just the two of us go out?" By following this line of questioning, she would have made clearer her intent to please him, and so would not have appeared manipulative.

When Sally found that Tom was reacting negatively to her idea, she could have backed off, remaining silent for a while to give him a chance to consider it. But because she assumed too much responsibility, she pressed too hard.

The next time the situation arose, Sally (after some coaching from me) used a different style of questioning.

SALLY: You look tired. Would you consider going to the movies or would you prefer to stay home?

TOM: Let me think about it . . . what would you prefer?

SALLY: Tonight I want to do what you want.

In this case, the dialogue was straightforward. Sally was clear that she was giving Tom his options. Tom in turn asked for time out to consider what he really wanted to do, but on the chance that she had hidden motives, he tested the waters by asking what she would prefer. She then was given the opportunity to make it clear to him that she sincerely wanted to follow his preference.

Sally might complain, "Why is it always necessary for me to say things just so? Why is he so touchy that he reacts negatively when I'm trying to be considerate?" The answer, of course, is that Tom is hypersensitive to being controlled. But by skillful questioning, Sally can build bonds of trust with Tom.

Flexibility

Some couples who have much in common, who are tender and loving when not fighting, flare up nonetheless when they have to make fairly simple decisions, such as arranging time together. They may be living by such rigid—though unspoken—rules that any resolution of their conflicts seems impossible. Take the following conversation I had with a couple, married for fifteen years, who were affectionate and loyal to each other, but unable to keep themselves free of endless petty arguments. Frances, a librarian, kept formulating rules and restrictions that Steven, an outgoing, smooth-talking audio equipment salesman, kept breaking.

FRANCES: We love each other a great deal, but we don't agree on anything.

STEVEN: We do agree on lots of things.

FRANCES: There you go again, disagreeing with me again! [Both laugh.]

ATB: Give me an example of your disagreement.

FRANCES: When I come home from work I'm famished, but Steven never comes home on time, so we end up eating late. If he really wanted to, he could rearrange his work schedule.

STEVEN: I can't rearrange it because most of my customers come in late in the day. When I can come home early, I do eat with her, but sometimes I simply have to eat late.

ATB (TO FRANCES): On the days Steven is late, how about just eating by yourself—I mean, you can eat when you get home and then Steven can eat later.

FRANCES: Oh, I couldn't do that . . . married people should eat together.

ATB: Of course it's good to eat together, but if your insistence is causing you to fight, aren't you better off without that rule?

In this instance, it took much effort for Frances to change her rules. She tended to see things in absolute terms. Any change in these *shoulds* was like a sin. As it turned out, her absolute rules led not only to bickering but also to a silent rebellion by Steven.

Steven had had a domineering mother. As a child, he had developed a whole array of strategies to undermine her, and he automatically used these same strategies with Frances. For instance, her strict insistence on eating together, keeping the house immaculate, and always being punctual irked Steven. In response, he would undercut her by being late when he did not need to, spending money more freely than she wanted, and putting off attending to household chores.

In their division of responsibilities, Frances took care of the budget and the credit and checking accounts. Every month she discovered that Steven had made various purchases without first discussing them with her. Steven, however, always professed ignorance of the charges —until Frances was able to demonstrate that he had made them. If Frances's standards were absolute and her actions domineering, Steven's response was what we call "passive-aggressive"—that is, in his own passive way, he was "aggressing" against Frances—frustrating and exasperating her.

In therapy, I was able to persuade them to adopt a different approach to each other. Frances ultimately agreed to test the hypothesis that if she would relax her standards, they would live more harmoniously together—a higher goal than meeting the standards themselves. Steven agreed to be less devious so that Frances would "get off my case."

Setting this up as an experiment meant that neither had to make a long-range commitment to the changes without knowing the pay-off first. If the experiment worked, these changes would then be an incentive for each of them to keep the new patterns alive. As it happens, the experiment did work, and Frances and Steven were able to get along much better.

RELAXING RIGID STANDARDS AND ABSOLUTE RULES

In a perfect world, we could have absolute, enlightened standards to guide us in leading our lives. As it happens, however, our standards are rarely enlightened, and our world is so complex that very few standards can be absolute. In fact, when people do have rigid standards, they are likely to be modeled on what they observed during their childhood—or rebelled against—or derived from "professional" advice (which may be of questionable validity), or from their own internal fears and doubts.

In fact, the more absolute the standards, the more likely they are to be based on fears and self-doubts, and so the more rigidly they are adhered to. Take the common areas in which couples are likely to clash: division of labor, expenditures, leisure activities, families and friends, children, and sex.

There are no absolute rules for how work at home should be divided. For example, Frances expected to do the domestic chores but insisted that Steven take care of the maintenance of the house and outside grounds. However, since Frances was home more often when plumbers, electricians, and other technical workers could come to the house, it would have been more efficient for her to take over these details occasionally. And even though Steven enjoyed cooking some-times, Frances clung to the notion that this was the wife's job.

When couples clash about expenditures, it is usually because one member of the couple is freer than the other at spending. Often, as in the case of Steven and Frances, this leads to one partner's nagging about overspending and the other's sabotaging the budget.

Some of the most common absolute standards concern child rear-ing. Drawing on their own past, each partner may have a very differ-ent view of how best to raise the children—how to handle issues like schoolwork, household chores, allowances, leisure time, and friends. In fact, the same sort of rules that cause clashes between the parents can also produce conflict between the parents and children.

Child rearing requires an enormous amount of flexibility. No two children are alike; what works well for one child may be counterpro-ductive for the next. Further, as children grow, old rules no longer apply, and once-successful strategies no longer work. Parents need to be flexible enough to change the rules and techniques they use. To do so, they need to be adaptable enough with each other in modifying their own rules.

HIDDEN FEARS AND SELF-DOUBTS

As we have seen, hidden fears and self-doubts are often at work when a person holds rigidly to a particular set of ideas. In setting policies for the children, for instance, Frances had the underlying catastrophic idea *"If I don't bring them up just right, they will be ruined for life."* Consequently, she had an overwhelming sense of responsibility. Ste-ven's point of view, on the other hand, was *"The children are only young once, and we should try to enjoy them as much as possible . . . if we are too hard on them, they'll have a bad time and won't like us."* Thus, Frances's rules were directed toward inculcating character and discipline, whereas Steven's goals were directed toward achieving pleasure and harmony.

As a couple's points of view become polarized, those views become harder to change. Each mate tends to see his or her point of view as "right" and the partner's as "wrong." This labeling may take on a moralistic hue, so that one partner perceives him- or herself as "good" and the other as "bad." Actually, Steven's and Frances's attitudes could have been reconciled as complementary rather than in opposi-tion to each other. Children need *both* discipline and fun—and if the parents can be flexible in merging their goals, they can provide the best mixture.

Concerns about money also may involve fears and self-doubts. Frances had a hidden fear: *"We will go broke the way Steven spends money."* Her own family had suffered financial reversals when she was young, and she feared that history would repeat itself. However, Steven's attitude was *"You should enjoy it while you can."* His hidden fear was that he might die prematurely, as had several of his uncles, or that he might become incapacitated and thus not be able to enjoy his money.

SELF-QUESTIONING

Most people who have hidden fears such as those of Frances or Steven are not aware how much these fears contribute to their rigid standards and expectations. With some effort, however, they can pinpoint these underlying fears and then judge their validity. Frances, for example, used the following line of questioning *on herself* (the *why* technique) to peel away layers in her thinking, until she got to the hidden fear at the center:

EXPECTATION: I have to be strict with the children.

Q: Why?

A: Because it's proper.

Q: Why?

A: Because children have to have good standards.

Q: Why?

A: Because they'll get into trouble if they don't.

Once the hidden fear ("they'll get into trouble") was uncovered, Frances had to ask herself a series of questions to test this fear against her actual experience with the children:

Q: What is the evidence that they will get into trouble if you aren't strict?

A: I don't know.

Q: Does strictness guarantee that children will stay out of trouble?

A: Not always.

Q: What happens when you're strict with the children?

A: They sometimes rebel.

Q: Do you think that an alternative method—such as setting a good example and being more flexible—could give them the proper values?

A: Possibly.

At this point, Frances and Steven tried an experiment: work together on being less strict (Frances) and less indulgent (Steven) to see how this new program works. Over the course of time, Frances did ease up and Steven became less indulgent with himself and the children —which made life more enjoyable for both spouses.

Compromise

Compromising can be difficult for a number of psychological reasons. For instance, if a person like Frances has particularly rigid standards, then any compromise means violating these standards, and so *doing something wrong*.

Among other psychological meanings, to compromise may mean to give in. To Frances, giving in meant not only sacrificing her own standards but surrendering control to Steven. She had a deep fear that if Steven was in control, his "sloppy attitude" would lead to chaos. The very rigidity of her rules "protected" her from ever again having to experience the disarray that had occurred in her family when her father lost his job and the children lost "direction."

To Steven, on the other hand, *any compromise meant a total victory for Frances*. According to his frame of reference, their differences represented a power struggle. If Frances won a concession, then he was "defeated." For him, such a "defeat" was demoralizing; it cut deeply into his own self-esteem, his image of himself. Thus, opposing Frances—even passively—was a way of keeping his self-esteem intact.

Both partners were governed by their fears and doubts. Frances's reaction to the idea of compromise was *"If I give in, he'll run all over me"* and *"If I am right and don't do what's right, something awful will happen."* Steven's thought was *"If she gets her own way, then I'm nothing."*

BEHIND THE POWER STRUGGLE

Another factor in inflexibility is the hardening of positions as partners jockey for power. It may be impossible to find a compromise until each becomes aware that he or she has a fixed perspective and tries to understand the perspective of the other.

Changing perspectives, of course, is often difficult. To one partner, such a change might mean *"I have lost the battle."* To another, changing perspectives may require much internal work. People are often irritated at having to make such a shift.

Interestingly, the more absolutely convinced partners are of the validity of their positions, the greater the possibility that they are overlooking something that contradicts their convictions. In this situation, it would be beneficial for each partner to try to take the stance *"I could be wrong."*

Accommodation

No couple is a perfect fit. As we have seen, differences in style or temperament are often the features that attract couples to each other in the first place. Later on, though, these same attractive differences can rub partners the wrong way. Thus, Karen's vivacity and impulsivity, which excited Ted early in their relationship, later troubled him; they came to represent frivolity and shallowness, disrupting his routine. And Ted's ability to organize their leisure time pleased Karen before marriage, while later these same organizational skills only suggested his stuffiness and stodginess.

As marriages mature, such differences can become blended in the relationship so that, for instance, the wife's impulsiveness melds neatly with her husband's need to plan in advance. In order to achieve such a blend, however, the spouses have to recognize the following:

1/There are, inevitably, significant differences between partners.

2/You need to accept the differences and overlook your partner's rough spots. When relationships are stormy, many of the idiosyncrasies and mannerisms that were once accepted or not even recognized seem to become continuous irritants.

3/When you view them from a different perspective—through reframing—you may find an attractive quality in these differences. For example, Sharon came to value the flip side of Paul's lack of seriousness: he could always make her laugh.

4/Capitalizing on the differences strengthens a partnership. For example, Ted could count on Karen's vivaciousness to add life to.their relationship; Karen could count on Ted's organization to make sure that their budget was balanced, that bills were paid on time, and that vacation plans were not left hanging in the air.

In successful relationships, couples learn to participate in each other's favored activities and to accept each other's peculiarities. In long-standing relationships, partners even come to resemble each other in their habits and preferences—even in their facial expressions and appearance.

Setting Priorities

The question of whose priorities are going to be honored in a particular situation is very delicate. When partners try to be accommodating, they may be misunderstood and thus feel abused or unjustly treated.

Most couples realize that neither partner can get his or her way all the time, that there must be some balance. However, the decisions can't be made simply on the basis of a rigid formula such as "Last time we did what *you* wanted, now it's *my* turn." A spouse might have very strong feelings about a given activity at one time, and at other times, he or she might have only mild feelings for or against it. Sensitive negotiations have to take into account not only the spouse's preference but also the *strength* of that preference.

It helps for each partner to state how strongly he or she feels about the options. For example, instead of asking his wife what she would like to do, a husband could state, "I am really in the mood to go to the movies tonight." If his wife demurs with the reply "I'm not much in the mood but I'll go if you want to," he can then return with a sincere comment like "It's really important for me" or "It's not really all that important." It is essential at this point that the husband give an honest answer, because if it is dishonest or sarcastic or cryptic, then further negotiations can get tangled up. By telling his wife what he believes she wants to hear rather than what he really feels, the husband sends a confusing message. Further, his wife may take this ambiguity as an indication that he is not being honest with her, and she may distrust the sincerity of his stated feelings in future discussions.

Although the term *negotiations* may seem to be impersonal or even imply a conflict, the fact remains that many decisions do involve negotiations. Often, particularly in the early stages of a relationship, the partners are sufficiently tuned in to each other's wishes—and sufficiently concerned with pleasing each other—to carry out these negotiations subtly and to quickly arrive at a mutually satisfactory decision.

Consider Cliff and Judy, whose negotiations got muddled:

CLIFF: Why don't we skip going to your parents for Christmas this year? We can either stay home, which would be a relief for me, or we could visit my parents.

JUDY: You never want to see my parents. You always avoid them, and you complain when we do see them.

CLIFF: [*She opposes me on everything.*] That's not true. We saw them last Christmas, and they already bunked in with us twice this year. [Raises voice] It's just that enough is enough. It's a drag.

JUDY: Stop yelling at me!

CLIFF: How am I yelling? I can't believe this. You try to control everything I say or do.

JUDY: There you go again. Always feeling sorry for yourself.

CLIFF: Stop picking on me!

JUDY: You're making me crazy!

How could they have done it differently? Cliff and Judy could have defused a potentially explosive problem by determining the relative importance of their desires:

HE: I wonder if we might skip going to your parents this year? I've been awfully tired lately and would appreciate having a breather around Christmas. If we want to celebrate, we can do it with my folks [who live just around the corner].

SHE: I would really like to see my parents this year.

HE: You know we went there last year, and we've already seen them twice this year.

SHE: I know. But it's not really Christmas unless I'm with my parents.

HE: How important is it to go to your parents this year?

SHE: On a ten-point scale, it's a ten. How important is it for you to stay home?

HE: On a ten-point scale, I guess it's about a five.

SHE: I guess the tens have it. [She laughs.]

HE: I guess you're right.

This chapter has presented some principles for resolving differences and making decisions in the course of a day's activities. In the next chapter, I will discuss how partners can clarify their differences in meetings that are especially set aside for such discussions.

TROUBLESHOOTING

Clarification of Differences

Some partners are angry at each other so much of the time that almost any exchange is likely to include some carry-over from previous fractious encounters. Chapter 17 will discuss ways to stem this overflow through "ventilation sessions," in which the grievances and accusations can be thoroughly aired. Such sessions include special rules for setting limits on the expression of hostility. If you and your mate are so continuously angry at each other that you can't talk things over without trading insults, you might want to read Chapter 17 first.

This chapter will give you guidelines on how to troubleshoot—that is, how to clarify and respond to your mate's complaints and requests. By following—and practicing—a number of techniques, you will be able to get a more specific picture of a problem and so better lay the groundwork for its solution. Complaints, conflicts, and problems are usually best dealt with at specially scheduled troubleshooting sessions.

Among the guidelines for clarifying your mate's grievance and understanding his or her perspective are the following:

1/ *Do not try to defend yourself, make excuses, or counterattack.*
Although your mate's complaint may be a gross exaggeration and seem unfair or unreasonable, try to be as objective as possible—assume the role of an investigator rather than a defendant.

2/ *Try to clarify precisely what you have done—or not done—that has upset your mate.*

This may take some detective work if your spouse makes vague, global statements such as "You never do what you promise" or "You're just a mean person" or "You're filled with hate." Asking a question like "Can you give me a specific example?" is the key to clarification. Reducing a global grievance to a specific problem puts you in a better position to deal with it.

3/ Give a capsule summary of your mate's complaints.

To be sure that you understand the precise nature of your mate's concerns, give him or her feedback, paraphrasing what seems to be the essence of the complaints. After further clarification, you should give your mate a *summary* of the complaints to determine whether you have understood them.

As practice in clarification, I gave Ted and Karen a summary of these principles and asked that they try them in my presence. Karen had been annoyed at Ted for several days but had postponed discussing her annoyance until their joint meeting with me. Their discussion went as follows:

KAREN: [angrily] You're a wet blanket. You don't like people. You only like to stay home and bury yourself in your books.

TED: [good-naturedly] Am I really that bad?

KAREN: [somewhat amused] You're much worse than that. I'm painting a rosy picture.

TED: Can you be more specific?

KAREN: You know when you're being antisocial.

TED: I'm not sure of that. [asking for specifics] Can you give me an example?

KAREN: Last week, I suggested that we call up the Browns to go to the movies with us, and you got annoyed with me because we hadn't already planned it out. If you haven't planned something years ahead, you never want to do it.

At this point, Ted might have responded defensively to Karen's criticism, but he tried to stick to the guideline about ferreting out what could be a legitimate grievance. By "keeping his eye on the ball," Ted was able to steer the conversation on a constructive course.

TED: [capsule summary] Are you saying that you would like me to be more flexible—do things on the spur of the moment?

KAREN: [still irritated] Yes, if you weren't so rigid, we'd both be happier.

TED: [holds his fire and tries to bring about a resolution] I actually wasn't in the mood to see other people that night. But I guess you thought I was being antisocial.

KAREN: [still won't give up] But it happens all the time.

TED: Perhaps this is something I can work on.

KAREN: [uncertain] Okay.

You may have noticed that Ted and Karen did not follow all the rules for clarifying—Ted offered an alibi prematurely. However, this was their first attempt, and it seemed important to Ted to explain how he really felt about social engagements. The solution would come later.

Part of the reason that Karen was unrelenting in her complaint was that Ted's strong emphasis on planning frustrated her desire to do things spontaneously. She did not as yet realize that her own impulsive style clashed with Ted's more studied, deliberate one. His style was actually no more rigid than hers—it was simply different—but Karen experienced Ted's failure to agree immediately to her suggestions as rigidity. As it turned out, it was easier for Ted to change his style than it was for Karen to change hers.

As their discussion continued, Ted revealed that though he wanted more of a social life, he frequently felt awkward around others. He believed he needed time to prepare himself when they were going to see people with whom he wasn't comfortable. Ted told Karen, "I was thinking about what you said about my being rigid. I don't think you understand. I *do* like people. It's just that I'm not secure socially."

There were two positive outcomes from this exchange. Ted was able to pinpoint precisely the pattern that upset Karen and was motivated to do something about it. Karen, for the first time, felt that Ted was "hearing" her. In later discussions Karen was to discover, to her relief, that Ted was willing to make social engagements on the spot even though his social anxiety dampened his enthusiasm in responding to her impromptu suggestions.

In summary, the art of clarification consists of the complaining mate's stating the grievance freely, with the other mate assuming the role of an investigator rather than a defendant. The steps consist of making no excuses or counterattacks, pinpointing the specific actions of the complaint, and reaching a consensus on the particulars of the upsetting incident. After the conflict has been clarified in this way, the next task is to seek solutions.

Understanding Your Mate's Perspective

Sometimes couples who follow the principles of good communication with the best of intentions still find that their discussions lead only to further frustration, futility, and antagonism. This occurs in part because they assess the problem and the roles they play in it from quite different perspectives. Instead of clarifying their differences, the discussions accentuate them.

Although reconciliation requires that each mate try to see the other's perspective, this can be difficult since the spouse's perspective can be hard to identify and even harder to comprehend. Further, clashing perspectives may arouse such antagonism that it seems impossible for each mate to assume an objective stance and question the other in a neutral way. Nonetheless, if one mate assumes the role of an investigator, not inquisitor, it may be possible to clarify the other's point of view.

"Data collection" can be facilitated if the investigating spouse motivates his or her partner to report automatic thoughts. In this way the mate can check out whether his or her mind reading, for example, is correct (Chapter 13). By using finesse—backed up by a reservoir of good will—mates should be able to get a grasp of each other's perspective. Once they have reached this goal, they are in a position to reconcile their differences and find a practical solution.

Let's tune in on Cliff and Judy. For the five years of their marriage, Cliff has been a salesman. Recently, he has been promoted to sales manager; consequently, he is spending part of his time selling and part of his time supervising other salesmen.

Week one: Judy complains that they have not been sharing enough good times and suggests that they spend more time together at home. She is feeling somewhat pessimistic. In the back of her mind is the recurrent worry *"Can Cliff really change?"* Cliff agrees with Judy's concerns and promises to modify his schedule so as to accommodate her desires. He pledges to reduce the number of his customers and to cut back on the number of hours away from home. At this point, their communication and intentions are good.

Two weeks later: Judy has become increasingly irritated at Cliff. Her recurring thoughts are *"Nothing has changed . . . things are getting worse instead of better . . . Cliff is stuck in the same old pattern . . . he will never change, no matter how often he promises."*

A dinnertime phone call for Cliff precipitates a breakdown in effective communication. Judy overhears the conversation, in which Cliff is apparently talking to another potential customer and seems willing to take him on. She thinks, *"Why does he keep on talking . . . the dinner is going to get cold . . . he knows I hate it when he interrupts our meals this way . . . he said he would reduce the number of his customers . . . I can't trust anything he says."*

After the phone call is over, Judy and Cliff have the following interchange (I had previously coached Cliff on being an investigator, and he tried to apply the principles as they talked):

JUDY: You said you were going to cut back on your accounts [scolding instead of clarifying].

CLIFF: But he is a very important account and can bring in a lot of income [being defensive].

JUDY: You're always making exceptions. You said that you were going to change, and you haven't changed at all [criticizing].

CLIFF: You never notice any of the positive things I do. I've changed in a lot of ways over the last couple of weeks, and you haven't noticed it [counterattacking, but also presenting new information—which is doomed because it is perceived as a counterattack].

JUDY: I haven't noticed it because it hasn't happened.

CLIFF: That's not fair. You know I am spending more time at home in the morning. Besides, I've turned down a lot of accounts in the past two weeks— you just didn't know about it [providing more new data].

JUDY: Just because you spend time at home doesn't mean anything to me. You are always working at your desk. You're just a body sitting there as far as I'm concerned [ignoring new data and still attacking].

CLIFF: All you want is for me to stay home—you never want me to go to work. I thought that if I worked at home, that would satisfy you [counterattacking].

JUDY: It doesn't satisfy me if I can't talk to you. You are married to your job. Even when you're home you're thinking about it all the time, and we never talk about anything besides your work.

CLIFF: You think that I only work for the fun of it. You don't realize that I'm doing this for both of us. You act as though I'm doing all this to spite you.

At this point, Cliff backs off to get a better perspective of what's happening, and he recognizes a number of problems. First, they have both been attacking each other's positions instead of clarifying their own. Second, he recognizes that he had not previously informed Judy of his efforts to cut back. Cliff had incorrectly assumed, as happens with many couples, that his partner had been aware of his constructive acts without his telling her about them. Also, he realizes his error in thinking that spending work time at home counts as time spent together. Finally, he tells himself that Judy's anger is understandable in view of her lack of information.

Fortunately, Cliff shifts to constructive problem solving and tries to get a feeling for Judy's position. He adopts an investigative role by paraphrasing her complaint:

CLIFF: The problem seems to be that you feel that I don't give you my undivided attention when I work at home. When I have long phone calls, that's not giving you attention. Is that right? [checking out his understanding]

JUDY: Well, it's not so much the attention. It means that I am less important to you than your business. If you really wanted to, you could arrange things better.

Judy is reassured that Cliff seems to understand her position. He then comes up with a constructive suggestion—that they make definite plans to do things together, perhaps to go out to dinner periodically and plan a vacation. Judy skeptically agrees.

There are several key aspects of their interchange: (1) Judy was able to describe the problem in terms that Cliff could comprehend, (2) Cliff was able to convey that he had already taken action on their agreement and thus modified Judy's belief that he could not change, (3) Cliff was able to understand Judy's perspective and to define their precise problem—the *quality* rather than quantity of their time together, (4) having defined the problem, Cliff and Judy agreed on a constructive course of action. Judy is still skeptical because she needs evidence that Cliff will follow through on the plan.

We should be aware that ideas like going out to dinner or scheduling a vacation are frequently proposed as solutions to such problems but do not necessarily solve them. They fail when the couple jumps at a solution without realizing exactly what the problem is. In some cases, for example, one of the spouses might feel too bound to the other and would like to have time alone. Sometimes premature solutions are worse than no solution at all, because when they fail to succeed, they are construed as "one more failure." Thus, it is essential during clarifying discussions to make sure that the solution is relevant to the problem.

Although there is no need for partners to act as psychiatrists toward each other, they can steer clear of some shoals in the relationship if they are aware of their mate's hypersensitivities and symbolic beliefs. One problem that was not addressed in the Cliff-Judy exchange was Judy's complaint of not being valued. Behind this lurked the hidden fear that if she desperately needed help, she could not count on Cliff. If not dealt with, such fears can thwart problem solving. In this case, Judy would have to describe her fear of abandonment, and Cliff would have to address it, in order for them to arrive at an effective solution.

Specific Rules for Troubleshooting Sessions

Many couples find it useful to set aside a specific time for discussing issues or problems. It is probably best to bring up just one or two problems at the first session lest you swamp your mate and start an unproductive, knock-down-drag-out fight. Below are general suggestions for the meetings.

1/Decide on a specific time for your troubleshooting sessions, a time when it is quiet and you can talk freely. Some couples find it valuable to go out to dinner and talk things over in a secluded part of the restaurant.

2/Do not bring up troublesome incidents each time that they occur during the week; instead, keep a list of things to discuss during the special session.

3/Agree on the agenda at the beginning of your session, listing the problems or requests. That way, you won't take your mate by surprise later in the session or forget to bring up any items for discussion.

4/Take turns and discuss one problem at a time. When it is your turn, state the problem clearly so that your partner can understand it. Restate it if necessary.

5/Suggest some possible solutions to the problem you present.

6/Brainstorm with your mate for other potential solutions. Try to come up with as many solutions as possible, and then do a cost-effectiveness analysis on these. For example, hiring household help might relieve some of the strain on a working couple but the cost might produce a financial deficit, creating more stress. Some suggestions might yield useful solutions in the long run but not the short run, and vice versa. For example, moving to a larger house may be a practical long-term goal when the family income has increased substantially, but it might be impractical in the near future.

One danger in focusing on problems and conflicts is that you can overlook the positive aspects of your marriage. In these troubleshooting sessions, you should find time to summarize some of the good things about your marriage or the pleasant events that have happened in the previous week, as described in Chapter 12.

Below is a checklist of specific rules for the troubleshooting sessions, followed by a discussion of each rule. These guidelines have been used with considerable success by me and other therapists. You and your partner should read the rules again before beginning the sessions. Then reread them a third time after each session and assess how well you followed each item on the checklist.

Checklist for Troubleshooting Sessions

Rules for the Speaker

_____1 / Be brief.

_____2 / Be specific.

_____3 / No insults, blaming, or accusations.

_____4 / No labels.

_____5 / No absolutes.

_____6 / State things positively.

_____7 / Check out your inferences about your mate's actions.

Rules for the Listener

_____1 / Listen attentively.

_____2 / Give feedback signals indicating that you are listening.

_____3 / Try to understand the kernel of what your partner is saying.

_____4 / Don't be defensive or counterattack.

_____5 / If indicated, clarify reasons for your behavior but do not make excuses.

_____6 / Do not analyze your partner's motives.

_____7 / Find points of agreement as well as disagreement.

_____8 / Apologize if you have clearly injured your mate.

_____9 / Summarize aloud what you think your partner means.

These rules are based on principles that you should understand in attempting to apply the rules.

PRINCIPLES FOR THE SPEAKER

▷ *Be brief.* Try to be as concise as possible in what you have to say. Stick to the essentials. I recommend the "two-sentence rule"—limiting your statement to two sentences—since it's often possible to pack the essentials into a few well-chosen words. This also minimizes counterproductive, hostile material.

▷ *Be specific.* Avoid vague, general remarks. For instance, instead of complaining, "I wish you were neater," say, "I would like you to hang up the towel after you use it."

▷ *Do not indulge in insults, accusations, or blaming.* It is better to follow the no-fault rule: "A problem exists. Let's see what we can do about solving it." Pretend you are a mechanic: you see that something is loose and needs tightening, and you simply suggest corrective action without blame.

▷ *Avoid the tendency to use labels* such as "sloppy," "selfish," or "careless," which are usually overgeneralizations and cloud the issue. Worse, they can be provocative and only sabotage the trouble-shooting session.

▷ *Avoid absolutes* like "never" or "always." These are usually inaccurate and only beg for rebuttal since it is the rare mate who *never* does a given thing or *always* does something else. If you use these absolute words, you may simply stir up an unproductive argument and get distracted from the point that you want to make.

▷ *Try to state what you would like rather than giving a criticism.* Say, for example, "I'd appreciate it if you would help with the dishes" rather than complain, "You never help with the dishes."

▷ *Do not try to read your mate's intentions.* Your inferences are likely to be wrong much of the time, which will only aggravate your mate. If you believe your mate is irritated at you, it is better to say, "I get the feeling you're annoyed at me" rather than accuse him or her of seeking revenge by not helping out. When you test your beliefs about things your mate has done, remember that these are inferences, not facts. It is pointless to indulge in pop-psychology analysis of your mate's motives.

PRINCIPLES FOR THE LISTENER

▷ *Find points of agreement or mutual understanding* so you don't sound like an opponent: "It's true that I have been preoccupied with my work lately." "I realize that my stopping for a drink on the way home upsets you."

▷ *Disregard your mate's negative statements.* When your mate is hurt or angry, he or she is likely to couch the problem in exaggerated, accusatory terms. Try to focus on *the cause of the anger* and ignore the expressions of blame and criticism.

▷ *Ask yourself questions.* Sometimes your mate's complaint may be crystal-clear to him or her but not to you. Ask yourself, "What is the point of what my mate is trying to tell me?"

▷ *Check out your understanding* of your mate's complaint. Say, for example, "I think you are telling me you won't put up with my mother's interference anymore" or "Are you telling me that you want me to start paying the bills?"

▷ *Clarify your motives* if you think your mate has incorrectly interpreted them. For instance, you could tell him or her, "I really did want to see you but I felt I had to finish the work before I left the office."

▷ *Don't be afraid to say you're sorry.* Loving includes expressing regret when you have unwittingly or deliberately hurt your mate. It is important to communicate this feeling.

TRANSLATING COMPLAINTS INTO REQUESTS

As your problem-solving sessions unfold, you will make more progress if you *focus on what it is that you want to achieve, rather than on what your partner does wrong.* In a meeting with Sally and Tom, I tried to show them how to approach their problems.

ATB: Now you both have grievances. Let's see if you can translate them into requests.

SALLY: It all has to do with going places. He's always late coming home, so he has to make up for lost time by racing there—

TOM: Are you kidding? When I come home, she's half naked and then she yells at me for being late.

SALLY: Well, the real problem is that his driving makes me crazy—he tailgates the car in front, passes in no-passing zones. The way he pushes his foot on the gas, we're lucky we're still alive.

TOM: You keep bugging me. You should sit in the back seat, where you belong, and do your back-seat driving from there.

SALLY: If I didn't say anything, I don't know what he'd do—he's always trying to jump ahead at the toll booths to see if he can crash into the bar before it goes up.

TOM: Well, one time the bar was slow in going up and I happened to hit it—

SALLY: You hit it because you stepped on the gas while you were tossing the coin in—

ATB: Let's hold on a second. Sally, just try to tell us what you would request from Tom.

SALLY: Simply that he drive slower, not pass like crazy, and plan to get there ten minutes later.

TOM: And you stop nagging.

ATB: Wait a minute. Is that going to be your major request for Sally?

TOM: Well . . . the girl is always running, running, running. There's never a relaxed moment. She has to be the All-American, dollar-a-year "yes" girl. She can't say no. . . . Anybody asks her to plan a program for a benefit or make arrangements for a class reunion—she has to do it.

ATB: Can you translate that into a wish?

TOM: Yes, I'd just like her to slow down from a fast blur.

SALLY: He's decided that what I do isn't important.

ATB: Is it possible to cut down on your commitments?

SALLY: He used to complain that I was never home at night, so when I stayed home, he spent every night at his workbench.

ATB: Sally, would it be feasible to spend more evenings at home?

SALLY: It's okay for him to volunteer coaching the Little League or the Boy Scouts—but when do *I* do what I want to do?

It should be evident that Sally and Tom were protecting their own interests. As the session progressed, however, they were able to settle for a trade—Tom to try to be more punctual and drive more slowly, and Sally to spend more evenings at home.

In most marriages the grievances accumulate over months and years. When they finally are voiced, it is usually in the form of a complaint, criticism, or accusation. In general, wives and husbands will find that they are more likely to get their partner's cooperation— and to reduce their own irritation—if they translate their complaints into requests. In fact, as part of the clarification sessions (see Chapter 15), it would be desirable for the partners to write down their specific requests. For example:

Complaint or Criticism	*Request*
It makes me sick to my stomach when you eat with your mouth open at the table.	Please chew your food with your mouth closed.
The kitchen looks like a pigsty.	Could you wash the dishes before you go to work in the morning?
I can't stand you when you've been drinking too much and then want to make love. You are disgusting.	I'd like to make love when you have not been drinking.
I can't stand your bad breath.	I bought some mouthwash that we can both use.
You're so sloppy. No matter how much I clean up the house, you make a mess.	Could you use the ashtray and be sure to hang up your clothes if you are not going to use them that day?
You always comb your hair over the sink, and it clogs it up.	Could you be more careful about not combing your hair over the sink?

Complaint or Criticism	Request
You've gotten so heavy that you've become really ugly.	How about going on a diet?
I can't stand when you wear curlers in your hair to dinner.	Would it be possible to wash your hair at some other time so you don't have to wear curlers to dinner?
You're so preoccupied with your work, we can never talk anymore.	Do you think we could set aside some time just to chat or go out for dinner some evening?

CONTAMINATED REQUESTS

In making requests, you should avoid put-downs or needling. For example, a wife says somewhat disdainfully, "I'd like you to take the trash out every morning—if you can spare a few minutes from your busy schedule." A husband says, "I'd like you to sit down and talk to me when I come home—if you can get off the phone." A wife says sarcastically, "I'd like you to help Andy with his homework—which I know is a tremendous burden to you." Such gratuitous jabs only sabotage the message that you're trying to get across.

Try to keep in mind the importance of using *I* statements rather than *you* statements. It is better to say, "I get upset when you come home late without calling" rather than "You always upset me by coming home late without calling." Similarly, it is better to say, "I would enjoy it more if you would tell me about what happened at work" rather than "You never tell me what happened at work." Starting the sentence with *I* instead of *you* tends to damp down the accusatory overtones.

Tom and Sally's discussion of how they spent time was filled with complaints and cross-complaints. But over the course of several weeks, they became quite adept at translating complaints into requests. I suggested that they write down their requests. Sally compiled the following list:

▷ Tell me what you did during the day without my having to ask you every time.

▷ Offer to go for a walk with me some nights.

▷ Talk to me while I'm folding the laundry.

▷ Offer to take the children out for a walk when you see that I am harassed —or else play with them.

▷ When you go to the refrigerator to get a drink, ask me if I'd like one.

▷ Meet me for lunch once or twice a month.

▷ Mow the lawn.

▷ Offer to drive the car pool to Sunday school.

Tom responded with his own list:

▷ Don't get involved in long telephone conversations with your mother when I am home.

▷ Don't close the door when you go into the study to work.

▷ Rub my back.

▷ Initiate love making.

▷ Check with me first before you make social engagements.

▷ Call me during the day.

▷ Balance the checkbook.

▷ Some nights put the children to bed before I come home so we can have drinks and dinner by ourselves.

Broad statements such as "Try to be more considerate" or "Act more loving" are not readily translated into action. It is better to be more specific. The symbolic meaning of a specific action matters the most, and unless you do what your spouse would like, you may never send the message that you care.

Even with the best intentions, you or your mate occasionally may continue to use put-downs in problem-solving discussions. During these times, it may be necessary to watch for your automatic thoughts and to remind yourself of the rules for the speaker and listener.

We next focus on Judy and Cliff, whose relationship also benefited from troubleshooting sessions. Cliff had received some marital counseling but Judy had gone to only one session. Nonetheless, Cliff was able to apply what he had learned in his therapy. Even though only one of the two partners was actively working on marital problems, good progress was made. The following conversation occurred one evening:

JUDY: I'm fed up doing all the housework, taking care of the garden, arranging to get things fixed, keeping everything going. You never take an interest in things anymore. You don't ever see things. You never see the clutter. You just rely on me for everything. I know you work, but at least when you are home I would like to rely on you to help out—like picking things up if they are messy, doing things without being asked to. You know what has to be done. I hate to have to nag you all the time. I'd like you to take the initiative.

CLIFF: [*There she goes, nagging me again, but I will try to be cool.*] That's okay with me. I'd like to help out. Let's sit down and you can tell me what you want me to do.

JUDY: Now, not only do I have to do everything myself, but I also have to tell you what to do. You should know after all this time what needs to be done. If you took an interest, you would know what to do [attributing bad motives for Cliff's behavior].

CLIFF: [*She loves to criticize but not focus on the problem.*] I *do* do some of these things. I do a lot of things, but I have to know what things you consider important. I've been doing more of the gardening—

JUDY: You just do the fun stuff.

At this point, they are still not connecting. Cliff is trying to follow the rules but, as will be seen in the next part of the dialogue, he gets derailed and becomes a participant in the exchange of digs.

CLIFF: [*Don't retaliate. Find out what she wants.*] Why don't you just tell me what you'd like me to do and let's see how it works out?

JUDY: You know all those boxes that are piled up in the living room? It really bothers me that they weren't put away—I just can't outlast you. How long was it going to take you to get bothered enough to move those boxes?

CLIFF: [*She's beating up on me.*] It would have taken forever . . . because it doesn't bother me. You're going to have to let me know what other things bother you.

JUDY: It doesn't bother you because you're not home all day looking at the mess.

CLIFF: [*Nothing is enough, no matter how much I try. There is always going to be something that bothers her.*] That sort of thing doesn't bother me because I don't consider it clutter. I'll be happy to move them if you want me to.

JUDY: That can't be true. I just can't believe that you don't see things.

Many people cannot believe that their mate is oblivious to certain things of which they themselves are acutely aware, and so they attribute the mate's actions to a lack of caring.

CLIFF: [*Hang in there.*] All right, I'll do what I can to try to see things better, but I don't like a lot of the things that you do.

JUDY: Such as what?

CLIFF: [checking out her motives] I noticed that you left my laundry on the top of the stairs. I assume you were testing me to see how long it would take for me to put it away.

JUDY: That's right.

CLIFF: [offering a solution] I just don't like playing games like that. I'll try to be more attentive to things, but I want you to stop testing me all the time.

Judy and Cliff then agreed to this trade-off. Ultimately, they got to the point in their clarification sessions of making request lists, as Sally and Tom had done. This kind of exchange worked well for Judy and Cliff: it undercut their pattern of bickering, nagging, and resentment.

It may seem from the previous dialogue that Judy was the more unreasonable partner. While she was more irritable than Cliff, she was actually under much more pressure. Besides her responsibility for the house and her art, she also worked part time in her home as a bookkeeper for several doctors. She thus experienced the double pressure of her own job and the responsibility for the domestic operations (see Chapter 18). Frequently the partner who assumes the primary responsibility—for example, the role of homemaker—experiences more strain than that imposed by the actual work to be done. Indeed, this sense of responsibility piled up to make Judy, who perceived herself as having primary responsibility for domestic duties, more irritable and less reasonable.

When they set up a new system for dividing the household chores, it helped to reverse Judy's negative image of Cliff. The symbolic meaning of Cliff's more active participation in domestic operations had a powerful effect on Judy. Knowing that Cliff was truly a partner and ally gave her added energy and increased her stress tolerance. Although her overall work load did not substantially decrease, she felt much calmer, which enabled her to adopt a more reasonable attitude toward Cliff. Cliff's patience was rewarded: it saw them through a difficult period.

17

TAMING
THE FURIES

"A good fight clears the air—that's what I used to think. We'd have a good fight, then we'd have tremendous sex. Now we have tremendous fights and no sex. . . . It used to be that after a fight we rediscovered ourselves, we felt closer, and we couldn't wait to jump into bed. But now the anger hangs on and on, and I don't want to ever see him again. I just can't forget the mean things that he says." Thus, Marjorie describes her built-up resentment of Ken.

Although the expression of anger may seem useful at one stage or another in marriage, at other times it can be disruptive. And when it carries over from one activity to the next, from hour to hour, day to day, and week to week, then it is destructive. At that point, a couple has to take action if their marriage is to survive.

The vast majority of unhappy marriages have been marred by mutual hostility. Continuous hostility changes a spouse's perception of his or her mate. As Marjorie said, "When I think of him, all I can see is his angry face and him yelling at me." When partners experience such anger, it feels natural for them to want to attack each other.

Of course, anger has its place. An idealistic attitude about anger—that it should never be expressed—is unrealistic. Sometimes the expression of anger may be adaptive, if not lifesaving. For instance, an abused, tormented spouse may find that being openly angry is a way she can protect herself. (Of course, the expression of anger by the victim often only further enrages the victimizer.)

Some people believe that expressing anger is the most effective way—in fact, the only way—to influence another person. They may not realize, however, that the expression of anger can cause substantially negative results. Further, it does not generally change the other person's attitudes and may suppress only temporarily an unwanted behavior—which resurfaces when the threat of punishment has been removed.

During the course of marriage, sentiments of gratitude, love, and affection sometimes seem to lose their influence. One mate may not feel there are enough pleasing interactions with his or her spouse—not enough time together or cuddling, for example. Or the spouse may take certain pleasing actions for granted and thus not consider them rewarding or worthy of a response. As expressions of pleasure (as a way of reinforcing desirable actions by the mates) decline, couples are more likely to resort to punishment as a means of control.

Another seeming "advantage" of expressing anger is the release of tension. After a good fight, both partners may feel relatively relaxed and be able to engage in more friendly, even erotic, activities. Still, the cost of fighting can be great; both partners may harbor memories of harsh words or even blows for years to come.

As heated arguments lead partners to withdraw from each other, their loving feelings seem to wane. This phenomenon results from the fact that negative attitudes generate negative emotions, such as resentment or sadness, whereas positive attitudes generate positive emotions, such as love or happiness. When attitudes change from positive to negative, the feelings change in the same direction.

But by cutting the roots of their hostility, or at least controlling its expression, many husbands and wives are able to switch their image of each other back from negative to positive. I have often been surprised to see the return of affectionate feelings and love that had seemed totally extinguished by the intensity of the partners' hostility.

In general, couples do best if they try to keep their outbursts of anger to a minimum. Since hostility is frequently based on misunderstandings or at least exaggerations, it is likely to aggravate rather than solve problems. In addition, the wounds that are inflicted cause much of the suffering in distressed marriages. When you do express your hostility, try to use ways of getting your point across that will minimize the undesirable effects on your partner. Some of these will be discussed later in this chapter.

Source of the Problem: You or Your Mate?

When they are engaged in a fight, spouses almost always see their mate as responsible for the problem. However, in systematic research, assessments by an impartial judge indicate that although the spouses believe that their mate is difficult, derelict, or antagonistic—and that *they* are the injured ones—both parties contribute to the arguments.

But the problem does not lie simply in how the mates behave toward each other. As we shall see, the hostility often (but not always) arises from *internal* sources (think, for example, of the misunderstandings and errors in judgment that stem from a clash of mates' perspectives).

When spouses fight, their clash is often attributed to a conflict of style or habit. "Karen and Ted fight because Karen is usually late and Ted can't stand being kept waiting." "Judy and Cliff fight because Cliff leaves his clothes around and Judy has to pick them up." On the surface, the arguments do seem to stem from such conflicts, which center on issues like promptness or neatness. Yet disagreement over such values or habits does not seem sufficient to produce the deadly serious fights that often occur. After all, it is not a tragedy if Ted has to wait for Karen—he often waits for other people without getting steamed up—or if Cliff leaves his sweater on the chair instead of hanging it up.

One paradox is that although conflicts like these *are* deadly serious, frequently neither mate realizes what he or she is actually fighting about. The questions of promptness versus tardiness, order versus disorder, although apparently at the center of the conflict, are only on the periphery. The eye of the storm is not the inconvenience of having to wait or of having to pick up clothes per se, but the *belief* that those events "prove" that the mate is irresponsible, insensitive, or disrespectful. Each partner is perceived as an offender: Ted and Judy, for being controlling and picky; Karen and Cliff, for being negligent and irresponsible. It is not the acts themselves that produce serious distress and rifts—it is the interpretations, or misinterpretations, the couple make.

As pointed out earlier, anger is aroused by the symbolic meanings partners attach to each other's actions. Ted believed that if Karen really respected him she would be on time, since she knew he worried when she was late. Because of his concerns about something happening to her, he concocted a rule: "She should not keep me waiting." When Karen was late, Ted became angry at her for breaking the rule—even when he knew that she may have been delayed for good reason. Ted thought, *"She knows how important it is to me that she be on time. Since she's late, it shows she doesn't give a damn about my feelings."*

The meanings that husbands and wives attach to events are shaped by the virtues and vices described in Chapter 2. By these standards a particular action, for example, may show a partner to be responsible, respectful, caring—*or* irresponsible, disrespectful, indifferent. Since the favorable behaviors seem to be taken for granted over a period of time, the unfavorable actions are more likely to be noticed and to receive a symbolic—and negative—interpretation. Thus, a spouse's missteps or misdemeanors, even though far less frequent than his or her helpful acts, may make a stronger and more lasting impression.

Although spouses often mind read, ascribing unworthy motives to their partner, they are in truth *blind* to the partner's actual thoughts and attitudes (see Chapter 1). Thus, many grave marital battles are staged by two blind combatants fighting against fantasized images they have projected onto each other. *Though directed at the fantasized image, the attacks pierce the real person.*

SOLVING THE INTERNAL PROBLEM

As a first step in reducing the mutual anger in your relationship, you should determine to what degree your own mental workings contribute to the problem. Because of the broad possibility of your having misinterpreted your spouse's actions, it is wise to take this step. You can assess the degree to which your anger stems from your own psyche by asking yourself specific questions and using techniques that I have already described in previous chapters.

1/When you start to feel angry, ask yourself, "Is my anger warranted? Is it appropriate or inappropriate? Is it based on my own problems or on a genuine problem in the relationship?" Often, you can answer these questions from your previous experiences, particularly those in which the anger seemed, at the time, to be warranted but later seemed either excessive, inappropriate, or ill advised.

2/Then ask yourself:

a/"What are my automatic thoughts?"

b/"How am I interpreting my partner's actions, reading meanings in them that may not exist?"

c/"Is my interpretation based on an objective appraisal of my spouse's behavior, or is it simply based on the *meaning* I attach to it? Does my interpretation logically follow from what has happened? Are there alternative explanations?"

Ways of dealing with these automatic thoughts have already been described in Chapter 13, and it might be helpful to refresh your memory on how to use the double-column technique in evaluating your anger toward your mate.

3/If your anger seems appropriate—that is, if you have interpreted your spouse's behavior accurately and it is clearly offensive—ask yourself whether it may be the result of errors in your thinking, such as tunnel vision, selective abstraction, either-or thinking, overgeneralization, exaggeration, mind reading, "awfulizing," "devilizing," and "catastrophizing."

4/Also, ask yourself if there is an element of satisfaction in finding a reason to attack your spouse. Perhaps you receive pleasure at seeing him or her squirm or appear hurt or guilty. You may also enjoy exacting revenge, showing your muscle, getting the upper hand. While all of these "satisfactions" are intrinsic features of obtaining victories, you will of course want to assess them in terms of your actual gains in the relationship.

CHANGING YOUR THINKING

Until now, we have been considering whether your own thinking—especially if it involves exaggerated meanings, misunderstanding, and errors in thinking—contributes to the intensity of your anger. Since such factors usually play a role, we should attempt to analyze the thoughts and meanings behind your anger.

To summarize the steps for applying cognitive therapy techniques to your own thinking:

1/Look at your automatic thoughts and note your responses. Look for errors in thinking.

2/Reframe your image of your spouse.

3/Attempt to see your spouse's perspective.

4/Distract yourself.

AUTOMATIC THOUGHTS AND RATIONAL RESPONSES (REFRAMING)

Listed below are negative automatic thoughts held by various husbands and wives. Their automatic thoughts represent "framing" the spouse—that is, interpreting the spouse's actions in such a way as to make him or her appear guilty of a "crime."

By attempting to find the best possible interpretation, the spouses were able to view these same crimes differently. Recasting your spouse's actions in a positive light has already been described as "reframing." Reframing does not refer to the "power of positive thinking" but to the process of achieving a more balanced—and therefore more realistic—picture of the spouse, taking into account the favorable as well as the unfavorable meanings of his or her actions. Going beyond this, you might find it useful to try to understand your spouse's perspective and to check the accuracy of your understanding with your spouse.

Automatic Thought	*Rational Response*
He's gone out drinking with the boys. This shows he doesn't care about me or the children.	This helps him to relax. He is always in a better mood if he has a beer with his friends before he comes home.
She is a lousy mother. She lets the kids push her around. They go wild and get away with murder.	She is very affectionate, and they love her. Besides, they're good kids and don't really cause any trouble. It's normal for kids to misbehave. There is nothing wrong with them.
She is such a nag about everything.	She is actually a great housekeeper with high standards. If she didn't have them, the house would probably be impossible to live in.
She talks to everybody when we travel. She's a perfect social butterfly.	She actually is very sociable. This makes trips more pleasant.
He is a tightwad. He begrudges every cent I spend.	He manages the finances very well. Somebody has to take charge of the budget.

Automatic thoughts and rational responses are illustrated in the following excerpt from the case record of Cliff and Judy.

SCENARIO: Cliff habitually left various things (boxes, magazines, old letters, clothes) on chairs, on the dining room table, or on the floor—instead of putting them away or throwing them out. Judy, fed up with picking up after him, decided to leave them where they were in the expectation that Cliff—realizing she was not his servant—would clean these things up himself. Judy believed Cliff was as aware of this mess as she was, and needed to be confronted with the fact that she would no longer "do his dirty work for him."

Cliff, on the other hand, was relatively oblivious to the mess. He customarily cleaned things up in spurts, usually when the accumulation exceeded his own, much higher threshold for noticing messes. Prior to marriage, Cliff cleaned about once a week, and he was inclined to continue the pattern after they were married. Judy, however, was more sensitive to disorder and followed a clean-as-you-go philosophy. When Judy told Cliff she could no longer stand picking up after him, he blew up at her and stalked out.

Their fights were not so much over conflicting styles or philosophies as over the meanings each attributed to what the other did. Thus, Cliff's initial "offense" was based on Judy's interpretation of his leaving things around the house. Judy had a number of automatic thoughts in response to Cliff's "mess." These thoughts then prompted her action, a criticism of Cliff. Cliff then reacted to her criticism with his own set of automatic thoughts. Both had learned, however, to label and evaluate their automatic thoughts. They recorded them, labeled them, and made rational responses, as shown here:

Judy's Automatic Thoughts	*Judy's Rational Responses*
He always leaves things around.	All-or-nothing thinking. He does pick things up sometimes. And he's probably right about not noticing them—since they really don't bother him.
He expects me to be his servant—do everything.	Mind reading. I don't know what he expects. I could ask him.
He doesn't care how I feel.	Personalizing. Just because he's sloppy doesn't mean he doesn't care about me.
When he withdraws, I can't tell him anything—he's filled with hostility.	Overgeneralizing. He is very sensitive to being told to do something. It reminds him of his mother. Most of the time he is loving and caring.

As Judy wrote down her automatic thoughts, she started to regain her objectivity, and when she started to work on rational responses, her perspective of Cliff—as self-centered, negligent, and uncaring—started to shift. She was able to see that she had fallen into the trap of all-or-nothing thinking, overgeneralizing, mind reading, and personalizing. And she was able to suggest alternative explanations for Cliff's behavior that seemed more plausible than those reasons she had automatically given herself.

As she completed this homework, she felt relieved and warmer toward Cliff. By recognizing her automatic thoughts and applying logic to them, she was able to change her perspective. Instead of seeing Cliff as all bad, she now viewed him for the most part as good, with some flaws.

Now, let's review Cliff's automatic thoughts and rational responses.

Cliff's Automatic Thoughts	Cliff's Rational Responses
She's always nagging me.	Overgeneralizing. She only does it when I haven't done something.
She enjoys putting me down.	Mind reading. There's no evidence she enjoys this. In fact, she gets upset. She says she hates to be a nag.
She treats me like a child. She expects me to do whatever she wants.	Mind reading. She doesn't want to treat me like a child, but I don't like her tone of voice. I can talk to her about this. Her main objection has to do with my neatness, rather than doing whatever she wants.

Both Judy and Cliff found that when they wrote down their automatic thoughts and responses, their anger was greatly reduced and they were able to talk over their problems without upsetting each other. In their discussions, Judy also asked herself—with a good deal of success—a series of questions that helped maintain her focus on their problem:

▷ What is Cliff trying to tell me?
▷ What is the real issue here?
▷ Is it necessary to answer every critical comment?
▷ What do I want to accomplish in this discussion?

At times their discussions got heated, and Judy found she had to ask herself other questions:

▷ Is the discussion becoming unproductive?
▷ Is it time to summarize our differences rather than argue about them?
▷ Should I try to clarify Cliff's perspective?
▷ Would it be better to have a time out now, or perhaps postpone the discussion?

The above approach has been supported in systematic research with distressed couples. Psychologists Donald Duffy and Tom Dowd, for example, found that clients trained in a method like this showed a much greater reduction in their anger than did a comparable group of clients who did not receive this instruction.

Gains and Losses
from Expressing Anger

You will have to decide for yourself whether, on balance, your marital fights are worthwhile. Remember that you *do* have options: you can choose to express your anger or not to express it at all. If you decide on the former, you can also choose *how* you express the anger. If expressed in a way that simply communicates that you are upset or troubled by your spouse's behavior, the anger will have fewer costs than if it is meant to threaten or humiliate your spouse.

Keep in mind that there is no rule stating that you *must* express anger. If you restrain yourself, your anger generally goes away—and you may be glad that you did not express it. Waiting for your anger to die down gives you a chance to evaluate whether it is based on your spouse's act itself or on the *meaning* you have attached to this act— i.e., you can better ascertain whether you want to punish your mate for what may simply have been an honest error or your misinterpretation of the event. For example, after his anger died down, Ken discovered he was wrong to think Marjorie didn't care about him simply because she had neglected to bring his suit to the cleaners— she had been worried about problems at work, and her preoccupation made her forgetful. Ken was then glad that he had not reproached Marjorie for her inattention to his request.

Before venting your anger at your spouse, ask yourself these questions:

1/What do I expect to *gain* by reproaching, punishing, or criticizing my spouse?

2/What do I *lose* by using these tactics? Even if there are good short-term results, are the long-term results likely to be bad? For example, even if my spouse gives in or capitulates right now, is there a likelihood that this is only going to make the relationship more disagreeable or emotionally distant in the future?

3/What is the point that I want to get across to my mate? What is the best way to make this point? Am I likely to do this by reproaching or blaming my spouse?

4/Are there better ways than punishment to influence my spouse— for example, by having a serious discussion about his or her actions, or by offering a "reward" (a smile or compliment) when he or she does what I like?

To help you assess the costs and benefits of expressing anger, I have prepared a checklist which you can use to estimate whether the gains from the anger will exceed the losses. The best way to determine the overall value of expressing anger is to evaluate your past experiences. Use this checklist to assess the gains and losses from episodes of fighting, continue to consult it, and update your answers after future fights.

Checklist for Value of Expression of Hostility

Think back to your most recent expression of anger and try to determine its positive and negative effects. You may have to check with your spouse to determine how to answer many of these questions, since part of each answer depends upon your spouse's reaction. Check those that are true:

Positive Effects of My Expression of Anger

_____1 / My partner behaved better after the episode.

_____2 / I felt better.

_____3 / My partner felt better.

_____4 / Fighting back protected me when my partner became abusive.

_____5 / I could tell that my partner really heard me, which doesn't happen when I just talk in a normal fashion.

_____6 / I experienced a relief of anger and a release of tension.

_____7 / It cleared the air, and we were able to turn our attention to other things.

_____8 / We loved each other more after having "a good fight."

_____9 / We settled our argument.

Negative Effects of My Expression of Anger

_____1 / I was less effective, more clumsy, or even incoherent in presenting my argument or complaint.

_____2 / I said or did things that I regretted afterward.

_____3 / My partner discounted or discredited the validity of what I said, dismissing my ideas as based on emotionality or irrationality.

_____4 / My partner did not even hear my message—because it was buried in a cloud of hostility.

_____5 / My partner responded only to my hostility, and retaliated.

_____6 / My partner was wounded by my attack.

_____7 / We got involved in a vicious cycle of attack and counterattack.

If you do decide to express your anger, you have a choice of tactics, some of which are more effective than others in simultaneously reducing your anger and getting your message across. For example, saying "I'm angry at you" may have a more constructive effect than attacking your partner's personality or giving him or her the silent treatment.

Even if you decide in favor of using nonhostile strategies (clarifying, problem solving, troubleshooting) to deal with your partner, this does not guarantee that he or she will also refrain from using hostile tactics. (The next section will provide suggestions on reducing your spouse's anger.)

It helps to learn to distinguish provocative statements from constructive ones. As a beginning, try to express yourself in a less provocative way: offer statements of fact rather than criticism. Try to assert yourself rather than put down your spouse. Here are some examples:

Provocative Statements	*Constructive Statements*
You're a louse for interrupting me when I'm talking to my mother on the phone.	It really bothers me when you interrupt my phone conversations.
You're a stinker for criticizing me in front of the kids.	When you criticize me in front of the kids, it upsets me and undermines my authority.
You're too lazy to turn off the lights when you leave the room.	I wish you would turn off the lights when you leave the room.
You've got a lot of nerve always making fun of the way I speak.	You make me mad when you tease me about my English.

Defusing Hostility
in Your Mate

When one mate is furious at the other, how is the second mate to react? If a husband starts yelling at his wife, should she yell back at him? Should she run out of the room? Or should she pick up a vase and throw it at him?

You need to deal with the fact that even if you have worked out your own excessive anger toward your mate, he or she may also have a problem with anger. You may choose to defuse your mate's anger on the basis that you find it unpleasant, that you are concerned about its potential escalation into serious abuse, and/or that the anger is not good for either of you. Don't forget that you do have choices and you'll be best served if you make the most responsible one. Your decision should be based less on what you feel like saying or doing than on what is best going to serve your long-range interests.

Listed below are some of the methods that can be used to defuse anger in your mate:

1/Clarify the problem, as described in Chapters 15 and 16. Try to decipher or get your mate to specify what is troubling him or her.

2/Cool off your mate. Acknowledge your mate's criticism (without necessarily agreeing with it) and insist on his or her quieting down so that you can help to solve the problem.

3/Focus on solving the problem.

4/Divert your mate's attention.

5/Schedule ventilation sessions.

6/Leave the room or the house.

CHOICE 1: CLARIFY THE PROBLEM

As indicated in Chapters 15 and 16, your partner's real problem may be so deeply buried in a cloud of accusations and criticism that you may miss it. If you simply respond to your partner's reproaches by counterattacking, it is unlikely that the problem will be solved. On the other hand, by ignoring the bluster and haranguing—and not responding to it with anger of your own—you will be in a better position to ferret out the source of the trouble. Not getting caught up in an exchange of shots may be one of the most difficult tasks that can be asked of you, but it may have the greatest pay-off for your marriage.

CHOICE 2: COOL OFF YOUR MATE

In dealing with angry patients, therapists have discovered ways of undercutting their anger that are also useful in marital fights. Basically, these methods consist of reducing your mate's level of anger by insisting that it is preventing you from understanding and helping with the problem. The following example of cooling off one's mate is illustrated by Marjorie, who had been instructed in dealing with Ken's flare-ups.

KEN: [in a very loud, angry voice, with a particularly menacing look] I'm really fed up with this. You never do anything that you are supposed to and I just can't count on you for anything!

MARJORIE: [cool, offering a direct suggestion] I know that you are angry, but I can't tell what you are angry about as long as you are yelling at me. Why don't we sit down, and we can talk about it.

KEN: That's all we do is talk about it. That's all you ever want to do is talk. All talk and no action!

MARJORIE: Look, I really do want to know what is bothering you, but I can't hear you when you're yelling at me. Why don't you sit down, and you can tell me without shouting.

KEN: I'm not shouting! I just want you to shape up around here.

MARJORIE: I'm willing to talk to you about this. Would you just sit down so that we can talk and stop screaming at me?

KEN: I can't keep stifling my feelings.

MARJORIE: Then let's talk about it later when you aren't so angry. I really do want to get this settled, but I can't do it if you are yelling at me.

KEN: I want to settle this right now!

MARJORIE: Then please sit down and stop yelling so we can settle it.

KEN: [much calmer] Okay. I'm sitting down and I'm not yelling. Now tell me, why aren't there any clean shirts in the drawer? You know that I have an appointment and need a clean shirt today.

In this instance, Marjorie was being *assertive,* not compliant—and not hostile. She stuck to her guns, seeking a resolution of the problem, and she refused to get involved in accusations and cross-accusations. Since she was the partner who was in control, she was able to achieve this goal. As Marjorie perfected this way of dealing with Ken's anger, she felt much less vulnerable; ultimately, through problem solving, she was able to reduce the frequency and intensity of Ken's outbursts.

Although one spouse might seem to be controlling the situation with yelling and criticizing, the other partner can take control by being calm and persistent. *The stronger person is not the one making the most noise but the one who can quietly direct the conversation toward defining and solving problems.*

CHOICE 3: FOCUS ON SOLVING THE PROBLEM

Many angry episodes consist of one mate's being upset over a problem and blaming the spouse, and the spouse responding to the blame rather than to the problem. Of course, a mate's habitual tendency to blame or accuse is a problem in itself, which should be brought up in a troubleshooting session. Unfortunately, when one mate is upset, the other usually becomes upset and hostile in response.

For example, Robert was in the middle of fixing a malfunctioning oven pilot light and could not find his screwdriver. He confronted Shelly, accusing her of misplacing it. She could have responded to the confrontation by engaging in a battle. At this point, they were heading for another fight about doing work around the house. However, she recognized that Robert was annoyed at her. By enacting a scenario in her mind, Shelly predicted his reaction if she retaliated; consequently, she decided to direct her efforts toward solving the problem instead of having a confrontation with him.

ROBERT: What happened to my screwdriver? You always take it and don't return it.

SHELLY: [*He's always blaming me. I feel like telling him, "I don't know what happened to your damn tool," but then he will answer back, "You don't know how to fix things. Why do you always take my screwdriver?" I would say, "You're always putting me down." He would then say, "I've got good reason." Then I would feel bad. It would be better simply to focus on the problem.*] Wait a minute, when did you last use it?

ROBERT: [distracted from his anger, and entering a questioning mode] I haven't used it since last week.

SHELLY: Weren't you doing some work around the house last night?

ROBERT: Errr—I guess I did use it last night.

SHELLY: Where did you use it?

ROBERT: I don't know . . . in the basement.

SHELLY: Why don't you look for it there?

As it happens, Robert found the screwdriver in the basement, where he had used it the night before. By shifting into questioning rather than counterattacking, Shelly was able simultaneously to defuse some of his anger and to find a solution to the problem. Her maneuver protected her from further scolding and relieved her anger toward Robert. In one of their troubleshooting sessions, Shelly brought up his tendency to blame her every time he had a problem at home. He acknowledged this and did make a constructive effort to try to solve problems rather than to blow up.

This case illustrates that it is not necessary to succumb to your impulse to retaliate when your spouse is annoyed. You will show more strength and mastery over yourself and the situation if you sidestep the confrontation and focus on the immediate problem. By keeping cool, you will help your mate recognize the inappropriateness of his or her outbursts.

CHOICE 4: DIVERT YOUR MATE'S ATTENTION

Many people in a state of white fury can calm down if their attention is shifted to another matter. A husband can, temporarily at least, divert his wife by changing the subject. Of course, she may protest that he is avoiding the sensitive issue, but he can offer to return to it later. Distraction does not alway work, however. As with other techniques, you have to rely on trial-and-error approaches.

Sometimes the judicious use of humor can help to break the tension of a highly charged moment. At other times, simply backing off—without responding to your mate—can de-escalate the conflict.

Other techniques, such as telling your spouse to stop yelling, to calm down, or to relax, are widely used, but they frequently backfire if the spouse resents being stifled. It is better to call a time out and suggest that neither of you speak for a while.

CHOICE 5: SCHEDULE VENTILATION SESSIONS

Sometimes the issues between a couple are so highly charged that neither mate can discuss them without feeling angry. Even if they both decide to discuss them "like two intelligent human beings," the sense of accompanying outrage may be so strong that as soon as they begin, their anger surfaces. Their carefully chosen words take on a sharp edge and, as the mutual provocation increases, they resort to fighting rather than clarifying or settling disputes. This is a signal that the partners should enter a session in which they can be more free to express their hostility—the ventilation session.

Another reason for having ventilation sessions is that some people cannot bring up bothersome problems except when they are angry. For example, a wife might be troubled by certain of her husband's actions but choose to ignore them. Yet repeated incidents of this sort may gnaw away at her until she finally is able to bring them out into the open.

In some cases, the wife may not even be aware that she is upset about specific actions—or inactions—by her husband. However, she may have a general sense of fatigue or low-level sadness or pessimism that she can't account for. (Such a case is described in Chapter 9.) Here are some practical steps to follow in ventilation sessions:

1/Set a specific time and place where you can both express yourselves without danger of being overheard.

2/ Set a limited time for each ventilation session. No more than fifteen to twenty minutes is probably best.

3/ There should be no interruption by either spouse while the other is talking.

4/ Take turns in speaking but decide in advance how much time each of you will speak. Setting a time limit—sometimes as brief as four or five minutes—can prevent the discussion from escalating into another round of fighting.

5/ Make provisions for time outs, which either spouse can call as needed.

WHAT TO DO IN VENTILATION SESSIONS

Recognize your anger. Many people are not aware of the early signs of their hostility. There are certain subjective clues that can be an indication. One woman, for example, discovered that when she started on a touchy subject, she would feel her heart skip a beat. Within a few minutes, she would be aware of feelings of anger. By observing her reactions closely, she was able to detect that the muscles in her arms, particularly the biceps, were becoming tense. She also began to feel shaky inside. Her stomach would churn a bit and at times she could feel her body become very tense all over. Sometimes she would even shake.

People can also train themselves to observe closely their tone of voice, how loudly they speak, and their selection of words and phrases. They often discover that they have been taking potshots at their spouse without being fully aware of it.

It is possible to experience the symptoms of hostility without really noticing them—until one is asked to do so. How can a person be hostile without realizing it? The answer lies in the fact that once a person gets into a fighting mode (Chapter 9), he or she will be so immersed in the mental and physical preparations (to attack or retreat) as to lose all self-awareness.

The attack mode is expressed partly through perception of the adversary in more negative terms, and partly through a mobilization of the body. Thus, the skipped heartbeat and muscle tension are part of the mobilization to attack. The angry words and the sharp edge are part of the attack itself.

WHAT TO AVOID IN VENTILATION SESSIONS

If the ventilation sessions are to be at all constructive, there has to be some agreement on controlling the degree of expression of hostility. If the hostility goes too far, it destroys the chance to make peace and can even lead to irreparable damage—either through bitterly angry words or an actual physical attack. The following are some ground rules for these sessions:

1/Try to avoid extreme condemnation of your mate. In general, it is better to say, "What you did the other day made me *very* angry" rather than "You are a total failure as a husband." Your mate can empathize with your being upset over some unpleasant action. He or she can relate to your feeling pained. What your mate cannot empathize with is denigration or contempt.

2/Try to refrain from insulting your mate.

3/Do not pounce on your mate's vulnerable areas. For example, if your mate is sensitive about his or her weight or drinking habits, don't attack these areas unless they are relevant to your complaint.

4/Don't dredge up past examples of your mate's misdemeanors unless they are essential to what you are trying to communicate.

Even though the ventilation sessions are designed to permit freer expression of anger, there must be some limits on that expression. Certainly, any form of physical attack is out of the question. But even verbal attacks can get out of control and lead to irreparable damage to your mate—as well as to the relationship. To prevent the escalation of the conflict to an undesirable level, you should be vigilant about keeping the expression of anger within limits. If one mate does go too far, the other must point this out and insist on restraint.

STAYING WITHIN THE PROPER ZONE

In the process of getting angry, husbands and wives can move—sometimes fairly rapidly—from a temperate zone, in which they are fairly clearheaded and objective about their mate, to a very hot zone, in which they have lost all objectivity and perspective, and can no longer think clearly. The zones can be defined by the mates' degree of anger and control. I have labeled them yellow for warm, red for the greatest degree of anger, and blue for temperate.

The Yellow (Warm) Zone

In this zone you feel angry toward your mate but are able to control your thinking and actions. You have some control over what you will say and how you will say it. Your goal is to demonstrate to your partner that you are angry and to get your grievances off your chest, but not at the cost of damaging the relationship. You can sense when you have gone too far and can pull back if necessary.

Although annoyed, you are able to consider reasonable statements that your spouse makes and show some capacity to see that your own thinking is illogical. If your spouse tells you something at odds with your own conclusions, you are able to evaluate this information without charging into a counterattack.

You recognize that the purpose of the session is to help the relationship, not to hurt your spouse. But you also know you can't discuss your disappointment and grievances without feeling and expressing anger.

It will help to follow policies that will keep you from passing into the hot zone. Among these are taking time outs (discussion to follow shortly) and changing the subject when things get too hot.

The Red (Hot) Zone

People who have entered this zone show an intensification of the symptoms of the yellow zone. Your thinking and actions are less controlled. You have an extremely negative view of your mate. Your thinking may be muddled, extreme, unreasonable, and illogical.

In this zone, the partners seem to have lost the capacity to recognize when they are being illogical or are distorting past and present events. Even when given corrective information that clearly contradicts their beliefs, they are unable to alter those beliefs. (One woman described her thought processes as follows: "My mind is like jelly. I really can't think straight; my thinking is jumbled.")

In the red zone, the content of what people say is marked by denunciations, accusations, and character assassinations. The angry words often progress to swearing, threats of violence, and/or intentions of breaking up the marriage. Sometimes the threats can extend to "I'm going to kill you." The other mate might then throw oil on the fire with the response "I know you'd like to do that."

In the hot zone, the rage may move into an actual attack, as described in Chapter 9. Gary, for example, would give himself permission to attack his wife when he was in the hot zone, thinking, *"She has it coming to her."*

The Blue (Temperate) Zone

Try to move into this zone before the ventilation session is over. The elements of the blue zone are the same as those of the troubleshooting session. You are able to hear your partner's complaints and to express your own in a coherent fashion, possibly translating those complaints into specific requests (Chapter 16). You are able to acknowledge when your partner's complaints are valid and to point out—in a reasonable, calm way—when they are erroneous or exaggerated.

The two of you direct your discussion toward establishing common grounds of agreement and trying to find ways of reconciling your disagreements. You discuss how to change your problem behaviors, and you lay the groundwork for resolving conflicts and solving problems in the future.

TAKING TIME OUT

During the ventilation sessions, you may experience difficulty controlling your thinking. You recognize that it is hard to think logically about what you want to say or to express yourself in a clear way. You may also have trouble following what your partner is saying.

If you start to experience some of these warning signals, then it is time for you to withdraw temporarily by taking a time out. I suggest that couples agree in advance on a particular length for time outs, usually about five minutes. Each partner must agree with the policy that either can call a time out whenever necessary. If five minutes isn't enough, of course, then the upset spouse should take longer.

If a ventilation session requires more than two time outs, it is probably best to terminate it and postpone the discussion until things have calmed down again.

CHOICE 6: LEAVE THE ROOM OR THE HOUSE

At times there is such a high risk of permanent physical or psychological damage that you may need to withdraw from your spouse until the anger has dissipated. You might choose to go into another room or, if your spouse follows you there, to leave the house.

If you are riding in a car during a heated discussion, it would be wise for the passenger to get into the back seat. As a last resort, one of you might leave the car. Incidentally, the automobile is probably the worst place to conduct a ventilation session not only because of the confined quarters but also because of the potential safety hazard if the driver gets too distracted. Your other options while in a car are to listen to the radio or agree not to talk for a period of time.

18

SPECIAL PROBLEMS

This chapter will explore a variety of special problems that exist in many, but not all, troubled marriages. Although these problems are often difficult and may contribute to the decline of the relationship, they can often be overcome when partners understand them and apply the kinds of cognitive techniques described in the earlier chapters.

Reduction of
Sexual Desire

The reduction or loss of sexual desire in marriage is far more common than most people realize. A research study found that even among happily married couples, at least 40 percent reported a reduction of sexual interest and desire over the course of time.

There are many reasons for this reduction. In general, the infatuation of courtship feeds the flames of desire; as the infatuation dies down, the intensity of the passion diminishes, too. As a marriage matures, other concerns of the partners, such as earning a living, making a home, and raising a family, become more pressing—absorbing some of the energy that had previously been channeled into romance. Gradually, the roles of wage earner and homemaker take primacy over the roles of lover. Finally, the fatigue and stress of work, child rearing, household duties, medical problems, and substance abuse tend to dampen sexual desire.

The major factors in reducing sexual desire after marriage, however, are psychological, stemming from attitudes toward oneself, toward sex, and toward one's partner. For instance, self-doubts involving a sense of inadequacy or a fear of failure can carry over into sexual activities. Or a person may have *specific* concerns about sex.

Some husbands and wives whose physical appearance does not measure up to their ideal may feel ashamed or self-critical, and they may avoid love making. A woman may dislike the size of her breasts or the shape of her thighs; a man may be self-conscious about the girth of his belly or about his spindly legs. Fearing that they do not appear womanly or manly enough—that they lack sex appeal—these individuals engage in a self-deprecation that interferes with the spontaneous expression of their sexual drive.

Further, many husbands and wives are concerned about their ability to perform adequately, to satisfy themselves and their spouse. This "performance anxiety" becomes a self-fulfilling prophecy: paying too much attention to their performance, they rob sex of much of its fun. Ultimately, sex may seem so much of a challenge or test that they lose desire for it.

Interpersonal problems between partners are a frequent source of trouble in their sex life. One of the most obvious problems is a discrepancy in their preferences—when, where, how, how long, and how often. Conflicting desires about timing, frequency, or variety of sex breed resentment, anxiety, or guilt. These unpleasant emotions can then pervade and contaminate their sexual contacts.

Negative feelings do not necessarily interfere with sexual desire. Many people find that sex is a welcome relief from feelings of anxiety, anger, or sadness. But when these feelings are directed toward the mate, they can be accentuated rather than relieved by sex. Sometimes they inhibit sexual arousal. There are exceptions, of course—when angry feelings are dispelled by fighting, for instance, and the partners' passions become aroused afterward.

A medley of attitudes toward your mate can encroach on your sexual feelings. For instance, people who regard sex as a "serious business" or who are depressed may experience an inhibition of sexual desire. Or, if you believe that your mate is using you, doesn't care about your feelings, or is undeserving, you may experience an automatic choking off of your sexual desire.

The loss of desire itself may lead to misunderstandings that further complicate the sexual as well as the nonsexual relationship. Ken, for example, interpreted Marjorie's loss of interest as a passive way of punishing him, of making him feel guilty for yelling at her. Martin believed that when Melanie turned off, she was trying to control the nature of their love making, to force him into being more romantic. Wendy interpreted Hal's waning sexual interest as a sign that he no longer cared for her. Of course in some cases, such interpretations may be valid, but usually they are wrong. Although people do not turn off voluntarily, they can turn on again voluntarily if they use the right methods.

I have listed in the next questionnaire some of the negative automatic thoughts reported by patients seen in our clinic. These kinds of thoughts occur to many husbands and wives during sex, and they interfere with their sexual desire and satisfaction. These ideas, which generally reflect attitudes about yourself, your mate, or sex in general, can be corrected by using the same techniques applied to the automatic thoughts described in Chapter 13. By correcting these negative attitudes and misinterpretations, couples find that their sexual desire can once again become active.

Review the statements in the questionnaire and select those thoughts and attitudes that represent your own thinking during sex. The techniques of cognitive therapy may be used to reduce the impact of these attitudes on your sexual life (see Chapter 13). An example of how cognitive methods can be used for this purpose follows on page 282.

Negative Automatic Thoughts during Sex

Read each statement and indicate how frequently you have these thoughts during sex:
    (0) *never*   (1) *rarely*   (2) *occasionally*   (3) *frequently*
    (4) *most of the time*   (5) *all the time*

Doubts about Self

_____ Parts of my body are not attractive.

_____ My body is not sexy enough.

_____ I am not good at this.

_____ I won't reach a climax.

_____ I won't satisfy my partner.

Doubts about Partner

_____ You're in too much of a hurry.

_____ You're only interested in your own pleasure.

_____ You're too mechanical.

_____ I wonder what you're thinking.

_____ I'm afraid I'll let you down.

_____ I'm worried that you'll be upset if we stop.

_____ I'm bothered that you're not turned on.

_____ How long is this going to take?

_____ That doesn't feel good but I'm afraid to tell you.

_____ You're trying too hard—I wish you'd relax.

_____ I'm concerned that you won't have a climax.

_____ I wish you enjoyed this more.

_____ You talk too much.

_____ If only this weren't so important.

_____ I'm not really enjoying this.

_____ This is all you're interested in.

Shoulds

_____ I feel I have to do whatever you want.

_____ I ought to enjoy this more.

_____ I'm expected to get turned on.

_____ We both should succeed at this.

_____ I feel obliged to give you an orgasm.

_____ I'm supposed to have an orgasm.

Negativity

_____ I'm just not in the mood.

_____ Why should I get interested?

_____ It's not going to work for me.

_____ I might as well give up.

_____ I'm only doing this to please you.

_____ I'm going through the motions but it means nothing to me.

_____ I'm too tired.

_____ It's too much effort.

_____ I'll be damned if I'll give in to your desire.

Whether you frequently have a large number of these thoughts and attitudes or whether only a few occur frequently, they can color your feelings about sex, damping down your normal sexual desire and possibly leading you to avoid sex completely. Use the techniques described in Chapter 13 to counteract the negative impact of these attitudes.

The anticipation of unpleasantness or indifference can increase over the years. It is fed by beliefs such as "I'm too old to get turned on" or "Sex is a burden" or "Sex is just for my partner—why should I get involved?" In the next section, I describe methods some partners have used to counteract those thoughts and attitudes that have interfered with their sexual satisfaction.

Self-Therapy for Sex Problems

There are certain obvious things that couples can do to increase sexual desire and enjoyment, such as use the methods proposed in Chapters 14, 15, and 16 for improving communication. Although it may be difficult at first, you can use these techniques to discuss each other's wishes concerning when and how often you will have sex. You can also bring up touchy subjects like differences in styles and each other's preferences regarding specifics such as foreplay, positions, and preferred kind of stimulation. As a way of breaking the ice, you could ask your partner about his or her likes and dislikes before plunging in with statements about your own preferences.

Some of the techniques for enhancing sex—such as relaxation, gradual bodily stimulation, focusing on sensations—or for overcoming specific problems are beyond the scope of this volume. Cognitive techniques that can resolve problems with sex include correcting faulty attitudes and misinterpretations, and using imagery to increase arousal.

Gary and Beverly had a satisfying marriage in many ways, but they ran into difficulties when he would spontaneously grab her, hold her in his arms, and caress her. Beverly would sometimes make a face and draw back. Gary would be hurt and puzzled—Beverly was usually warm and affectionate with him.

This simple description, though, doesn't tell what caused their problem—what they were thinking. During a session, I drew out the following information: Beverly was concerned that sometimes when Gary hugged her, he wanted to "go all the way." Instead of enjoying the closeness, she would wonder, *"What next?"* Since she did not want the "love making" to go any further at that time, she would draw away, thinking, *"He's not doing this for affection. All he wants is sex."*

Her interpretation was wrong. To Gary, playful hugging meant affection, not an invitation to love making. When Beverly drew back, he thought, *"She doesn't care for me,"* and he would withdraw, sulk, and not talk to her. As a result, they both lost much of their desire for intimacy. I suggested that they note their automatic thoughts the next time an incident occurred and then try to make a rational response. At the next appointment, each brought in a sheet of paper showing their responses:

Beverly's Thought Record

Situation	Automatic Thought	Feeling	Rational response
Gary made a pass at me.	He wants to have intercourse. He's damned inconsiderate. Can't he see I'm busy?	Angry	He's just trying to be affectionate. I don't know if he wants to go further. If I don't want to, I can tell him.

Gary's Thought Record

Situation	Automatic Thought	Feeling	Rational Response
Beverly pulled away from me when I gave her a little hug.	I was just giving her a hug. She's just not affectionate. What's the matter with her? Maybe she doesn't really love me.	Hurt	She's affectionate at other times. She just doesn't want to fool around now. It doesn't mean anything.

After Beverly and Gary wrote down their automatic thoughts and rational responses, they discussed their reactions with each other. They realized that they had misunderstood each other's behavior. They agreed that Gary should continue to express affection freely. If he was interested in more, he could watch for a signal from Beverly that she also was interested.

Gary and Beverly illustrate one of the ways in which mates often differ. One partner may react to an affectionate interchange with the desire for a more erotic exchange, while the other may feel the show of affection is satisfying in itself. If the husband occasionally presses for sexual intimacy after the initial overture, the wife may then experience *every* affectionate gesture as a seduction, thinking, *"All he's interested in is sex."*

Below are some typical automatic thoughts that people have during sex, and the rational responses they have made to those thoughts:

Automatic Thought	Rational Response
My breasts are too small.	It doesn't bother him. Why should it bother me?
I'm not enjoying this very much.	I often enjoy it a lot. I can't expect to enjoy it every time.

Automatic Thought	*Rational Response*
I wish she would have an orgasm.	She's told me many times she gets pleasure from being close. It puts pressure on her if I expect her to come.
He's so uptight about this. I wish he'd relax.	I can talk to him later about relaxing more and not being so serious.
She's taking forever to get warmed up. What's the matter with her?	Different people have different rhythms. I can pace myself until she's ready.

Some people with reduced sexual desire do not have any sexual fantasies during the initial phase of love making, though they have them when masturbating. Others believe that sexual fantasies are an important source of sexual stimulation. If you have difficulty in warming up, it might be helpful to experiment with conjuring up a fantasy during the preliminaries. Some people feel guilty or disloyal if they have romantic fantasies about someone other than their mate; however, such fantasies are generally normal and need not stir up guilty feelings.

Some couples read erotic material as a source of stimulation. Others find that watching X-rated movies arouses them. If these suggestions are not effective, it would be advisable to consider seeking professional help.

Infidelity

In the 1983 book *American Couples,* sociologists Philip Blumstein and Pepper Schwartz estimate that at least 21 percent of women and 37 percent of men have had an extramarital affair within ten years of marriage. The authors point out, however, that even partners who have had affairs still regard monogamy as an ideal.

Despite the fact that extramarital affairs appear to be fairly common, they can have a devastating effect on the other mate—and on the marriage itself—if they are discovered. Of course, such affairs not only undermine an already shaky marriage but may also be a symptom of it. Marriage counselors and divorce attorneys report that the overwhelming majority of their clients acknowledge having had affairs prior to or in association with the disruption of their relationship.

Why does an affair have such a traumatic effect on the aggrieved partner, particularly when the incident is so often described by the unfaithful mate as trivial? The answer lies in the symbolic meaning

of the affair. Nowhere is all-or-nothing thinking more clearly drama-
tized than in issues related to fidelity: a spouse is either faithful or
unfaithful. There is nothing in between. A single affair suffices to
label him (or her) as unfaithful, just as a person who has stolen once
is branded a thief, or a person caught in a single lie may forever be
seen as a liar.

Just as the bond of matrimony represents love, we get a sense of
the symbolic meaning of an extramarital affair from descriptive words
used by the offended spouse: *betrayal, treachery, deceit.* Even these
words don't completely capture the devastation that some aggrieved
mates experience—it's as though the entire fabric of their life has
been irreparably torn apart. Beyond this sense of devastation, doubts
about their own desirability, adequacy, or worthiness arise: "I obviously failed in some way . . . I guess nobody wants me," one injured
spouse said with tears. In addition, these spouses often experience a
deep wound to their pride or feel a prized possession has been stolen
from them.

Without condoning or accepting infidelity, the aggrieved spouse
can attempt to put this trauma in perspective. Polarized, all-or-nothing thinking makes the "betrayed" spouse likely to perceive the situation as a far greater threat to the marriage than it often is. This is
particularly true in those instances where the husband, for example,
has had a succession of one-night stands.

Of course, it is important to recognize that the threat is not imaginary: a single liaison *can* develop into something much more lasting
and present a serious threat to the marriage. However, the betrayed
spouse may react to *any* such offense as though it were such a major
threat.

Many couples come to counseling after infidelity has been discovered. When such behavior is a symptom of a disturbance in the marriage, a counselor can often help the couple unravel their problems
and thus reduce the likelihood of such an act's reoccurrence.

For example, Dan was a very busy salesman who spent almost all
of his waking hours on the job. He would usually leave the house at
6:00 in the morning and not return until after 8:00 or 9:00 at night. His
wife, Barbara, worked shorter hours, and she became increasingly
unhappy with his schedule, which deprived them of needed time
together. Their sexual relations drastically waned, leaving her feeling
empty and bored, and longing for satisfaction.

Barbara joined a number of organizations. Over the course of time,
she became friendly with another organization member who had recently been separated from his wife. As their relationship developed,
her new friend made sexual advances. At this point, Barbara's urges
for closeness and intimacy, which had not been fulfilled by Dan, came

to the fore. In addition, Barbara was a compliant person who had an inordinate need to please other people. These factors overrode her prudence: she and her friend had a single sexual liaison, after which she felt very guilty.

Dan began to suspect that Barbara had more than a platonic relationship with this other man. After he interrogated her, she felt so guilty that she burst into tears and told him exactly what had happened. Dan was "destroyed" and told her that he could not continue in a marriage in which he was unable to trust his own wife. After his hurt and fury had abated, however, they decided to seek marriage counseling.

When they consulted me, it was clear that a substantial change in their priorities and planning would be required to repair the damage to their relationship. Dan agreed to cut down on his work at the office. Barbara, in the meantime, was encouraged to find other sources of satisfaction. She started to take courses at a local college—something she had wanted to do for a long time.

Dan's reaction was typical of that of many aggrieved spouses, whose perspective shifts so as to make the errant partner seem all bad (see Chapter 8). Every action of the offender is weighed anew through this frame. Suddenly, qualities that had previously been admired are now seen as negative, superficial, or deceptive.

One of the first corrective steps is to attempt to reframe the injured mate's perspective of the offending spouse. Is the offense really an unpardonable sin? It initially seemed that way to Dan. But when he tried to look at it differently, he had to acknowledge that the offense wasn't as terrible as it first appeared. He realized that several of his married friends had "slept around," and he had considered this acceptable—as long as they didn't get caught. In fact, on several occasions he had been tempted to have an affair, though circumstances did not allow it. He also admitted that once he had *talked* to Barbara half jokingly about his having an affair—as a way of getting "prior consent" from her in the event that a future opportunity should arise. But he never expected that this conversation might open the door for *her* to have an affair.

As a matter of fact, such conversations between husbands and wives are not infrequent. Blumstein and Schwartz note in their case reports that husbands and wives often interpret these conversations completely differently; the husbands infer that they have received consent from their wives, while the wives believe they have made known their opposition to their husband's having an affair.

Dan realized that if *he* had had an affair, he would not feel that he was really disloyal or treacherous. Hence, he could not logically apply these labels to Barbara. This recognition helped him to "de-awfulize" the event: Barbara's actions were not "terrible." Even though he clung to the belief that Barbara had seriously wronged him—betrayed his trust—he acknowledged that her actions were understandable, given the real defect in their marriage. When he recognized the cause of Barbara's act, Dan was somewhat relieved—it did not mean that he was unlovable.

It is also important to "de-catastrophize" the event. Dan had said, "I will never be able to trust her again." He thought that once she crossed the line of fidelity, she could do it again—and again. But he was able to reason with himself: if she honestly meant to devote herself to improving the relationship, there would be no reason for her to look outside the marriage for satisfaction.

As Dan began to reframe his negative image of Barbara, he shifted from seeing her as unreliable, irresponsible, and completely self-indulgent to someone who had made a mistake and was truly sorry. He decided that he could still live with her—even though he would never forget her transgression. Before he reached this point, however, he had to explore the deep meanings of her infidelity and to overcome his need for revenge. As he reflected on the symbolic meaning, he realized that her affair made him feel helpless, as though she were completely out of his control, and that if she decided to do something, he had no influence whatsoever on her actions.

Dan's helpless reaction is not so farfetched as it may seem. Married people need to have a sense not only that their mate won't step over certain bounds but also that they have some control—that they can influence their mate not to do something that will hurt them. Basic trust, described in Chapter 11, gives a partner the security that the relationship comes foremost and won't be sacrificed for a whim or self-indulgence.

Dan also recognized that Barbara's affair had forced him to question himself. Was he as desirable as he thought? If she could do this to him, perhaps he wasn't basically likable; perhaps he was personally unattractive, would never be able to have an intimate relationship, and would end up abandoned and alone. He realized that his pain and desire for revenge stemmed largely from these feelings of unworthiness. When he was able to quell his self-doubts by looking at himself more realistically, his desire to punish Barbara for inflicting this pain decreased.

I urged Dan to try to understand Barbara's perspective, to see how loneliness in the marriage had made her vulnerable. As he was able to identify himself with her, he felt more forgiving. Such forgiveness is essential to reconciliation.

Dan still remained somewhat mistrustful of Barbara, but they agreed that she would take pains to allay his suspicions. Barbara agreed that when she had a meeting or engagement, she would let him know precisely where she was going and with whom, and would call him if she was going to be late. At the same time, Dan had to learn to tolerate the uncertainty of not knowing where Barbara was every minute. Barbara and Dan also reviewed ways they could please each other and show that they cared (Chapter 12). For instance, they started to buy each other presents, to eat breakfast out frequently, and to plan improvements on their house. They also made plans to go away together for long weekends. But most important, they agreed to have regular troubleshooting sessions that would allow them to air—and solve—their conflicts.

Stress

There are many stress points in a marriage, any combination of which may upset the relationship. In the early years, mates who previously have not been living together need to make innumerable decisions, from the smallest details (such as the allocation of shelf space in the bathroom) to large ones (such as where they will live). Questions of adjusting their work schedules, meals, and budgets also arise. Since there are invariably some differences in preferences, habits, and styles, the continual decision making, concessions, and compromises may produce friction. Couples living near the parents of one partner confront the standard in-law and child-parent problems, adding to the difficulties of this period of adjustment.

The next stress point usually occurs with the birth of the first child, an event that can dislocate the marital relationship in a number of ways. The birth and care of the first child produce an obvious burden for the mother. Less obvious are the effects on the father, who may experience depressed feelings over the dislocation of his marital relationship.

The new mother frequently experiences an upset in her "give-get balance." For many women, pregnancy, birth, and early child care require giving up some important sources of satisfaction and security without receiving equivalent replacements. The expectant mother may have to curtail her involvement in her job, in social engagements, and in sports and other recreational activities. As she diverts her attention and energy to the newborn, the sheer amount of time spent with her husband, particularly affectionate periods, may be diminished.

While there are obvious compensations in having a child, the new mother often experiences a net loss in immediate satisfaction and control over her life, and a simultaneous increase in pressures and responsibility. Despite the gradual shifts in the traditional roles of the mother and father, the lion's share of household duties and child care is borne by the mother.

For many women, this discrepancy between what they must sustain—the physical and psychological load—and what they receive in return—appreciation and support—may be expressed in an emotional disturbance, such as depression. Husbands are not immune to these shifts in the relationship. They may feel a loss of affection, interest, and empathy—and usually a reduction in their sexual relations. Research has shown that a large proportion of husbands and wives experience mild depression during this transition. On the other hand, many husbands feel closer to their wives. They participate by attending classes for prospective parents, by being present during the delivery of the baby, and by sharing in child care activities such as changing diapers, feeding, and bathing. Husbands often become more demonstrative to their wives after the birth of the first child (although not necessarily for subsequent births).

Other difficult periods occur in child rearing, such as the children's teenage years and the movement of grown-up children from the house. Increased involvement or changes in careers for one or both spouses, illness or death of the spouses' parents, and, finally, retirement are also likely to create marital stress points.

The *timing* of a given stress may have a profound effect on a marriage. Take, for example, wives pursuing advanced degrees. Investigators have found that when a certain factor was present, the marriages of women who went to graduate school tended to break up after they began their studies. Those women who had children prior to or during graduate school were more likely to be divorced than those who had children after graduate school. Having a supportive husband, however, tended to neutralize the stress for wives in graduate school—but did not reduce it for those wives who already had children. The investigators concluded that the marital disruption was caused in part by the strain that resulted when the wives tried to balance career and mothering roles. Other contributing factors undoubtedly included the husbands' difficulties in coping with the changes in their wives' roles.

In sum, each phase of marriage has its own specific pressures, losses, and stresses. And the strain itself often impairs the partners' capacity to deal with these problems.

STRESS AND FAULTY THINKING

We all know that when under strain, we are more irritable and more apt to lose control of our tempers. What we may not realize, though, is that we are also more subject to faulty thinking, and that this is partly responsible for our irritability and excessive anger. The same kinds of erroneous thinking at play when one partner negatively frames the other—tunnel vision, overgeneralization, "catastrophizing"—come to the fore when we are under stress.

This process is illustrated by Laura—head of the PR department for a division of city government that was frequently attacked by the media—who told me, "When my job is going well, nothing about Fred bothers me. He can do no wrong. When my job is going poorly and I'm under a lot of stress, he can do no right. I can only see his faults and the bad things he does. Everything he does is wrong."

At times like this, the stressed mate seems to be at her most unreasonable. Laura recounted an exchange with Fred that occurred when she was under considerable pressure at work. Fred had promised to fix a chair but had repeatedly forgotten to purchase the right tool.

FRED: Oh, no! I forgot it again.

LAURA: What do you mean you forgot it? You already forgot it once, and this time I even went to the trouble of calling you about it.

FRED: I'm sorry. I got busy and I forgot it. I'm absentminded about these things.

LAURA: You shouldn't have forgotten it!

FRED: I had an emergency patient right after you called, and it just went right out of my head.

LAURA: You care more about your patients than you care about me!

FRED: [getting angry] That's not true! You're overreacting.

When a person is this upset, he or she tends to discount benign explanations ("absentminded," "emergency patient") and clings to negative interpretations such as *"You don't care about me."* (Interestingly, individuals who are not themselves absentminded are particularly dubious about the "absentminded" explanation offered by their mates.)

Another effect of stress is a slippage of control over your thinking and behavior. People who are strained find it more difficult to moderate their extreme interpretations, to correct their distortions, and to regulate how they express their feelings. At times like these, they are more likely to slip into using abusive language—even physically assaulting their partner—or withdrawing totally. When stress leads to drinking, the combination of the two may be explosive—generating a violent display of anger.

People under stress also exhibit childish patterns of thinking and acting, also known as regression. Laura observed, "When my job is going well, I enjoy my relationship with Fred. I don't feel pressured. I can go my own way. But when I'm all stressed, I cling to him, I depend completely on him, I need him constantly."

ANTIDOTE TO STRESS

What should you do when you're "stressed out"? The first bit of advice is to try to avoid becoming stressed in the first place. By applying some of the principles of cognitive therapy described in this book, you may be able to prevent stress more often. For instance, many people slide into this state because they "awfulize" and "catastrophize" particular disappointments or frustrations. "It's terrible that my staff didn't get the work done in time" and "Jon's mediocre report card shows he'll never make it in life" are two examples. Such exaggerated interpretations are registered as increased tension in your body and eventually deplete your resources—you no longer have the psychic energy to temper your emotions or correct your extreme thinking. You can also head off stress by countering your automatic thoughts with rational responses.

The *shoulds* are another mental mechanism that drains your resources: the continual "do this," "don't do that" takes its toll. Confronting your *shoulds* and damping them down to realistic levels will take a great deal of needless pressure off you.

When you are already under stress, there are steps you can take to minimize its impact on you. You should first of all recognize the signs of strain—tension, distractibility, irritability, difficulties in sleeping. By realizing that you are prone to overreact or misinterpret what people say or do, you can guard against trouble by giving people the benefit of the doubt, by avoiding unnecessary confrontations, and by steering clear of controversial topics with your mate—until you are more rested and relaxed.

There are several ways in which you can calm down and help restore your mental resources. Taking time off to get away completely from your problems is one. Some people find that even taking a long walk helps to settle them down. Certain forms of relaxation or meditation, such as those recommended by Dr. Herbert Benson in *The Relaxation Response*, are helpful to many people.

What can you do when your mate is stressed? First, you need to recognize some of the previously mentioned telltale signs: a short fuse, restlessness, and a tendency to misinterpret what you say. During this period, avoid getting into unnecessary conflicts or confrontations. Also, try to offer some type of diversion—some favorite form of recreation or entertainment.

When both of you are under stress, it may be best to postpone addressing important concerns or making major decisions. This is also a good time to practice giving your partner the benefit of the doubt. If you have to deal with particularly obnoxious behavior, for instance, arrive at benign explanations (*"He's really worn out"*) instead of more negative explanations (*"She's always putting me down"*).

Two-Job Families

Increasing numbers—more than half—of all married women are now in the work force. As a result, growing attention is being paid to the problems of the two-job family. In a sense, the term *two-job* is a misnomer, because there are at least three jobs in such families—two are paid and the third, homemaking, is not. (In some families, of course, homemaking—both housekeeping and child care—is done to some extent by hired help: maid, housekeeper, babysitter.)

Social psychologists Rena Repetti and Carol Piotrkowski did research on the two-career, three-job family. They found that when wives are satisfied with their jobs, they are more content within marriage and feel better about the children than do those who stay at home with the children. Nonetheless, working wives report—as do working husbands—that they tend to carry home the tensions, disappointments, and frustrations of work. One wife said, "When I open the door at night, I'm different from the person who left in the morning."

In a study of working wives, Blumstein and Schwartz found that in most cases the wives continued to be responsible for much of the housework in addition to their full-time jobs. Even when husbands were unemployed, they did substantially less housework than the average working wife. In addition, when husbands agreed to share household responsibilities equally, they still trailed their wives in time spent on typical chores such as cooking, laundry, and grocery shopping. Blumstein and Schwartz concluded, "The idea of shared responsibilities [has] turned out to be a myth."

PSYCHOLOGICAL PROBLEMS

Although double paychecks contribute to the material comforts of a couple and offer greater flexibility in spending, the two jobs can aggravate the partners' psychological and interpersonal problems. Laura, for example, was content with the way she did her housework when she got a job, but became upset over Fred's desultory attention to the domestic chores he had taken on. And Fred secretly harbored resentment over Laura's telling him what to do and looking over his shoulder while he was doing it.

Laura told me, "The only area I have control over is the kitchen. There's a right way and a wrong way to do things. He never puts away the dishes properly on the shelf. He mixes the tall glasses and the short glasses and the cups. And he won't stack the dishes properly in the dishwasher. And he doesn't rinse the dishes well enough before putting them in the dishwasher."

So far this may seem to be a simple conflict of standards, which could be resolved by Fred's paying more attention to his tasks or by Laura's relaxing her standards. But beneath the practical problem is a psychological difficulty. Look at the meaning for Laura:

I think he considers it beneath him to do the job. He does it, but he doesn't really care about *how* he does it. It's all right for me to do it but it's not all right for him. Basically, he doesn't think much of me.

We see here that questions of status and respect are involved. Now, let's hear Fred's complaint:

She's a fanatic about the housekeeping. She's always looking over my shoulder to see that I do it properly. I'll admit my heart isn't in it—I already have a boss at work. But I'm willing to pitch in. The main thing, though, is that Laura's hung up on this equality thing. Everything has to be equal. When I come home from work and she's in the middle of a job, like diapering the baby, she stops in midair and says it's my turn—even before I have time to put my coat away!

Let's tune in on their dialogue:

LAURA: Fred, you don't treat me like an equal. You're always trying to get out of things so that I have the most work to do. I'm not your inferior.

FRED: I'm willing to do this for you.

LAURA: You're not doing it for me, you're doing it for *us*.

FRED: I'm willing to cut it down the middle. But seeing as that you're not happy with the way I do things, I'll take my half and hire a maid to do it.

LAURA: You already have a maid—me! You're always using me. It's okay for me to do my share of the work, but you can go off and hire another servant to do your share. That's not equality.

FRED: Equality doesn't mean telling me what to do all the time.

What we see here is not a simple fight over the division of labor but a clash of personalities. As part of her own personal growth and desire to be more independent of Fred, Laura got a full-time job. Nonetheless, the personality conflict was not solved by her independence at work; it was played out in the arena of domestic duties, where their bristles and sensitivities came to the fore.

Laura was sensitive in two areas: she wanted assurance that Fred valued her contributions, and she wanted to be respected—as well as treated—as "an equal human being." Fred, on the other hand, was sensitive to anything resembling domination or control on her part. He rebelled in response to Laura's checking on how he performed his duties. Consequently, he did his share halfheartedly, undermining the agreed-on plan.

My strategy in counseling was twofold. Laura was shown that although she subscribed to equality in principle, she was not treating Fred as an equal when she monitored his performance or told him, "It's your turn now." Laura came to see that despite the division of labor, she still took command to see that things were done properly. She then saw how her approach to housework was dominated by *shoulds* and how she applied these *shoulds* to Fred.

I pointed out to her that Fred was willing and capable of doing his job, but that her overseeing his work undermined his morale—and thus his motivation. Fred, on the other hand, had to overcome his sensitivity to Laura's feedback. Ultimately, he was able to see that she wasn't trying to dominate him but to ensure that the job was done reasonably well.

Over time, Fred found that he could negotiate arrangements with Laura without sacrificing any autonomy. Similarly, when Laura was able to see the situation from Fred's perspective—that he experienced her as being too bossy—she was able to relax her surveillance. She realized that it was Fred's sensitivity to being controlled rather than any perception of her as inferior that made him defiant.

In summary, when both mates are breadwinners, they can resolve conflicts by using the same analytic tools that I have described in previous chapters. First, define the specific points of conflict. Second, ascertain the meanings of the conflicts to yourself *and* to your spouse. Third, try to revise your own perspectives. Fourth, think of solutions.

"GROWING AWAY FROM EACH OTHER"

A problem may arise—particularly in two-job families—as one or both partners change and mature over the years. Thus, a couple who had been in a close relationship may grow apart when one or both become more independent or develop new interests, tastes, or values not shared by the other. Such differences sometimes cause the partners to lose interest in each other.

Marie, a thirty-five-year-old woman in a two-job household, consulted me about divorcing her husband. She told the following story: "I worshiped my husband at first. Michael was everything I had dreamed about. He was tall and strong and very sure of himself. When I saw him across the room, I would turn to mush. We were married for about ten years when I got a job in a publishing company. I met new and exciting people every day, and I looked forward to going to work. But when I got home, we didn't have anything to talk about. I started to really see Michael for the first time. He was dull and boring. All I could see was him sitting in front of the TV with a beer can in his hand or sprawled out on the sofa. I still love him, in a way, but I don't respect him anymore."

Marie had changed her criteria for judging Michael, and with this change her admiration for him lessened. Marie had come from a Puerto Rican family that was traditional and patriarchal. When Michael and Marie married, they re-created the patriarchy, with Michael in the authoritarian role and Marie in the subservient one. But after she started to work, their roles equalized. Marie no longer looked up to Michael as a symbol of authority, and she became acutely conscious of his flaws.

My counseling with Marie consisted of two parts: first, assessing Michael's good and bad qualities, and second, determining what Marie wanted out of life and how best to attain it. Marie listed Michael's desirable and undesirable qualities:

Undesirable Qualities	*Desirable Qualities*
He's a slob.	He loves me.
He has no interests except sports.	He supported me in getting a job.
He never helps with the housework.	He's gentle.
He's uncouth at times.	He's a good father.
	He works hard at his job.
	He's handy at fixing things.
	He's reliable.
	He never gets mad.

In the course of reevaluating Michael, Marie realized that his strong points outweighted his "bad" ones. As she compared him in a systematic way with the men at work—whom she admired—she saw them as lacking Michael's "sterling" qualities. In one of her comparisons, she told me, "Joe is exciting and very intelligent, but he's highly neurotic, very emotional, and has no respect at all for his wife. I'm sure he plays around. Living with him would be an adventure, but it could never last."

As Marie reexamined her new values and reassessed Michael, she began to give greater weight to his virtues—and her respect for him increased once again. She also came to realize that it was unnecessary for her to meet all her needs through one person. She could maintain an affectionate marital relationship and at the same time enjoy the intellectual stimulation of other people.

I spoke to Marie only twice, but if the problem had not been worked out somewhat readily, I would have seen Michael and then counseled them together. It is possible that Michael had withdrawn from Marie because he felt unwanted and unappreciated, and that part of Marie's dissatisfaction was a result of this distancing. At the second interview, Marie said that she had decided to put more into her relationship with Michael. She realized that he was a "diamond in the rough," and she resolved to improve her own attitude toward him.

In another case, Harold's reactions to changes in his wife, Carol, posed a different kind of problem. He complained, "All she does is talk about the wonderful people she's met at work. I've met them—they're a bunch of creeps. She can't talk about anything else but her work. And she invites those people over all the time. They act like they belong to a cult or something."

In this case, Carol was not interested in ending the marriage—in fact, she saw nothing wrong with it. But Harold felt left out and regarded her co-workers as "aliens." The counseling incorporated three steps to help them restructure their personal and social life: (1) Carol was to put a limit on the amount of time she discussed her job, (2) Harold was to have equal time to discuss his work, and (3) they were to take turns in deciding whose friends to invite to the house.

RELIEVING THE STRESS OF TWO-JOB FAMILIES

Inevitably, the strain experienced by one partner spills over into the relationship. In the case of working parents, an effective way to reduce stress would be for the husband/father to lessen the work overload on the wife/mother, and to help resolve her conflict between working and mothering. He can, for example, explain that he doesn't expect her to do a "perfect job" as a wife and mother at the same time that she is holding a part-time or full-time job—and that she can't expect this of herself. Further, by participating more actively at home, he can alleviate her distress over "neglecting" her children and household duties. At the same time, the husband/father has to resolve his conflict between his job and the responsibilities of home life.

A number of stress programs have been successful in reducing the strain of dual-career marriages. Part of one program aims to restore a proper give-get balance. The key steps follow:

1/*Emphasize the positive.* Concentrate on the benefits you get from having a job: a greater sense of personal fulfillment, an increased standard of living, an ability to provide more cultural and educational opportunities for the children, and greater equality between husband and wife. Studies have shown that working mothers express more contentment with their lives than do nonworking mothers.

2/*Set priorities.* Since conflicts between family and job demands are inevitable, you need some principle to guide you in resolving the conflict. For example, some people follow the maxim "Family needs come first."

3/*Be ready to compromise with yourself.* It is impossible to reach an ideal in both family and job. A series of compromises is necessary—for example, spending less time with the children or on the job than you would like, or possibly sacrificing opportunities for advancement at work. Keep in mind that you can't realistically get the best of everything but should aim for the best balance among your various activities.

4/*Separate your family and work roles.* Try to achieve this as much as possible. For example, Marjorie would feel guilty while at work, thinking she should be spending more time with her children. But when she was with her children, she felt guilty about not working on assignments taken home from the office. She had to train herself to block off her office time from her time at home—not to think about the children when she was at work, and not to worry about work when she was with the children.

5/*Be realistic about your standards.* Some people believe that their homes should be just as immaculate after they have children as before, or when both spouses, instead of one, work. It may be necessary to lower your standards and to accept some degree of disorder.

6/ *Organize domestic duties*. The dilemma of the domestic overload sometimes can be resolved by reassigning who does what, with the husband and children taking on more of what traditionally has been the wife's responsibility. Be as concrete as possible in dividing household responsibilities. Many families profit from writing down everyone's assignments on a job chart. Try to clarify ambiguous areas, such as which parent has responsibility for putting the children to bed.

7/ *Cultivate a sharing attitude with your spouse*. This is the place to put into practice the kind of helping relationship I cited in previous chapters. Sit down with your spouse periodically and discuss what you can do to help each other in your respective jobs—at home and at work. Home problems deserve as much respect and attention as do work problems. Many husbands and wives report great relief when their partners lend an ear to their complaints, offer a sounding board, and give advice and encouragement.

8/ *Try to maintain a balance between responsibilities and recreation*. Remember that if you are both working in order to increase your standard of living, you should use some of the extra income to enhance your enjoyment of life. If you spend all your psychological resources on job and home responsibilities, you will have little energy left over to do the things that will make your life more balanced and enjoyable.

Problems in Remarriage

In view of the fact that more than half of all marriages end in divorce, and that 83 percent of all divorced men and 75 percent of all divorced women remarry, the problems of the remarried couple deserve special attention.

Remarried families have a unique set of difficulties, no matter how compatible the spouses are. One common problem for many of them involves where the family members' loyalties lie. Who is "inside" the family and who is "outside" may be unclear, and may vary in the minds of different family members. For example, children may regard themselves as disloyal to their absent natural parent if they enjoy being with their stepparent. On the other hand, a stepfather may feel guilty for spending more time and establishing a closer relationship with his stepchildren than with his natural children. Such an arrangement can also lead to resentment on the part of his own children.

The issue of loyalty is compounded by the tendency of children of different parents living under one roof to regard themselves not as one family but two. They may say things such as "You're not my brother" or "Don't talk to my mother that way." They tend to maintain boundaries based on loyalty to their earlier families.

Closely related to the issue of loyalty is the problem of competition, which can take many forms. For example, struggles arise among natural children and stepchildren for the attention of a parent. In addition, the natural father and mother may compete with each other for the favor of their child. Charges of favoritism are often heard—for example, that the stepmother favors her biological children.

Remarried parents may also differ in their policies about child rearing. They must deal with stepchildren without having had the opportunity to develop and agree on sets of rules and routines when those children were younger. They are suddenly expected to collaborate as parents, without having had time to prepare themselves.

Even though remarried parents may want to work as a team, they are often hampered by the tendency of the natural parent to assume the role of disciplinarian with the natural children. He or she may say, "She's *my* child—I'll handle it." When the stepparent attempts to enforce a rule, the stepchildren may challenge his or her right to impose it when it differs from those rules established by the natural parent—thus triggering a fight.

Remarried couples also must agree on such questions as how much autonomy to allow the children, curfew and bedtime restrictions, and the degree to which a child is allowed to express anger toward a parent.

Conflicts that arise from child-rearing differences between the remarried parents can lead to shifting coalitions: the wife siding with her husband against her natural child in one instance, the natural children and stepchildren ganging up on one parent another time, or the husband siding with his natural children against the wife.

One remarried couple ran into conflict when the husband's teenage children, who were living with their mother, would drop in unexpectedly after school. The stepmother felt that they should call first, while the father believed the children should be free to come over whenever they wanted. The husband and wife each felt aggrieved by the other's position, and they accused each other of not caring.

The many problems that arise in the lives of remarried couples can be dealt with successfully, but they require a high level of decision making and fine tuning by the new couple. Frequent decision-making meetings, such as those described in the previous chapters, are extremely helpful. In addition, the new spouses should try hard not to allow their conflicts to interfere with their work as co-parents.

Some experts say that the percentage of divorce in remarriages is almost as high as in first marriages. However, I believe that if the partners are prepared for the psychological problems that occur, they can solve them. Some of these problems revolve around the basic beliefs of remarried families about family life and their explanations for the causes of problems among family members. Among these expectations and beliefs are the following:

▷ Our new family unit should be happier than the old one.

▷ My stepchildren should view me as their "new mommy" (or "daddy").

▷ My children are disloyal if they become attached to their stepparent.

▷ If my children care about their natural (absent) parent, they can't care for me.

▷ Our new marriage should be free of conflict.

▷ We should try to be perfect parents and stepparents.

The tendency to assign blame when difficulties arise is more complicated in remarried families. Often the blame is leveled against the ex-spouse: "Your son would be all right if your ex-wife would leave him alone" or "Your ex-husband gives in too much to your daughter." Remarried couples need to stop blaming and, instead, to treat each difficulty as a problem to be solved. When the partners differ, they have to negotiate. Even more than is the case in the original families, remarried couples must clarify the division of responsibilities, make systematic schedules, and set priorities.

Remarried life demands many compromises, but these can be achieved if the partners apply themselves. They must be sensitive to each other's pressures and needs, and cultivate an extraordinary degree of patience and tolerance. Given this good will, remarried couples can attain a substantially better degree of stability and happiness than in their first marriages.

NOTES

Introduction

N.B.: Several studies have shown the effectiveness of the cognitive approach to marital problems. Such programs emphasize problem-solving skills; improving communication; and clarifying unrealistic expectations, faulty attributions, and misinterpretations. Some programs have been successful in *preventing* marital distress.

D. Duffy and T. Dowd, "The Effect of Cognitive-Behavioral Assertion Training on Aggressive Individuals and Their Partners," *Southern Psychologist* 3 (1987): 45–50.

H. J. Markman et al., "Prevention of Marital Distress: A Longitudinal Investigation," *Journal of Consulting and Clinical Psychology* 56 (1988): 210–217.

P. 3: Most couples are aware that there is a continuing crisis in marriage; that between 40 and 55 percent of marriages are likely to end in divorce. *Newsweek* (July 15, 1987): 15.

Chapter 1
The Power of Negative Thinking

P. 25: Research studies have shown that couples in distressed marriages can be reasonably objective in the motives they attribute to other couples; but, in the same situations, they inaccurately attribute negative motives to their own spouses.

P. Noller, "Misunderstandings in Marital Communication: Study of Nonverbal Communication," *Journal of Personality and Social Psychology* 39 (1980): 1135–1148.

P. Noller, "Gender and Marital Adjustment Level Differences in Decoding Messages from Spouses and Strangers," *Journal of Personality and Social Psychology* 41 (1981): 272–278.

P. Noller, *Nonverbal Communication and Marital Interaction* (New York: Pergamon Press, 1984).

J. M. Gottman, *Marital Interaction: Experimental Investigations* (New York: Academic Press, 1979).

P. 26: The power of the negative is shown in a number of research studies. What most of all distinguishes distressed marriages from satisfactory marriages is not so much the absence of pleasant experiences but the larger number of unpleasant experiences (or ones given that interpretation).

C. Schaap, "A Comparison of the Interaction of Distressed and Nondistressed Married Couples in a Laboratory Situation," in K. Halweg and N. S. Jacobson, eds., *Marital Interaction: Analysis and Modification* (New York: Guilford), pp. 133–158.

Chapter 2
The Light and the Darkness

P. 31: Infatuation has been likened to an addiction by social psychologist Stanton Peele.

S. Peele, *Love and Addiction* (New York: New American Library, 1976).

Chapter 3
The Clash of Perspectives

P. 45: For example, Carol Gilligan, a psychologist at Harvard University, has shown that wives tend to be more involved in personal relationships (sociotropic), whereas husbands are likely to be more independent.

C. Gilligan, *In a Different Voice: Psychological Theory and Women's Development* (Cambridge, MA: Harvard University Press, 1982).

P. 46: Research by University of Maryland psychologist Norman Epstein and his colleagues indicates that during misunderstandings, distressed partners are more likely to attribute negative motives to each other than are nondistressed couples.

R. Berley and N. Jacobson, "Causal Attributions in Intimate Relationships," in P. Kendall, ed., *Advances in Cognitive-Behavioral Research and Therapy*, vol. 3. (New York: Academic Press, 1984).

N. Epstein, "Depression and Marital Dysfunction: Cognitive and Behavioral Vantages," *International Journal of Mental Health* 13 (1984): 86–104.

N. Epstein, J. L. Pretzer, and B. Fleming, "The Role of Cognitive Appraisal in Self-Reports of Marital Communication," *Behavior Therapy* 18 (1987): 51–69.

Chapter 4
Breaking the Rules

P. 62: Psychoanalyst Karen Horney, in a series of books on the "neurotic personality," introduced the concept of the "tyranny of the *shoulds*."

K. Horney, *Neurosis and Human Growth* (New York: W. W. Norton, 1950).

P. 63: They think, *"He has no right to treat me this way," "I deserve better than this," "She let me down."*

A. Ellis, *Reason and Emotion in Psychotherapy* (New York: Lyle Stuart, 1962).

P. 66: Some studies have shown that at this time, husbands as well as wives are prone to experience symptoms of depression and increased irritability.

J. Fawcett and R. York, "Spouses' Strength of Identification and Reports of Symptoms during Pregnancy and the Postpartum Period," *Florida Nursing Review* 2 (1987): 1–10.

P. 67: Psychologists Norman Epstein, James Pretzer, and Barbara Fleming have found that individuals in distressed marriages tend to get high scores on questionnaires like this one.
Epstein, Pretzer, and Fleming, "The Role of Cognitive Appraisal."

Chapter 5
Static in Communication

P. 74: The couples with unhappy marriages were less accurate in decoding what their spouses meant than were the happily married spouses.
Noller, "Gender and Marital Adjustment Level Differences."

P. 75: But as anthropologists Daniel Maltz and Ruth Borker point out, women take these feedback utterances to mean *"I am listening."*
D. Maltz and R. Borker, "A Cultural Approach to Male-Female Miscommunications," in J. J. Gumperz, ed., *Language and Social Identity* (Cambridge, England: Cambridge University Press, 1982) pp. 196–216.

P. 77: This is a prime example of how a difference in conversational style leads to misunderstanding, anger, and criticism.
D. Tannen, *That's Not What I Meant* (New York: Ballantine Books, 1986).

P. 79: Although a given person may have essentially the same style as the spouse, in most instances where there is a difference in style, the wife adopts a culturally defined, "feminine" conversational style; the husband, a "masculine" style.
Maltz and Borker, "A Cultural Approach to Male-Female Miscommunications."

P. 80: This conversational device may also represent their greater involvement in personal relations.
Tannen, *That's Not What I Meant.*

P. 83: A poll by *Family Circle* magazine had illuminating results: the respondents indicated that women are much more willing to talk about the intimate details of their lives with other women than they are with men.
C. Rubenstein and M. Jaworski, "When Husbands Rate Second," *Family Circle* (May 1987).

Chapter 6
Breakdown of the Partnership

P. 90: Without realizing it, people have a tendency to interpret events in a way that puts them in the most favorable light, or serves their own self-interest.
T. R. Tyler and V. Devinitz, "Self-Serving Bias in the Attribution of Responsibility: Cognitive vs. Motivational Explanations," *Journal of Experimental Social Psychology* 17 (1981): 408–416.

Chapter 8
Tricks of the Mind

P. 127: Polarized thinking is, in part, a carry-over from the kind of categorical thinking typical of childhood.

J. Piaget, *The Moral Judgment of the Child* (Glencoe, IL: Free Press, 1965).

P. 129: In identical circumstances, distressed couples are more likely to make negative attributions toward their mate than they would toward someone else, according to several research studies.

F. Fincham et al., "Attribution Processes in Distressed and Nondistressed Marriages," *Journal of Abnormal Psychology* 94 (1985): 183–190.

H. Jacobson et al., "Attributional Processes in Distressed and Nondistressed Married Couples," *Cognitive Therapy and Research* 9 (1985): 35–50.

Noller, "Gender and Marital Adjustment Level Differences."

P. 130: *"If I am sad, it means my spouse doesn't like me."*

D. Burns, *Feeling Good* (New York: New American Library, 1980).

Chapter 9
In Mortal Combat

P. 147: George Bach, for example, has advocated that couples "express their anger" and has offered techniques for doing so.

G. Bach and P. Wyden, *The Intimate Enemy* (New York: Avon Books, 1968).

P. 147: These prescriptions have been criticized by authors like psychologists Albert Ellis and Carol Tavris.

A. Ellis, *How to Live with and without Anger* (New York: Reader's Digest Press, 1977).

C. Tavris, *Anger: The Misunderstood Emotion* (New York: Simon & Schuster, 1982).

Chapter 10
Can Your Relationship Improve?

P. 160: Research indicates that when partners continually and unrealistically blame each other, their marriage is distressed.

Fincham, "Attribution Processes," pp. 183–190.

A. Hollyworth-Monroe and H. Jacobson, "Causal Attributions of Married Couples," *Journal of Personality and Social Psychology* 48 (1985): 1398–1412.

Jacobson et al., "Attributional Processes."

P.163: Problems arise when the match between two mates is not good.

W. Ickes, "Sex-Role Differences and Compatibility in Relationships," in W. Ickes, ed., *Compatible and Incompatible Relationships* (New York: Springer-Verlag, 1985) pp. 187–208.

Chapter 11
Reinforcing the Foundations

P. 177: Erik Erikson has noted that this attitude starts to develop out of a child's experiences with major figures in the family.

E. Erikson, *Childhood and Society* (New York: W. W. Norton, 1964).

Chapter 12
Tuning Up the Relationship

P. 188: Most husbands, by contrast, regard their wife as their best friend.

Rubenstein and Jaworski, "When Husbands Rate Second."

P. 193: Dr. Goldstein found that 70 percent of the couples who tried this simple method reported an improvement in their relationship.

M. K. Goldstein, "Research Report: Annual Meeting of the Association for the Advancement of Behavior Therapy." (New York, October 1972).

P. 194: For example, avoid making conditional requests—veiled attacks, really—such as "I'd like you to help me with the dishes, but take that pained expression off your face" or "I'd like you to talk to me when you come home from the office instead of dashing in to watch the six o'clock news."

R. Stuart, *Helping Couples Change* (New York: Guilford Press, 1980).

Chapter 13
Changing Your Own Distortions

P. 208: By reexamining this positive side, Sharon and Paul were able to recapture some of the good feelings they originally had for each other.

A number of cognitive therapists have used "flip-side analysis." Janis Abrahms, Susan Joseph, and Norman Epstein have all used this approach effectively. The most complete description has been provided by Janis Abrahms in a workshop at the Annual Meeting of the Association for the Advancement of Behavior Therapy, Boston, November 1987.

Chapter 14
The Art of Conversation

P. 213: Even couples who were well tuned in to each other in the early years may later find that their simplest conversations are jarred by misinterpretations leading to the complaint "That's not what I meant."

Tannen, *That's Not What I Meant.*

P. 221: A number of authors regard men's reticence about their feelings as an inevitable male shortcoming.

For example: L. Rubin, *Intimate Strangers: Men and Women Together* (New York: Harper & Row, 1984).

P. 222: A "marrying judge" found that when she asked couples what drew them together, a great many replied, "We laugh together."

Personal communication from Judge Phyllis W. Beck, Superior Court, Commonwealth of Pennsylvania.

P. 222: Other possibilities are suggested in psychiatrist William Betcher's book *Intimate Play*.

W. Betcher, *Intimate Play: Creating Romance in Everyday Life* (New York: Viking, 1987).

Chapter 16
Troubleshooting

P. 254: CONTAMINATED REQUESTS

R. Stuart, *Helping Couples Change* (New York: W. W. Norton, 1985).

Chapter 17
Taming the Furies

PP. 259–260: However, in systematic research, assessments by an impartial judge indicate that although the spouses believe that their mate is difficult, derelict, or antagonistic—and that *they* are the injured ones—both contribute to the arguments.

Gottman, *Marital Interaction*.

Rosenstorf et al., "Interaction Analysis of Marital Conflict," in K. Halweg and N. S. Jacobson, eds., *Marital Interaction: Analysis and Modification* (New York: Guilford Press) pp. 159–181.

PP. 265–266: Psychologists Donald Duffy and Tom Dowd, for example, found that clients trained in a method like this showed a much greater reduction in their anger than did a comparable group of clients who did not receive this instruction.

Duffy and Dowd, "The Effect of Cognitive-Behavioral Assertion Training."

Chapter 18
Special Problems

P. 278: A research study found that even among happily married couples, at least 40 percent reported a reduction of sexual interest and desire over the course of time.

E. Frank, C. Anderson, and D. Rubenstein, "Frequency of Sexual Dysfunction in 'Normal' Couples," *New England Journal of Medicine* 299(3) (1978): 111–115.

P. 282: Some of the techniques for enhancing sex—such as relaxation, gradual bodily stimulation, focusing on sensations—or for overcoming specific problems are beyond the scope of this volume.

L. G. Barbach, *For Yourself: The Fulfillment of Female Sexuality* (Garden City, NY: Anchor Books, 1976).

H. S. Kaplan, *The New Sex Therapy: Active Treatment of Sexual Dysfunction* (New York: Brunner/Mazel, 1974).

M. Scarf, *Intimate Partners: Patterns in Love and Marriage* (New York: Random House, 1987).

B. Zilbergeld, *Male Sexuality* (New York: Bantam Books, 1978).

P. 284: In the 1983 book *American Couples,* sociologists Philip Blumstein and Pepper Schwartz estimate that at least 21 percent of women and 37 percent of men have had an extramarital affair within ten years of marriage.

P. Blumstein and P. Schwartz, *American Couples* (New York: William Morrow, 1983) p. 583.

P. 286: But he never expected that this conversation might open the door for *her* to have an affair.

Blumstein and Schwartz, *American Couples.*

P. 289: Despite the gradual shifts in the traditional roles of the mother and father, the lion's share of household duties and child care is borne by the mother.

Blumstein and Schwartz, *American Couples.*

P.289: The investigators concluded that the marital disruption was caused in part by the strain that resulted when the wives tried to balance career and mothering roles.

S. K. Houseknecht, S. Vaughn, and A. S. Macke, "Marital Disruption among Professional Women: The Timing of Career and Family Events," *Social Problems* 31(3) (1984): 273–284.

P. 291: Certain forms of relaxation or meditation, such as those recommended by Dr. Herbert Benson in *The Relaxation Response,* are helpful to many people.

H. Benson, *The Relaxation Response* (New York: William Morrow, 1975).

P. 292: Increasing numbers—more than half—of all married women are now in the work force.

Blumstein and Schwartz, *American Couples,* p. 118.

P. 292: Nonetheless, working wives report—as do working husbands—that they tend to carry home the tensions, disappointments, and frustrations of work.

C. S. Piotrkowski and R. L. Repetti, "Dual-Earner Families," *Marriage and Family Review* 7(2/3) (1984): 99–124.

P. 292: Blumstein and Schwartz concluded, "The idea of shared responsibilities [has] turned out to be a myth."

Blumstein and Schwartz, *American Couples,* p. 118.

P. 297: A number of stress programs have been successful in reducing the strain of dual-career marriages.

D. A. Skinner, "The Stressors and Coping Patterns of Dual-Career Families," in H. I. McCubbin, A. E. Cauble, and J. M. Patterson, eds., *Family Stress, Coping, and Social Support* (Springfield, IL: Charles Thomas, 1982) pp. 136–150.

P. 298: In view of the fact that more than half of all marriages end in divorce, and that 83 percent of all divorced men and 75 percent of all divorced women remarry, the problems of the remarried couple deserve special attention.

A. J. Cherlin, *Marriage, Divorce, Remarriage* (Cambridge, MA: Harvard University Press, 1981) p. 29.

P. 299: They may say things such as "You're not my brother" or "Don't talk to my mother that way."

L. A. Leslie and N. Epstein, "Cognitive-Behavioral Treatment of Remarried Families," in N. Epstein, S. E. Schlesinger, and W. Dryden, eds., *Cognitive-Behavioral Therapy with Families* (New York: Brunner/Mazel, 1988).

P. 299: They tend to maintain boundaries based on loyalty to their earlier families.

E. B. Visher and J. S. Visher, *A Guide to Working with Stepchildren* (New York: Brunner/Mazel, 1979).

PP. 299–300: Some experts say that the percentage of divorce in remarriages is almost as high as in first marriages.

R. Stuart and B. Jacobson, *Second Marriage: Make It Happy! Make It Last!* (New York: W. W. Norton, 1985).

P. 300: Some of these problems revolve around the basic beliefs of remarried families about family life and their explanations for the causes of problems among family members.

C. J. Sager et al., *Treating the Remarried Family* (New York: Brunner/Mazel, 1983).

BIBLIOGRAPHY

Bach, G., and Wyden, P. *The Intimate Enemy*. New York: Avon Books, 1968.

Barbach, L. G. *For Yourself: The Fulfillment of Female Sexuality*. Garden City, NY: Anchor Books, 1976.

Benson, H. *The Relaxation Response*. New York: William Morrow, 1975.

Berley, R., and Jacobson, N. "Causal Attributions in Intimate Relationships." In *Advances in Cognitive-Behavioral Research and Therapy*, vol. 3, edited by P. Kendall. New York: Academic Press, 1984.

Betcher, W. *Intimate Play: Creating Romance in Everyday Life*. New York: Viking, 1987.

Blumstein, P., and Schwartz, P. *American Couples*. New York: William Morrow, 1983.

Burns, D. *Feeling Good*. New York: New American Library, 1980.

Cherlin, A. J. *Marriage, Divorce, Remarriage*. Cambridge: Harvard University Press, 1981.

Duffy, D., and Dowd, T. "The Effect of Cognitive-Behavioral Assertion Training on Aggressive Individuals and Their Partners." *Southern Psychologist* 3: 45–50.

Ellis, A. *How to Live with and without Anger*. New York: Reader's Digest Press, 1977.

Epstein, N. "Depression and Marital Dysfunction: Cognitive and Behavioral Vantages." *International Journal of Mental Health* 13: 86–104.

Epstein, N.; Pretzer, J. L.; and Fleming, B. "The Role of Cognitive Appraisal in Self-Reports of Marital Communication." *Behavior Therapy* 18: 51–69.

Erikson, E. *Childhood and Society*. New York: W. W. Norton, 1964.

Fawcett, J., and York, R. "Spouses' Strength of Identification and Reports of Symptoms during Pregnancy and the Postpartum Period." *Florida Nursing Review* 2: 1–10.

Fincham, F.; Beach, S.; and Nelson, G. "Attribution Processes in Distressed and Non-distressed Marriages." *Journal of Abnormal Psychology* 94: 183–190.

Frank, E.; Anderson, C.; and Rubenstein, D. "Frequency of Sexual Dysfunction in 'Normal' Couples." *New England Journal of Medicine* 299(3): 111–115.

Gilligan, C. *In a Different Voice: Psychological Theory and Women's Development*. Cambridge, Harvard University Press, 1982.

Gottman, J. M. *Marital Interaction: Experimental Investigations.* New York: Academic Press, 1979.

Hollyworth-Monroe, A., and Jacobson, H. "Causal Attributions of Married Couples." *Journal of Personality and Social Psychology* 48: 1398–1412.

Horney, K. *Neurosis and Human Growth.* New York: W. W. Norton, 1950.

Houseknecht, S. K.; Vaughn, S.; and Macke, A. S. "Marital Disruption among Professional Women: The Timing of Career and Family Events." *Social Problems* 31(3): 273–284.

Ickes, W. "Sex-Role Differences and Compatibility in Relationships." In *Compatible and Incompatible Relationships,* edited by W. Ickes. New York: Springer-Verlag, 1985.

Jacobson, H., et al. "Attributional Processes in Distressed and Nondistressed Married Couples." *Cognitive Therapy and Research* 9: 35–50.

Kaplan, H. S. *The New Sex Therapy: Active Treatment of Sexual Dysfunction.* New York: Brunner/Mazel, 1974.

Leslie, L. A., and Epstein, N. "Cognitive-Behavioral Treatment of Remarried Families." In *Cognitive-Behavioral Therapy with Families,* edited by N. Epstein, S. E. Schlesinger, and W. Dryden. New York: Brunner/Mazel, 1988.

Maltz, D., and Borker, R. "A Cultural Approach to Male-Female Miscommunications." In *Language and Social Identity,* edited by J. J. Gumperz. England: Cambridge University Press, 1982.

Markman, H. J., et al. "Prevention of Marital Distress: A Longitudinal Investigation." *Journal of Consulting and Clinical Psychology* 56: 210–217.

Noller, P. "Misunderstandings in Marital Communication: Study of Nonverbal Communication." *Journal of Personality and Social Psychology* 39: 1135–1148.

Noller, P. "Gender and Marital Adjustment Level Differences in Decoding Messages from Spouses and Strangers." *Journal of Personality and Social Psychology* 41: 272–278.

Noller, P. *Nonverbal Communication and Marital Interaction.* New York: Pergamon Press, 1984.

Peele, S. *Love and Addiction.* New York: New American Library, 1976.

Piaget, J. *The Moral Judgment of the Child* (M. Gabain, trans.). Glencoe, IL: Free Press, 1965.

Piotrkowski, C. S., and Repetti, R. L. "Dual-Earner Families." *Marriage and Family Review* 7(2/3): 99–124.

Rosenstorf, O., et al. "Interaction Analysis of Marital Conflict." In *Marital Interaction: Analysis and Modification,* edited by K. Halweg and N. S. Jacobson. New York: Guilford Press, 1984.

Rubenstein, C., and Jaworski, M. "When Husbands Rate Second." *Family Circle,* May 1987.

Rubin, L. *Intimate Strangers: Men and Women Together.* New York: Harper & Row, 1984.

Sager, C. J., et al. *Treating the Remarried Family.* New York: Brunner/Mazel, 1983.

Scarf, M. *Intimate Partners: Patterns in Love and Marriage.* New York: Random House, 1987.

Schaap, C. "A Comparison of the Interaction of Distressed and Nondistressed Married Couples in a Laboratory Situation." In *Marital Interaction: Analysis and Modification,* edited by K. Halweg and N. S. Jacobson. New York: Guilford Press, 1984.

Skinner, D. A. "The Stressors and Coping Patterns of Dual-Career Families." In *Family*

Stress, Coping, and Social Support, edited by H. I. McCubbin, A. E. Cauble, and J. M. Patterson. Springfield, IL: Charles Thomas, 1982.

Stuart, R. *Helping Couples Change.* New York: Guilford Press, 1980.

Stuart, R., and Jacobson, B. *Second Marriage: Make It Happy! Make It Last!* New York: W. W. Norton, 1985.

Tannen, D. *That's Not What I Meant.* New York: Ballantine Books, 1986.

Tavris, C. *Anger: The Misunderstood Emotion.* New York: Simon & Schuster, 1982.

Tyler, T. R., and Devinitz, V. "Self-Serving Bias in the Attribution of Responsibility: Cognitive vs. Motivational Explanations." *Journal of Experimental Social Psychology* 17: 408–416.

Visher, E. B., and Visher, J. S. *A Guide to Working with Stepchildren.* New York: Brunner/ Mazel, 1979.

Zilbergeld, B. *Male Sexuality.* New York: Bantam Books, 1978.

INDEX